BLUE INK

MOLLY RIGGS

NEW DEGREE PRESS

COPYRIGHT © 2021 MOLLY RIGGS

All rights reserved.

BLUE INK

ISBN   978-1-63730-347-4   *Paperback*
        978-1-63730-348-1   *Kindle Ebook*
        978-1-63730-349-8   *Ebook*

BLUE INK

To everyone who has supported me on this journey toward my dream.

TABLE OF CONTENTS

AUTHOR'S NOTE — 11

PART I. — **17**
CHAPTER 1. BROTHER — 19
CHAPTER 2. CLOUD WATCHING — 29
CHAPTER 3. CLOSED DOOR — 35
CHAPTER 4. A FUNERAL — 53
CHAPTER 5. A PARTY — 63
CHAPTER 6. PANCAKES — 75
CHAPTER 7. MOVING IN — 87
CHAPTER 8. GIRLFRIEND — 97
CHAPTER 9. LOCKED DOOR — 117
CHAPTER 10. ONE HAPPY STORY — 127
CHAPTER 11. ROAD TRIP — 141
CHAPTER 12. ANOTHER FUNERAL — 157

PART II. — **173**
CHAPTER 13. SISTER — 175
CHAPTER 14. STARGAZING — 189
CHAPTER 15. VISITING HOME — 201
CHAPTER 16. SICK — 217
CHAPTER 17. ALONE — 227
CHAPTER 18. AN ADDICTION — 241
CHAPTER 19. SILENCE — 251
CHAPTER 20. NOISE — 259
CHAPTER 21. TRUCK ARMS — 267

CHAPTER 22. BAD TRIP   277
CHAPTER 23. CLEAN   283

EPILOGUE: ONE MORE HAPPY STORY   295
ACKNOWLEDGMENTS   299
APPENDIX   303

"... things get broken, and sometimes they get repaired, and in most cases, you realize that no matter what gets damaged, life rearranges itself to compensate for your loss, sometimes wonderfully."

—HANYA YANAGIHARA, *A LITTLE LIFE*

AUTHOR'S NOTE

Dear Readers,

It was the spring semester of 2019 when the characters of this story appeared to me in an Intermediate Poetry class at the University of Northern Colorado. There were two boys in that class who seemed like they were complete opposites yet struck up a close friendship that saw them leaving class together every day. One of the boys, my inspiration for Levi, was extremely sociable. He would sit at the back of the room with his feet up on the desk in front of him and talk with whoever happened to be around him. The other, who inspired Charlie, sat in the first row, and didn't speak unless it was to read his poetry.

As a writer, I have an especially perceptive personality. I tend to observe the people around me and analyze the root of their mannerisms. I took what I saw from the outside of this friendship and created a novel that explores the bond two very different individuals can form.

Although inspired by real people, the characters of Charlie and Levi are completely fictitious. Similarly, while my novel is set in existing locations, I took creative liberties with the setting to fit the needs of my story. My goal was to portray the often-difficult struggles of real life through a work of fiction.

I have always been interested in heavy subject matter. Although I had a relatively happy childhood, I began to struggle with my mental health when I entered high school. During this time, I looked for stories that would help me explore the darkness I was facing internally. I became obsessed with the author, Ellen Hopkins, whose books tackle themes like addiction, mental health, and trauma. These are themes that I latched onto in my first feeble attempts at writing stories, and they are still themes that interest me today.

Even as my taste in literature matured, my obsession with dark themes continued. My favorite book of all time is *A Little Life* by Hanya Yanagihara. This book is about four men who meet in college, and it follows their paths to adulthood through their struggles with addiction, sexuality, success, and most notably, trauma. *A Little Life* is the saddest book I've ever read, and its themes inform my own novel. I wanted to implement the trauma wrought throughout that book into my own work.

My character Charlie demonstrates how trauma can infuse itself into all aspects of our everyday lives, including how we react to our surroundings and build relationships. With this story, I wanted to expel the belief that we need to bury our trauma to overcome it. I believe we owe it to ourselves to mourn and reflect on our trauma—how Charlie does by writing out his story—to make sense of it. But unlike Charlie, we cannot fixate on our trauma or try to bury it to the point it interferes with our ability to form positive relationships. The point is to recognize the way our past trauma affects our present lives so that we can learn to live with it.

Another theme I wanted to touch on in this story was sexual identity. I feel that there is still a gap in the publishing sphere of books that depict the fluidity of sexuality. I refrained from explicitly defining the characters' sexual orientation because I believe it is natural to experiment with all genders, especially at the college age. I want to destigmatize and bring visibility to bisexual attraction, especially for men, whose sexuality is often equated to their masculinity. Even before Levi recognizes his attraction to Charlie, the two share a healthy, affectionate relationship at no expense to their "manhood."

Finally, I tackled the topic of addiction because it has always been a subject of interest to me. The descent into addiction is often subtle, but the impacts on both the addict and those around them can be devastating. I wanted to show both sides in this story. We witness addiction from the outside in Charlie's chapters, watching the continued fall of his brother, and with Levi's chapters, we see the chaos from within. I chose to take some creative risks in the style of my story for the purpose of accurately depicting the emotional turmoil of addiction, including unconventional shifts in point of view, changes in tense, and even the omission of punctuation in the later chapters.

Although the themes of addiction and sexuality can be difficult for some to confront, they are pertinent to telling a story set in the modern college landscape. Jeffrey Juergens of the Addiction Center found college students are at a higher risk for substance abuse, with around 80 percent having abused alcohol at some point in their education. And where the national average of LGBTQ+ identification sits around 4.5 percent based on a 2017 study, Eric Duran and Brooke Sopelsa of NBCNews cite that around 20 percent of incoming college freshmen identify as something other than heterosexual. *Blue Ink* offers a conscientious representation of these real experiences.

Ultimately, this book is for readers interested in digging into the complexities of human emotion—including the darker side. As is true with most fans of literary fiction, readers must be able to accept a story that isn't necessarily happy but feels realistic to the human experience.

While the story may feel like a hopeless journey, I hope it reminds readers that although life can be traumatic, if you let people in, they can help uplift you from your darkest moments.

PART I

1

BROTHER

Charlie was alone at the kitchen table, working with a determined focus to capture the image of a perfect family. With his teacher's permission, he had borrowed a piece of red construction paper and a box of crayons from his first-grade classroom on Friday. Now, he plucked each individual crayon carefully from the box as he needed it and slipped the color back into its designated spot before choosing a different one. He didn't want to make a mess on the table—the only clean space in the otherwise cluttered apartment—and he wanted to return the box just as he had gotten it to the classroom on Monday.

He had started by drawing his dad, the tallest of the four. He used the tan crayon to draw his big, rough hands and the brown crayon for his thick, angry eyebrows and his boots, set in an intimidating stance. His mom's hair required the same brown, and he drew it messy like it was when she had just gotten out of bed. Of course, he had to put her in her silky red pajamas and make her eyes wide and watery with a dark blue. His brother was next, slouched in a dark green jacket with a distant half-smile in gray. Charlie positioned one of his brother's hands near the half-smile, holding a little, smoldering cigarette. The other was holding hands with the shortest of the bunch: Charlie himself. He used a lot of the same colors he had on his brother, finishing off the eyes in a bright blue. Then, he began coloring in the sunny sky with the same crayon. An involuntary grin slipped onto his lips, proud of the four smiles he had drawn and the way they made his family look.

That grin wavered as the sound of his parents' yelling broke into his focus. They had been fighting behind the closed door of their bedroom for a while, but Charlie was so used to the sound that he had gotten good at tuning it out. As he filled in the background behind the four smiles, the argument continued to escalate in volume, becoming impossible to ignore. Charlie pressed the crayon harder against the paper. The light blue was starting to feel like the wrong choice. He wanted the drawing to be accurate.

He abandoned the blue crayon without returning it to the box and quickly snatched up the black instead. He began sounding out the curse words he was hearing and wrote them as best he could in shaky letters across the sky. He had heard these words plenty of times, and although he did not understand what they meant besides being something to shout when you're angry, he was able to guess how to spell them.

His teacher had complimented his spelling earlier in the year and told him she would write it on his report card so his parents would be proud. That report card was lost somewhere in the mountainous stacks of unread mail and dirty dishes on the kitchen counters, always on the verge of collapse. There were already a few fallen stacks scattered across the dirty linoleum floor.

The sky in Charlie's drawing was quickly becoming dark and messy with his handwriting. It looked like a thunderstorm. He jerked his head up in frustration so he didn't have to look at the picture any longer. He had hoped maybe writing the words above his family would help him figure out why his parents were using them against each other, but the dark sky just revealed how unrealistic the four smiles were. The picture's story was confused. And there was no way to change it. It was ruined.

So Charlie focused his attention fully on the argument, which was leaking from beneath the crack in the door like a spill. It was the same fight they always had. His dad was mad because his mom hadn't gotten out of bed in a few days, and he thought she was "mentally unstable." His mom was mad that his dad was going on another business trip where he would "fuck other women." Charlie didn't get any of it, but the angry tones they were using made him feel nervous. He bit his lip, fiddling with the black crayon between his fingertips as he stared at the door's crack and wished for it to end.

This wish did not come true, but the sound of his brother's door opening down the hall pulled his attention momentarily away. He released the black crayon, which hit the table beside the blue one with a pitiful click, and turned his head to watch his brother emerge in a thin cloud of skunky smoke. At first, he was facing their parent's room, shaking his head, but when he caught sight of Charlie from the corner of his eye, he turned fully to the kitchen and skipped toward him with an animated smile pasted on his face. Charlie smiled shyly in return, feeling comforted when his brother sat down in the chair beside him.

"Whatcha colorin', Charlie boy?" His brother slid the piece of red construction paper toward him and picked it up to examine it.

Immediately, Charlie's cheeks stung with embarrassment at the confused drawing, and to avoid the feeling, he returned his focus to his parents' feud. He wished he was old enough to understand where their anger for each other came from. His brother knew—his eyes naturally drifting back over to him, studying the paper with a furrowed brow—but he refused to explain it.

His brother wanted to protect Charlie—that's what he told him anyway. And a lot of the time, he did feel safer with his brother around. He held Charlie's hand when he needed reassurance. He let him crawl into his bed at night when he felt afraid. He made him smiley-face pancakes when he was upset. But there were other times when it was his brother who upset him. He would leave for days without explanation and return with a faraway look on his face, which always started up a bout of shouting between their parents.

Charlie didn't know where he went or what he did when he was gone. All he took from those fights was that his brother was dirty and refused to get clean, which didn't seem like that big of a deal considering nothing about their family was clean. With them, it was always messy.

A curious Charlie stared up at his brother, who had cast the drawing aside and was dragging his hands down the sides of his face, the corners of his mouth drooping into an exaggerated frown. His fingers slipped off the edge of his chin, and the skin bounced back into its resting gloom—faint on the surface but deeply hollow behind. But from that more neutral position, it appeared easier for him to mechanically shift his lips up into a soft smile.

"Let's go somewhere, huh?" He placed a hand on Charlie's tightened shoulder, which eased immediately at the touch.

But although the comforting hand made Charlie believe this was one of those times when he could feel safe, there was a certain faraway quality to his brother's gaze that made him unsure. But he wanted to get away from his parents and forget about the drawing, so he hesitantly nodded.

Charlie's brother took his hand, intertwining each finger and squeezing tightly. He used the other one to fish a cigarette from his jacket pocket and stuck it between his chapped lips. Then, he led them out of the small apartment, through the echoing stairwell, and into the bright day, putting two doors and three flights of stairs between them and the fight.

Charlie was caught up in the glowing end of his brother's cigarette as they began walking through the streets of Rockford, Illinois. They moved from the chain-link fences, cracked sidewalks, construction signs, and weed-ridden dirt fields of their neighborhood toward the part of town with thriving greenery, freshly paved roads, and popular storefronts of bright red brick. He was fascinated by the flaring ember when his brother breathed in and the white cloud he blew from the back of his throat a few seconds later.

Unlike the stinky haze that drifted from his brother's bedroom earlier, Charlie loved the smell of cigarettes. They left a scent on his brother's fingertips that he found comforting. Sometimes, when they held hands like they were doing, Charlie's fingers would come away with the smell. It made him feel closer to his brother.

There was a fourteen-year age gap between the two of them, so Charlie often felt distant from his brother. It had mostly to do with the faraway look, which descended like a thick fog whenever the kind of smoke he didn't like filled his nose or when he saw his brother pull the little baggy of white pills from his combat boot and swallow one. His brother's focus would start to wander, and his words would become all jumbled up on each other. When his brother was faraway, Charlie didn't feel as safe.

Although he felt comforted by the cigarette smell as they moved farther and farther from the apartment, he also kept checking his brother's eyes for any sign of the dreaded far-awayness. He knew they were heading in the direction of a restaurant that served special drinks, which had the same effect on his brother: creating a storm of clouds in his eyes. Charlie hardened, preparing himself for rain.

But his brother stopped unexpectedly, tossing the now-tiny cigarette onto the sidewalk and extinguishing it with his toe. They were standing in front of Charlie's favorite breakfast restaurant. His mouth hung open for a moment in disbelief, and then he beamed at his brother, who grinned in return and led them inside.

While his brother went up to the line at the front counter to order, Charlie slipped into their usual booth and sank comfortably into the vinyl cushion. He bounced with excitement. This was his favorite place because their smiley-face pancakes were the most similar to the ones his brother would make on the nights Charlie felt least like smiling. They didn't try to overcomplicate it like other restaurants. They used just two chocolate chips for the eyes and a line of them for the smile. That's all he needed.

He peered around the back of the booth to see if his brother was at the register yet, and the excitement immediately drained out of him when he saw his brother bent down, pretending to tie his shoe while he slipped a white pill in his mouth. Charlie felt betrayed. He slumped back in the booth, fighting off tears, and began picking at a blueberry syrup stain on the marbled table to keep from crying.

His brother returned with a tray of pancakes in his hand and sat down across from Charlie, placing a plate in front of him. Charlie pushed it out of his way and continued scratching at the stain with his finger. He purposefully did not look at his brother, but he could already feel him drifting away. He doubled his effort against the crusty blue spot, and when he finished that one, he found more. But it didn't take long for him to pick his side of the table completely clean.

Charlie had no choice but to glance up at what was happening on his brother's side of the table. He didn't like what he saw. Just like his own plate, his brother's pancake remained untouched. He had his head tilted back against the booth, and he seemed hypnotized by the skylight in the ceiling above them.

He was also mumbling to himself. "A six-year-old shouldn't be coloring cuss words across the sky. They're supposed to draw zoo animals, or flowers, or dogs and birds and shit like that. What have we done to you?"

Charlie moved his focus to the floor, his brother's words twisting his gut in a funny way, making him feel queasy. He began counting all the spills he could find in the black and white checkered pattern to distract himself. He was at twenty-two when he heard his name:

"Charlie?"

His brother was looking directly at him, that faraway look on his face but also tears in his eyes. He had his hand resting on the table between them, and Charlie put his own hand on top, wanting so badly to feel close to him and safe.

"You're always looking down at the ground," his brother whispered. "Why?"

Charlie rested his chin on the table, feeling tired, and shrugged. "I like the shapes a spill can make. I come up with stories out of them."

His brother sighed and looked back up at the skylight, where a cloud was passing by, momentarily blocking out the stream of sun. He sniffed, rubbing away the tears with the back of his fist, and came back down to the table, pointing at the forgotten plates.

"We can't leave our friends here to get cold. They get lonely too, you know."

Charlie tried to conceal a giggle as he pulled the smile back in front of him, cut into it with his fork, and brought a bite to his mouth. The inside was still warm and fluffy. The chocolate melted on his tongue.

"I think these may be our happiest pancakes yet," his brother said through a mouthful of his own bite.

When both of their plates had been licked clean, Charlie's brother stood and extended another hand. Charlie felt a bit unsure about taking it but was encouraged when his brother had situated another cigarette in his mouth.

Hand in hand, they walked out of the restaurant and even farther from their home to a pleasant little park with a colorful metal playground, a baseball diamond, and a big hill of green. It was a beautiful day. The sky was a bright blue and full of puffy clouds.

His brother led them to the top of the hill. He let go of Charlie's hand and threw himself down in the grass with a gentle laugh.

"Come on," he encouraged Charlie to join him. Charlie had his hands crossed behind his back. He was swaying slightly and nervously kicking his toe into the ground. He didn't want to get hurt by his brother again if the baggy came back out or somehow the bad smoke appeared.

His brother was reaching out for him, though, and Charlie couldn't help but give in to the idea of their intertwined fingers. He took his brother's hand and lay down beside him, scooting close so that he didn't have to see his face but could smell the cigarettes on his clothes.

"Have you ever tried looking for shapes in the clouds?" his brother asked.

Charlie shook his head at the canvas of clouds in front of him.

"Why don't you give it a try?" He paused, giving Charlie a chance to look around. Immediately, all sorts of pictures began appearing to him. "What do you see?"

"I'm not sure what it means," Charlie muttered, his eyes darting back and forth trying to read all the images for some sort of bigger story.

"That's okay. Just describe one thing."

"There's a big monster truck that's running down a whole line of people." He strained his eyes to make out who was behind the wheel. He couldn't tell. He shifted his body a few inches from his brother so he had room to turn his head. "What do you see?" he asked curiously.

"Two boys holding on to each other for dear life." He lifted their clasped hands in the air to point. Charlie found the cloud he was referring to easily.

When his brother brought their hands down again, he pulled Charlie's over to his lips and kissed it softly. Then, he closed his eyes, and soon, he was snoring.

Charlie thought about doing the same because he felt drained from the day, but he couldn't stop studying the story he was seeing spread out above him. A few times, he felt close to putting it all together, but his thoughts were fleeting with nothing to hold them down, and as quickly as the ideas came to him, they floated off to join the clouds.

Eventually, the sky began to dim. That was when his brother woke up. He let go of Charlie's hand to push himself into a sitting position and put a cigarette in his mouth. Charlie smiled. His brother's eyes had cleared. He was no longer far away.

And he took back up Charlie's hand once his cigarette was lit. "One more stop, and then we'll head home."

They ended up at a little shop full of books. Charlie had never been there before, and he scanned the towering shelves in awe. But his brother led them away from the books and straight to the front counter, where there was a display of journals. He bought Charlie a red-leather one and a fountain pen with blue ink.

"Keep looking up, Charlie boy. And write what you see. Soon, the stories will start to make sense."

By the time they got back to the apartment, the fight had long since ended. The door to their parents' bedroom was still closed, but there was silence behind it, and the lights were off. That meant their mom was back in bed. The car keys were gone from the hook by the door. That meant their dad had left for his business trip. His brother went to his room, and soon, the smoke Charlie didn't like emerged from the crack beneath the door.

Charlie returned the black and blue crayons to their places in the box and set it aside. He flicked his drawing off the table so that it fluttered to the floor and sat down in the same spot at the kitchen table as earlier, opening his new journal to the first page. He began to write out the story he had seen in the clouds in blue ink.

2

CLOUD WATCHING

———

I gotta be honest. I had dropped two tabs of acid on the day he and I became friends.

There's a chance I might not have even approached him if I wasn't tripping. I mean, I was a pretty social person. I just knew he wasn't. We had been in classes together throughout our first year at St. John's College, but he was the kind of kid who sat in the first row and only spoke when called on by the professor. I was more the type of person to drop acid in the middle of the day. Sober me probably would've assumed someone like him didn't want to be bothered by someone like me.

But I had always been curious about him. Whenever he did speak in class, his low, rugged voice was never insecure. And though his broad shoulders were perpetually slumped—his neck bent toward the ground—he had a quiet courage in the way he moved: firm, secure. He carried a journal with him everywhere and always had it open, writing furiously away with a blue fountain pen.

That day, the journal was lying closed in the grass beside him. It was a Saturday afternoon in Annapolis, and everyone else was in their dorm rooms trying to sleep through their hangovers from Friday night's parties. He was a lone, dark body in the wide expanse of unruly green that made up the lawn in front of the English building. From where I stood on the crooked brick path down the hill, he was just a speck against the ancient, twisting oaks and the building itself, which towered behind him with its deep umber brick and the many-paneled windows trimmed in stark white. The sky was similarly intimidating, dark with a coming storm.

Still, his sure presence made him seem big, beyond his sturdy frame—especially as I approached him, feeling cagey from the kaleidoscope of colors coiling down my skinny arms.

He flicked his blue eyes momentarily my way when I stopped above him but didn't say anything, promptly returning his gaze to the storm. I didn't linger long on him either, instead circling the crimson cover of his journal—like a big, red self-destruct button asking to be pressed. I was tempted. I imagined slipping it open would be like taking a scalpel to his chest and peeling back the thick skin to find a fleshy, throbbing heart. He would feel exposed, but I knew I'd find it beautiful.

Looking at him then, I could see through his thick wall of muscle to the fragile bones below, but I could also see him stiffen. It was an intrusion, looking inside of him. Just like it would be if I opened his journal.

So, I abandoned the thought. I decided instead to plop down beside him in the grass and look up to see what he was seeing—what had pulled his attention away from the journal. The clouds were menacing: ink-black and traumatic.

If I had been sober, they probably would've intimidated me. The far-reaching darkness might have left me hollow inside, desolate, lonely even. But with my altered state of mind, I was confident barreling down the violence before me. I believed the storm was under my control. And even though I didn't know him yet, I believed myself unstoppable with him by my side. He would save me if I did start to lose control. I was sure.

"What do you see in the clouds, Levi?" he asked me, the comfort of his steady voice reaffirming my assumption that I was safe with him.

My lips fell open in an awed smile. I hadn't expected him to speak first between us, but I was glad he did. I had been struggling to find the words to articulate my experience.

His question opened me up. "Wow," I sighed, "a lot. It's a bit grim. Isn't it? Like I thought you were only supposed to see pictures in the clouds when they're all puffed up and positive. But no, these dark ones are painting pictures extra vivid: a funeral at the zoo where all the animals are in their best suits; a sunflower squirting out seeds for children who refuse to grow; some sexually explicit content between a dog and a crow. You know what I mean." I shook my head, chuckling. Then I turned to him suddenly. "Do you know what I mean? I'm tripping pretty hard right now."

"I see it," he nodded. Then, he closed his eyes serenely.

A warmness flushed through my veins at his affirmation. He could have disregarded my ramblings; he knew I was high. Instead, he listened and even attempted to understand. I had the urge to roll on top of him and kiss him sloppily on the cheek to show my gratitude, but I knew he'd hate that. Out of respect, I took his lead and closed my eyes too.

We stayed suspended there longer than two other strangers might. I don't know how long it was. Minutes, hours? Time was the calm before the storm. It was a still pond before the rippling. We were the aimless wandering before a major discovery.

I was extra attuned to the world around me. A low rumbling of thunder rolled across the horizon. The electricity of nearby lightning was raising the hairs on my arms, stippled with goosebumps from a brisk breeze. My tongue was parched, and I had to peel it from the roof of my mouth, prepared to thrust it from my cracked lips at the first drop of rain. The fresh honeysuckle scent of his detergent, mixed with the stale nicotine-tinge of my own clothes, amassed into an oddly syrupy smell.

A thick drop of rain splashed between my eyebrows. I opened my eyes, and the rain had begun. Just a sprinkle at first. Neither of us moved, and he kept his eyes closed. But soon, it became a steady downpour.

I laughed in the face of it. It was coming down hard, but I was only going up. And the animals at the funeral got out their umbrellas, and the sunflower seeds finally bloomed, and the dog and the crow climaxed. And I still believed I had complete control over everything.

But then I noticed his journal lying in the soggy grass. It was blurry in my sight, obscured by the sheets of water spilling from the clouds, but still a bright red signal reading, *Help*. Usually, it was being poured into. Now, it was being poured onto.

His eyes were still closed.

"Hey," I grasped on to his forearm and shook it, trying to get his attention. "Your journal's being ruined! Your blue ink is probably bleeding all over the place."

He didn't stir. "It's fine," he said quietly, barely moving his lips. His hair was usually messy on top, but the brown strands were now plastered in flat lines to his forehead.

My own long, wavy black locks were hanging in front of my eyes, giving the already dim scene an even darker vignette around the edges. I was crawling outside of my skin at the thought of everything he had hidden behind that leather cover being erased. I waited for him to shed his sturdy exterior, for an unbounded panic to expose itself—for him to bolt upright and cry with me over the soiled pages. It never came.

And finally, I couldn't contain myself. I threw my body over his, reaching for the journal and flipping desperately through the sodden pages. But it was too late. All that blue ink, all those words, had spread into meaningless stains.

Tears welled up and edged themselves toward my bottom lashes.

"This doesn't hurt?" I squeaked, feeling my own stomach bottoming out at the loss.

He finally opened his eyes and looked over at me. I was fully crying, and he could tell, even though the tears were getting all jumbled up with the rain. Both of us were drenched.

He sat up and sighed. "They're just words."

"But what if you can never get them back?" I shook my head in confusion, trying to rationalize the lack of grief he displayed as a physical piece of himself disappeared from existence. I couldn't. And it made me feel cold.

Earlier, I had wanted to hug him. Now, I wished he would hug me. I knew he wouldn't.

"It's nothing new." He shrugged. "Anyway, it's not the words, but the stories I wish would wash away." He took the journal gently from my hands and closed it, so I didn't have to look at those oceans of indiscernible ink any longer.

But I couldn't quite let go. "Aren't you sad about everything you've lost?"

He placed his hand on my shoulder. It wasn't a hug, but still, his handprint was like a center of heat in my freezing body. I was shivering, and my teeth chattered violently.

He stood, his sneakers squelching on the mushy lawn, and extended a hand to help me up. I took it, sniffling.

He led me back to his dorm room, which was pleasantly stuffy—feeling almost like the hug I'd been craving with the way its thick humidity pressed against my stippled skin. But the muted sound of the rain pounding against the window outside kept my paranoid brain from sighing in relief. Instead, I eyed the basic furniture set—identical to my own—suspiciously, as if at any moment it could smear like his pages, only for me to realize l was inside his story all along.

He guided me to the bathroom and sat me down on the toilet seat, handing me a scruffy red towel. I rubbed harshly at my dripping cheeks. Then he gave me some dry clothes to change into. He turned his back while I took off my own.

And then he let me sweat out the next eight hours of my trip in his bed—caught in some dream state between a horrifying past I didn't recognize and a tumultuous future I hadn't yet experienced.

On the other side, I still felt a bit strange, the phantom grief lingering like a weighted blanket against my tingling skin. It was the next day. There were two Ibuprofen and a glass of water on the nightstand, and he was at his desk, writing beneath lamp light. My pulsing heart lifted to my throat.

I realized he was writing over the blue stains, now dry, with new words. Nothing that had been lost couldn't be created again.

3

CLOSED DOOR

———

The window of his dorm room was north-facing, and though the morning sun trickled through the closed blinds, with no direct light streaming in, the room was brisk. I burrowed further under his comforter, pulling the thin, gray fabric up to my nose, inhaling the fresh scent of his bargain detergent, and taking stock of the room. I started at the angry, red alarm clock on the nightstand, which read 6:30 a.m. Early. And at him, wide awake and writing furiously at the desk. He hadn't noticed me wake up. The tips of his messy brown hair were damp, and there was a towel draped over the back of his chair, so he had already showered. How long had he been awake?

I found a pair of running shoes positioned neatly beside the door, facing out toward the hall as if ready for a quick escape. Maybe he had been for a sunrise run around the campus, but there was no indication in the form of discarded athletic gear. If it had been me—which it never would because I didn't wake up early unless hungover and didn't run unless being chased—I would have tossed my dirty clothes on the floor. But, besides the natural wear of past tenants, the floor was spotless, the entire room meticulously organized.

Everything had its place: on the dresser next to his desk, a neat bag of toiletries zipped; the hamper beside it with no stray sleeves poking out; a shelf of books above his head arranged alphabetically by author—Burroughs, Kerouac, Nietzsche, and so on. The messiest thing about the room was me.

And on the other side of the barren carpet was a second set of everything, only empty—a nightstand without an alarm clock, a desk without books, a bed without sheets. Had he slept there?

"You don't have a roommate?" I sat up, plunging myself into the chill. I slipped the Ibuprofen in my mouth for good measure and downed the glass of water he had set out for me. "Me neither."

He flinched at my voice but regained his quiet composure quickly. He closed his journal and turned to face me.

"How are you?" he asked, his voice flat.

"Definitely one of my stranger trips." I shrugged. I noticed my clothes folded neatly on the end of the bed, and I crawled forward to get the pack of cigarettes and lighter from my jacket pocket. I offered one up to him, but he shook his head, so I leaned back against the wall and lit just one for me. He stood up to open the blinds and pop the window.

"Oh, sorry." I breathed out smoke. "Is this okay?"

He was eyeing the two fingers that sandwiched my cigarette, but he looked with more nostalgia than concern. Maybe he had quit?

"It's fine." His tone remained even, so I couldn't tell if it was actually fine. I finished the cigarette quickly, just in case, and put it out with the tips of my licked fingers, pocketing the stub to throw out somewhere else.

But still, he kept his eyes locked dubiously on me like I was doing something wrong. I wiggled my eyebrows at him, grinning mischievously to catch him off guard, and his look retreated, embarrassed, to the unaccompanied carpet.

"So, what are you doing with your day? Should we get food or something?" I felt bad for making him uncomfortable. "It's on me, really. I appreciate you helping me out."

"I was actually going to head over to the library to get some work done." He shifted in his seat as if to get up, a classic move that meant to cast an uneasiness over the room, encouraging me to leave. But my threshold for withstanding social discomfort was already pretty high—sort of came with the territory of being the wildcard at a party. And I'd already embarrassed myself in front of him. As far as I was concerned, there was no room for awkwardness between us.

So I played dumb: "On a Sunday? Come on! Let's just go lounge around in the grass and chat. I bet it's a real nice day after that storm."

"I've got a paper to write." He deepened his excuse, but I was relentless.

"The one for ENG 344? We're in that class together. It's not due until Friday!" I could see him running out of excuses, desperately searching the recesses of his brain for one. I was nearly there—had nearly broken him. It was a special talent of mine, getting people to open up who didn't particularly want to. Something about my smile and carefree attitude, even introverts just couldn't resist. I went for the final blow: "I'll buy us some coffees, and we can brainstorm together. Maybe get to know each other a little bit afterward. How about that?"

Although I had felt progress being made, suddenly, something in the room shifted, and a thick wall went up between him and me, not three feet apart from bed to desk.

"Sorry. No." Now he really did get up from his seat, turning his chin toward the door.

I blinked in surprise, not sure what had just happened. I tried to read his face to see if I had done something to offend him, but he refused to display even a hint of what he was feeling. He had forced himself cold and closed.

Disappointed, I accepted my defeat. I stood up and began putting on my clothes. Once I was dressed, he led me to the door.

I stepped out into the hall with a "Thanks aga—" but the door was shut before I could finish my thought.

I trudged back to my own dorm room across campus, perturbed. The air was beginning to get muggy as the rising sun boiled away yesterday's puddles into a thick humidity. The twisting brick paths were quiet in the early hour but for the echo of birds flirting with each other between the highest tree branches. My brain whirred through our interaction over and over, trying to make sense of its abrupt end. Was he really that stressed about his paper? Did he not like coffee? Or was it just the thought of getting to know me that turned him off the idea?

I smacked at a desirous mosquito on my forearm and burst into my building, expecting a relief of cool air. But it was just as sticky. The RA manning the front desk was dozing, his snoring upper lip moist with sweat. In front of him was a printer paper sign scotch-taped to the counter: *AC broken, Repairman coming Monday.*

I groaned, longing for the chill I'd left behind in his room, and started down the hall, deserted and stifling.

I swung open my door, pausing in the doorway as if someone were waiting for me on the other side. Unfortunately, but of course, there was no one there. I was alone with the hot mess of my room. There were dirty clothes scattered across my floor, an ashtray overflowing on my nightstand, my bed was unmade, and the vacant bed was piled high with various boxes of snacks my mom had sent me and books I would never bother to read for class. I threw myself onto my unwashed sheets and tried to sleep. It was still so early.

But I couldn't get him out of my head. Had I said something to offend him? I tossed back and forth in yesterday's damp clothes, increasingly wet with my collecting sweat, and slapped at my dilapidated pillow in an attempt to get comfortable. Maybe something had happened during my trip. I pictured the scene behind my thick eyelids, trying to parse through what I might've done to upset him. But I kept getting distracted by the odor of my unclean bedding, the suffocating quality of the room without air conditioning, and the burden I felt from the sloppiness of my floor.

Finally, I gave up and decided to take a cold shower instead. But I made a mental note to get to the bottom of it. I'd ask him directly what I'd done wrong and apologize extravagantly until he had no choice but to forgive me.

"I'll win him over," I said to myself as the brisk water washed away all traces of the previous day—a few pieces of grass that had dried to the backs of my arms circling down the drain.

Once I was all clean, and the clock read a more reasonable hour, I ended up on the lawn just like I had proposed to him. Only, it was to smoke with a group of people who I wouldn't quite consider friends but did hang around a lot because they had good weed. I didn't really have any friends although I could get along and have a good time with almost anyone. It was the beginning of my second year at St. John's, and there just wasn't anyone I felt close to.

That was the story of my life. The high school I went to, which was only a few minutes away, was full of people who liked to invite me to their parties but who I never really got to know intimately out of that setting. A rager isn't really the place to form lasting bonds with someone, and anyway, a lot of the time, people become different versions of themselves after a few drinks. But it started to feel like nobody really wanted to get to know me outside of my intoxicated persona. I was the life of the party. That role didn't allow for anything serious from me.

And that feeling carried itself through to the college party scene. Whatever deep conversations I struck up sharing a smoke on the back porch with a stranger remained an oasis of the blurred night. Even when I woke up in bed beside a naked girl, whatever intimacy we might've shared scattered as soon as she opened her eyes, collected her clothes, and left me alone in my dorm room. To be fair, that's the nature of a hookup, and there were plenty of times I didn't want to get to know the girl either. But still, that didn't mean I wasn't left feeling empty when she was gone. It's how I had felt that morning when he closed the door in my nose.

But I want to get to know him, I thought as I took a hit of the joint that was being passed around the group. For no reason at all, he had taken care of me yesterday. He had let me sleep in his bed. Yet, this morning, he had all but thrown me out when I proposed we do something together. He hadn't seemed angry but just… scared?

From what I could tell, like me, he didn't have any friends. He was always sitting alone, and in class, he never talked to anyone. Maybe he liked his alone time—fine—but who didn't want at least one person to be close with? I craved it.

I lay back in the grass and closed my eyes, the summer sun bathing my face in a fresh sheen of sweat, drowning me. I remembered the way the rain fell down on his journal, soaking the pages. What did he write in there? There was a joke floating around the pretentious side of the English department—those who advocated for a full course load of classic literature—that he wrote soft porn.

I bet that shit is absolutely twisted, someone had whispered to me in the back of our poetry class when the professor had prompted him to read out his piece. He had written a poem about his running shoes that somehow managed to be violent—positioning them as slaves to his feet.

From what he had shared in class, I didn't view his work as dark or twisted. He just seemed reflective. And honestly, he was a good fucking writer. In my opinion, the best at St. John's.

That just made me want to get to know him even more. I wanted to know what inspired his work. I wanted to know how he could have so much to write about. I especially wanted to know what it was that washed away in the storm the previous night—what he had been rewriting that morning. *It's not the words, but the stories I wish would wash away.* What did that mean?

Usually, I committed my efforts to drinking. The main draw of college for me had been partying. I liked learning as much as the next person, but I didn't really care for academia. And I already knew I wouldn't use my English degree in a career—suitable job prospects for me included mostly menial nine-to-five cubicle work with decent benefits. I had come to college to enjoy the last years of my carefree youth before that bleak future, and that's where I devoted all my efforts. But there on the lawn, enjoying the lazy high of an indica strain, I recommitted myself to him. We would be friends, I vowed, and I would see for myself the stories hidden in that rain-stained journal of his.

My half-formed plan was to sit next to him in class, where there would be no escape. I'd get to the room early to take the seat right next to his usual desk at the front, waving at him stupidly when he walked in the door and winning his heart.

That was what I had devised on the lawn in the afternoon anyway—before the group had dispersed and I had followed a couple of them to a shitty punk concert in a downtown hole-in-the-wall venue. We got absolutely smashed on vodka shooters we'd snuck in, plus some miscellaneous white powder in the handicapped stall of the grungy bathroom. I hadn't stumbled back to my still air-condition-less dorm and fallen into my BO-soaked sheets until around 3 a.m. So unfortunately, but not surprisingly, I overslept.

And by the time I got to class—drenched in sweat, out of breath, hungover, and ten minutes late—the desks on either side of him were already occupied. I had to resort to my typical seat at the back of the room.

I spent the entire class zeroing in on the back of his head and not paying attention to the lecture. I tried to imagine what was going on behind that strategically mussed hairdo of his. Presumably, he was thinking about Allen Ginsberg, the topic of the lecture I was neglecting. But I had the idea that as focused a student as he seemed, maybe his mind wandered to bigger things than *Howl*—a pretty lengthy poem, to be fair—during class. Selfishly, I hoped he was thinking about the weekend, about the storm we'd experienced together and the way we left things the next day. Realistically, he was probably planning out his next story, which he'd be busy writing as soon as class was over.

I wanted to catch him before that, so I began clearing my desk five minutes before the hypothetical bell rang, and as soon as the professor dismissed us, I threw my backpack over my shoulder and weaved through the maze of desks. I stood in front of him as he thoughtfully placed his books in his bag from biggest to smallest. He didn't notice me until he had zipped up his bag and stood to leave, and I could tell I startled him although he tried to suppress the alarm that flashed across his features.

"Hey there!" I greeted him obnoxiously. "Pretty interesting stuff on that Alvin Ginseng, don't you think?" We were walking by the professor, and she gave me a stink eye, shaking her long, gray braid in disapproval. I winked as we popped out the door and broke away from the funnel of students.

"I actually think you'd like the poem if you read it," he said quietly, stifling a smile at my sarcastic remarks.

"Wow, you assume I haven't read it?" I mocked offense.

He ignored me. "It's about pleasure, and art, and sex… and drugs." We were outside of the building, and he squinted up at the sun. I watched him shade his eyes with the back of his hand and avoid mine. "It's a great poem."

"It does sound pretty good." I dropped the goofy act at the way he said *drugs*. "Look, I'm sorry you had to deal with me on Saturday in that state. I swear, I'm usually pretty fun."

"I don't doubt it."

We walked along the path toward the dining hall. All classes let out at the same time, so college students were buzzing at every corner: backpack-clad freshmen hurrying to the next class here; careless seniors lounging beneath the tree cover there; a bible thumper shouting about the end of times and pressing pocket New Testaments into the hands of budding Marxists; and a group of three old men in athletic gear taking a round of frisbee golf way too seriously.

He wasn't taking any of it in, his head down, focused on the consistent rhythm of his feet against the brick. I was trying my best to focus on him, but people kept coming up to me, slapping my back and asking if I knew of any party going on that night. Still, I managed to keep up with him.

"Did you ever get that paper done? Maybe we could get some lunch, and you can read Albert Gingivitis to me, so I see what all the fuss is about." I tried to be as nonchalant about my proposal as I could.

"Look, Levi," he stopped abruptly. We were in front of his dorm. He was looking at me with a note of affection, but his tone was that of a partner delivering the dreaded break-up clichés. "I don't want you to feel bad about Saturday. I'm fine. I just don't think we have very much in common, okay? No hard feelings."

Before I could object to the end of our nonexistent relationship, he slipped inside, the door closing with a click behind him. For a moment, I considered going after him, to keep up the pursuit. But breaking down his wall was already turning out to be more difficult than I had initially thought. I guess he just liked being closed off—keeping others at a comfortable distance. And I wasn't one to work too hard at anything. So, I decided to chalk the attempt up to a loss and forget about the whole thing. Was I still curious about the stories? Sure. And I really did believe we could be close friends. But he didn't think so, so what could I do but shrug and drink away the whole ordeal that night at the party I had known was going on.

I swam through the same drunk montage as always, start-ing with a shot of whiskey. Then two, then three. A solo cup of beer to sip on through the idle chitchat. Then ten more in a lost game of beer pong. A shot with him, a shot with her, a shot with a group of them who called out my name, knowing I wouldn't refuse. The count ended somewhere after that, but the drinking didn't. I smoked through a pack of ciga-rettes. I got into a friendly fight with someone over politics. I might've even done a keg stand. Things got blurry.

But still, I couldn't shake him from my mind. All night I talked myself in circles about him to anyone who would listen—which was mostly unlucky women who thought I was cute and approached me to flirt.

"What did he mean we don't have anything in common? He doesn't know me! I don't know him either, like *at all*. But isn't that the point? You get close to someone, and you learn all their stories. I got stories. Maybe I'll write them down one day. And I won't share them with him! I'll just let the rain wash them away. How about that?" I raised my finger knowingly as if I had just made a groundbreaking point that would blow away whoever had ended up on the sullied brown couch with me.

But when I looked to my left and my right, I realized I was alone. The only one around was a stoner guy with long, shaggy hair standing in front of me with his arms crossed.

"Look, man," he said, "I don't know about all that, but you gotta leave. It's 6 a.m., dude. The sun's coming up."

Now I noticed the entire house was empty. There were a few stragglers passed out on the floor, but other than that, it was only empty bottles and me.

"No one can hang these days," I slurred, standing up unsteadily. I bid the random stoner adieu and was off, wandering around the campus in the early morning light. There was a welcome chill to the air, and I longed for the comfort of his bed, safer than my own.

I considered just giving up—lying down in the grass and waiting until someone found me on their way to class. Maybe it'd be him. Maybe whoever it was would call the campus police. I didn't care. I was tired of being alone. An entire party of people and I had ended up on the couch all by myself, talking to no one. I wanted someone to hear me when I spoke. I wanted someone to listen.

Just then, I saw a shadow jogging steadily along the path leading into campus. I squinted my eyes to try and make out whether it was him—believing no one else would be up running so early, but also aware that I was pretty drunk, with a pill or two thrown into the mix, so I could be imagining it. But it was definitely him—the slouch of his shoulders, the messy quaff of his hair. I began running to catch up.

He was fast, and even though I had a bit of drunk stamina stored up, I couldn't quite close the distance between us.

"Hey!" I yelled so he'd slow down. He glanced back at me, and surprise spread across his face.

"Levi?" He slowed enough for me to reach him but didn't stop running like I was hoping—my temples already beading sweat and my chest aching at the exertion.

"What makes you think we don't have anything in common?" I accused, the alcohol obliterating my filter and renewing my sense of determination for this chance at a real friendship. My muscles burned, and I felt a smoldering in my stomach like yearning.

"What?" He was caught off guard by my forwardness and probably also at the general sight of my wasted running form.

"I think we could be close *friends*." I tried to state it confidently but tripped over the tip of my shoe, nearly wiping out. I caught myself at the last second, but the scare mangled the word *friends* into incomprehensible mush. "Could you stop running for a second?" I begged.

He seemed to digest what I said, muddled as it was, but he shook his head and didn't stop. "I can't."

He pressed forward, and I had to give up, my legs on the verge of giving out. I bent over my knees, heaving in breaths, coughing my lungs up, and trying not to vomit other organs all over the pavement.

I could hear the stupid click of the dorm door closing.

What was his problem with me? As friendless as I felt sometimes, people generally liked me. I had never been outright rejected by someone. It only made me more desperate to convince him my friendship would be worth it.

As soon as I had my breath, I started running again, into his dorm building, his hall, and then bursting into his room.

"What the hell, Levi?" His shirt was off, and he was using it to wipe the sweat from his forehead. His running shoes were positioned neatly by the door, just as they had been on Sunday morning. He tossed the dirty shirt into the hamper where it belonged.

I reached into the hamper and pulled it back out, throwing it onto the spotless floor. "You have a place for everything. Don't you?"

"So what?" he said, both defensive and genuinely confused as to why that had come out of my mouth as an insult. "I don't like a mess." He picked the shirt right back up from the floor and threw it into the hamper again.

"And that's why you don't like me," I reasoned. There was no accusation in my voice, only curiosity as my mind performed a mental gymnastics high beam routine trying to solve the sporadic equation in front of me: Where x was him and y was me, and I couldn't figure out how to balance the two sides because I was much too drunk for math or acrobatics.

"I never said I didn't like you." He upturned my entire system of equations with that revelation, leaving me further from the answer than ever. Even though the statement was wrought with vulnerability, his physical presence remained unreadable. I could've roared with frustration. "I just think it would be a bad idea for us to get close."

Why? was the question I wanted to ask more than anything. But he turned away from me, and the word caught in my throat. I felt the same self-doubt as I had trudging across campus the morning after the storm. What was inherent in my character that convinced him so adamantly that he didn't want to know me? Was it the same thing that had always kept others at a distance? Why hadn't I figured it out before? There was a reason I was alone—there had to be. Something invisible but irrefutably off-putting, like the odor of unwashed sheets or a broken AC.

I hung my head, prepared to exit out of the open door and back to my own lonely room, dejected. But then, recognition flashed in my eyes. The door was still open. Last time, he'd shut me out completely. This time, I was in, and I was getting something out of him, vague as it was. He didn't *not* like me; it was the closeness that presented a problem for him and the idea of a mess.

The contorted thoughts of my intoxicated brain stuck the landing.

"You think my mess will become yours if we get close," I proposed my conclusion gently, but despite the softness of my voice, confidence surged through me. "But my question is, what's wrong with being a mess every once in a while? It seems you could stand to be a bit more messy." I turned my head to each compulsively clean corner of his room as Exhibit Type A.

He followed my gaze, crossing his arms uneasily. His shoulders hunched up in his insecurity, and I imagined it was a sign that he was just about ready to give in. His pursed lips twitched to one side in consideration. But then his eyes landed on me, my surely disheveled appearance, and the flicker of affectionate longing I caught was immediately snuffed out, leaving him blank.

"I've seen how easily it can get out of hand." His voice was brittle, his wall up and fortified. "I can't risk it."

"But isn't that what life's all about?" I chuckled, incredulous. Our perspectives were so different. But that was exactly what convinced me we needed each other. "Especially college! Taking risks, forming relationships, failing? It's messy, sure, but it can also be beautiful, and that's why we put ourselves through it."

Impassioned, I stepped toward him. He stepped back. I leaped forward to close the space between us and grabbed the sides of his face, impulsively but delicately, trying to shake loose the foundation that had closed him off to the exquisite disorder of humanity and me among them. His eyes were wide, his body tense, but he didn't yell at me or try to break away.

So I took the opportunity, and I quoted Allen Ginsberg in his face. I had read it before the party, not once but twenty times, mesmerized by the love and the suffering and the kinship wrought in its story and the words, they stuck with me.

Especially the end—what I recited to him: where imaginary walls collapse.

I stopped shaking him then, and there was a short lull where the only sound in the room was the subtle whistle of his nose with each breath in. I believed I could see that glimmer of affection return at that moment, spreading pink across his pale cheeks, into my palms, down my arms, into me.

I thought he would comment on the poem, but he took one more deep breath in and said instead, "Your hands smell like cigarettes."

"Let me in." I fought one last time. "It'll be fun. The most fun mess you've ever experienced."

Holding deep eye contact, and with a broad smile across my lips, I took one hand from his cheek and removed the shirt from the hamper, tossing it on the ground once again.

I could see him cracking, the left corner of his mouth turning up in an act of mutiny. I took that as him wanting to open up to me. But his eyes were scanning my face dubiously—his agoraphobic brain no doubt preparing to shut me out. But my sweaty palms were still pressed warm against his cheeks, my fingertips brushing the wisps of his hair, causing his confliction.

So where he ended up was somewhere in the middle, balancing precariously between letting me in and shutting himself off, which took the physical form of his face softening but his "All right," coming out stiff.

But I refused to let go until I got a more definitive answer that I had won him over. "We can be friends then?" I double-checked.

"Yeah, we can be friends," he said, a little more sure. He nodded in reassurance for both of us.

I laughed, planting a sloppy, wet kiss on the center of his forehead before finally releasing him. He fell back on the bed and wiped away my spit, pretending to be disgusted. But I saw a slight ease in his shoulders, which counteracted whatever wariness I could still hear in his voice. I knew I wasn't completely behind his wall. Not even close. But the door was open to me. After that morning, I just walked right in.

4

A FUNERAL

———

Charlie didn't cry at his mom's funeral. But not because he was a ten-year-old boy who believed himself too tough for tears. He had shed plenty at the last funeral he'd been to: same tacky glossed wood of the hosting funeral home; same depressing bundles of wilting lilies; same black suit, although the jacket had gotten tight in two years and the pants no longer hit his ankle.

The only difference was the body in the casket.

He could only see the very tips of her nose and lips unbreathing from his place in the front pew, and still, his eyes were dry.

His dad's girlfriend, on the other hand, was crying uncontrollably. His dad told him it was the hormones and not to say anything because it would only upset her more, which wasn't good for the baby. Charlie hadn't even brought it up in the first place. But he guessed his dad was uncomfortable by the whole thing because, after all, it was his wife's funeral they were attending.

So Charlie didn't say a word. But then, he never did say much.

He was especially quiet after his mom had been admitted to the mental health facility three months ago. She had been the one crying on the car ride there, begging his dad to take her back to their home, to her bed.

"I'm not allowed to be sad?" she asked helplessly, head resting against the passenger-side window. His dad had plucked her right out of bed, so she was still in her pajamas, her hair mussed in the back. Charlie had a few vague memories of her in long floral skirts, soft sweaters, necklaces bulky with jewels, and deep red lipstick. Those memories were warm. But what she wore on that car ride was more familiar to Charlie. It was the uniform of her endless days in bed; it was the compliment to her quivering lip and empty stare; it was the chill Charlie knew much better than the warmth.

His dad didn't respond. He kept his hardened stare on the cracks in the road ahead.

"You're just trying to get rid of me." She sniffled.

From the backseat, Charlie couldn't see the tears streaking her face, but he could hear the thickness of her sorrow. And the weight of her pain was evident as he watched her robed shoulders wilt.

When he finally saw her face—after his dad was finished filling out the paperwork and they were preparing to leave her in the hospital—she was pale like a corpse, and her eyes were already dead.

In the coffin, her eyes were closed. He stood over her and experienced the same numb sense of absence he had felt leaving her behind that day, only amplified. Someone had attempted to make her the mom he could only vaguely remember. She was in a red turtleneck dress that matched the shade on her lips. They were trying to hide something behind a wall of makeup. But Charlie could see the truth he had known since her first stint in a mental ward—when he was three, and his brother had tried his best to explain her depression in simple terms: like when your head goes under the water in the bathtub. It was written in the dark circles around her eyes, the way her cheeks sagged over her fragile bones, and the blue veins scrawled across her paper skin.

Charlie tugged at his tie. He felt like he was being strangled. His mom looked like she was being strangled, her head propped up on a stand, her neck encased in red wool. He wanted to pull down the turtleneck so she could breathe, but he knew there was a thick red mark running beneath. And anyway, she wasn't breathing.

She had not been able to breathe for a long time, according to her. She described it as drowning, an ocean of choppy waves swallowing her whole, encasing her body in a dark blue, descending.

At first, Charlie didn't understand what that meant. He had never been to the ocean, and so his brother's description made a little more sense to him. But in both cases, he had a hard time imagining how it was possible to stop breathing when the entire space between the grass and the blue sky was full of air, not water. But then he had discovered that sometimes your air is taken away. You don't always have a choice.

He watched as his mom was lowered into the ground, and his breath was stolen. He couldn't breathe, and he couldn't cry. Beside him, his dad's girlfriend wept. And beside her, his dad had that hardened stare of his fixed on the hole in the ground. He was already burying her, just like he buried everything else.

Like at the reception, when he drank glasses upon glasses of whiskey. Charlie knew this was another way to drown. There was plenty of food slopped into tin trays on the battered folding tables lined against the wood-paneled wall of the funeral parlor: congealed pasta dishes, little cheeses stacked on stale crackers, and soggy fruit bowls. But his dad stayed by the bar, cradling his drink like a precious child.

Charlie didn't go for the spread either, and not just because it was so unappealing—especially seeing the crumbs that missed the paper plates and ended up ground into the Berber carpet by the various dress shoes.

Even more than at the burial, Charlie found it difficult to breathe watching his dad drink at the bar and his dad's girlfriend snivel on the shabby burgundy sofa in the center of the room.

So he slipped out undetected and retreated to the stairwell. The black leather dress shoes that were pinching his feet echoed off the unpainted walls as he descended, but once he had crawled beneath the steps where they ended in the basement, it became a quiet place to hide. It was dingy and freezing, with blackened pieces of chewing gum imprinted into the icy concrete floor. But Charlie preferred this stripped-back space to the gaudy décor upstairs. The air felt less heavy.

He completely undid his tie and took his journal out of the back of his pants, where he had hidden it while getting dressed in his too-small suit that morning. His dad had told him he couldn't bring it: "I'm not going to have you distracted by that thing all day. I want you present for her."

But who was his dad to talk about being present, especially when it came to her?

And what he didn't realize was the writing helped Charlie breathe. It helped him cope with what was happening—helped him understand it. The words were painful to form, but afterward, he was always reminded to look up instead of down. So, Charlie had actively disobeyed his dad, even though the number of times he'd done so fit neatly onto one hand.

He reached into his right pant pocket with a fistful of defiance and found that his pen had leaked everywhere. The lining of the pocket was stained. He imagined his skin beneath was awash with blue.

He could already hear his dad yelling. Charlie had ignored him, and now there was a mess that couldn't be cleaned up simply. And even though the suit was too small anyway, it had cost a small fortune, and Charlie had been expected to wear it more than twice.

Even though his dad's anger would be justified, Charlie still resented it. And he resented the stain even more. Though not immediately visible, it would always be there, and Charlie knew it would affect how he felt at all significant future events—good or bad.

He took a page from his dad's book and buried the anger burning up from his right thigh. He refocused his emotion onto the pages of his journal, and that's where he stayed for the entirety of his mom's funeral reception.

His dad found him there a few hours later. His words were thick and reeked of alcohol, but they weren't angry like Charlie expected. His usual steely gaze was soft and blurry, grazing gently over the forbidden journal.

"I suspected this was what you were doing." He wavered on his feet and, with a slight delay, decided to plop down on the floor beside Charlie, whose entire right side stiffened like a wall against him.

His dad didn't notice the change in his body language, and similarly, didn't spot the soiled suit pocket. His drunkenness fixed upon the full pages resting in Charlie's lap.

"What do you write about?" his dad asked, a hint of his natural anger slipping into the question from his desperation to know.

Usually, Charlie didn't like to share. He used to show his brother sometimes, but now, he thought the stories were his burden to carry alone. But today, he wanted his dad to bear some of the weight.

He was writing a story about his mom, Charlie told him. A memory.

He was seven, and she was in the kitchen smiling so widely it was almost inconceivable, considering how little she smiled during the course of her motherhood.

She was at the stove, cooking up pancakes. Besides the bag of semisweet chocolate chips next to her, spilling out, the countertops were unusually clean—the garbage bin full of unwanted mail and the dishes washed and stacked in their proper cabinets. She chose each chip carefully and crafted an army of smiles in a stack of pancakes. He watched her from behind: her sunflower skirt flowing as she moved between the stack and the stove, the bangles on her wrists clanking with each flick of the spatula, the rare presence of a glint in her eyes foretelling an unexpected warmth. He didn't know whether to trust it. Part of him felt wary of her smile.

He had woken up to it that morning, her hand shaking him gently awake, asking if he wanted smiley-face pancakes for breakfast. His first thought was that something was wrong if she was out of bed and dressed. But she held his hand to the kitchen, poured him a glass of orange juice, and started cooking as if it were an everyday routine. He let himself believe it might be. He abandoned his doubt and prepared himself to devour the joy.

"Get 'em while they're hot," his mom sing-songed cheerfully. She set the stack down on the table and sat beside him, taking a single smile for herself. He took four, greedy for them. Starving.

But he didn't dig in right away. He took a moment to study each of the pancakes' distinct smiles.

The largest one had a number of burns that encircled its smile like frown lines. It was as if its smile was conditional. There was anger bubbling beneath the surface, the uncooked interior soggy inside the thick pancake. He knew as soon as he sliced through the tough exterior, the wet batter would leak out onto the plate.

There was a pancake with a smile that felt artificial. The chocolate chip eyes were dull, and the edges were pale. Drowned in syrup, he might forget that this pancake had been neglected in its time on the stove, but the taste of its faults would linger on his tongue.

One of the pancakes was thin and fragile. It already had a few cracks, and its smile would break easily. It was trying hard to hold onto its warmth, but the cracks allowed the steam to escape, and he could already see how it was getting cold.

There was one pancake smile that was unfamiliar. Yet, it was the only smile he wanted to save. He didn't know if he could. He was starving.

He drowned them all in syrup and began to eat. She nibbled on her pancake beside him, oblivious to the way he was observing her in his peripheral while he chewed, still expecting the worst.

He had made it all the way to his third pancake when he decided to just ask. "Mom, why are you so happy today?"

She put her fork down, having made it through only a couple of bites. "Is there something wrong with that?"

"No…" he stabbed one of his fork prongs into a chocolate chip, "it's just you're usually sad." He pulled the fork back and found the silver clouded with brown. He looked up at her, and her face had emptied to its normal, dulled shade.

"Did I not make you a whole plate of smiles?" she said through gritted teeth. With her demeanor, the room had drained of the stove's heat and was now icy cold. He stared at the mess of pancake remains on his plate.

"Yes," he mumbled. "I just want to know if you'll make them again." He knew her happiness was wearing thin. He wanted to hug her. He wanted her to hold him. He wanted to be a warm pancake on the stovetop, smiling. He felt his ears burning. "Is it my fault you're sad?"

"Why would you ask that?" Her lip quivered.

"I'm sorry," he backtracked quickly, feeling the beautiful morning spiraling out of his grasp. "Let's just enjoy breakfast."

She shook her head, wordless. She stood up, abandoning what was left on her plate, and grabbed a pack of cigarettes from the counter. She went out to the porch to smoke.

As soon as she closed the sliding glass door, the apartment felt thick with absence. He watched her from his lonely seat at the table and tried to breathe. It was a familiar feeling. He shouldn't have expected any different.

When his mom came in from the porch, she shut herself into the bedroom. He wandered outside and found her cigarette, still smoldering. Curious, he picked it up and gave it a sniff. The smell was almost comforting. And there was a ring of her red lipstick around the end. He put his lips in the same place, maybe hoping it would feel like a kiss. He breathed in as if it were air.

Fire filled his lungs, and he threw the cigarette away, choking. He coughed so violently the pancake smiles came back up and all over the ground. He sat back and stared at the mess he had made.

———

Charlie's dad looked up from the blue ink when he had finished reading.

"That's not you in the memory. Is it?"

"No," Charlie said, self-consciously. Generally, he did try to write about himself, but he had wanted a warm story of his mom, and he couldn't recall any of his own in enough detail. But he remembered vividly when his brother had told him that story, at the stove making pancakes for three-year-old Charlie after that first time she was put away.

His dad closed the notebook and set it down on the concrete between them.

"She made them for me too," he whispered, falling into his own memory. "Before we had your brother. When we were young. In love. When she was happy."

He wallowed in the glow of his nostalgia only momentarily, pressing it back down with a manly grunt. "I know it's tough right now, Charlie, but we're going to have to find a way to move on." He placed his large, calloused hand on top of Charlie's, speckled in blue from his furious writing.

Moving on was easier for his dad. He already had both of them buried and replaced. What he was really saying was that Charlie had to paste on a smile if he didn't want to get left behind when the new baby came. He knew it would probably happen anyway. He was always getting left behind. This second funeral was proof.

As were the pages of his journal, still so full of stories he didn't understand, even now that he was older. Why so much absence? And whose fault was it?

His brother had asked their mom if it was his fault. But now that they were both gone, it was clear it couldn't be either of theirs. That left only one option.

Charlie ripped his hand from beneath his dad's and brought it close to his chest, sure not to breathe in because he knew it would smell like nicotine, and he didn't want to start associating that with loss or his dad.

At first, his dad's drunk eyes were big and watery—so much like his mom's—but he blinked that emotion away harshly, and the anger Charlie had expected all along surfaced. "Just put that stupid journal away and come join the party. Okay?"

His dad pushed himself off of the ground and stormed up the stairs, the sharp echo of his shoes flooding down and drowning Charlie in his loneliness.

He picked up his journal once the silence settled again and skimmed through the story, convinced he now understood the catalyst for every stain in their family history. He shoved the journal back in his pants and the pen in his ruined pocket and followed after his dad. He didn't consider that there had been a fourth pancake left on his brother's plate.

5

A PARTY

"C'mon, all you ever do is write and look serious. Let loose for a night!"

I was sitting crisscross on his perfectly made bed with my shoes off, trying to convince him to join me at a party. We were a few Fridays into our friendship, and he hadn't tagged along to a single one. Every weekend I begged him for at least an hour, working a number of different angles—anything I thought would win him over. I told him that most of the parties were essentially just large book club meetings, with lively but civil debates and a glass or two of red wine at most. I told him I was actually going to the parties to scout members for the literary movement I was planning and needed his help finding the next Beat Generation. I told him the party scene exclusively consisted of big-breasted intellectuals who would ride him while simultaneously giving him tips on how to market his writing.

The truth was much simpler, but I couldn't tell him directly because it was embarrassing: I was thrilled to have him as my friend. In the weeks since he had agreed to the friendship, we had spent almost all our time together. He wasn't a big talker, but that was perfect because I was, and he was a great listener. He made me feel heard, always chiming in to my rants at the perfect moment with a counterpoint that made me rethink everything in the best way. I would talk his ear off late into the night and end up passing out in his bed. The next day I would wake to his calming presence. I never felt alone when I was with him.

The only time I ever felt lonely anymore was at the parties, which was why I wanted him to come with me. I wanted to show him my world. I wanted him to be a part of it. And I wanted to show him off to that world—like *yes, I have a best friend who's smart and fun and cares about getting me home safe at the end of the night. Look at me.* Plus, I thought I was a better version of myself at parties, and I wanted him to see that.

But I hadn't been able to convince him yet. Every Friday, I ended up leaving the room on my own. I would return hours later, completely wasted, and he'd be in the exact same position.

He was in that position now: hunched over his desk, writing and looking serious under the dim light of his lamp. He didn't respond—didn't even shake his head. I guessed he figured he had told me *no* enough times. Clearly, he didn't know me well enough yet because I wouldn't give up on the idea until I got my way. And I had already popped an upper, so I wasn't going to leave the room without him this time.

"I need an accomplishment to hang my hat on." I shifted onto my stomach and held my chin with my fists, looking up at the shadowed side of his face. The blinds were open, but the sky outside was rapidly darkening, and he rarely turned on any of the dorm room's lights aside from the dinky desk lamp. "You'll make a name for yourself with your writing.

No doubt. I'll just be pumping gas and drinking myself to death. So you gotta let me have this." I paused but still got no reaction. "Let me take you to your first party. And you can write a best seller about it later."

"I've been to a party before," he said into his journal.

"What?" I popped up off the bed and spun him around in his chair so he couldn't ignore me in his journal pages anymore. "So it's just your best friend you refuse to party with?"

"Pretty much." He gave enough of a subtle grin for me to know he was being sarcastic before spinning back around in his chair to return to his writing.

I laughed, taking a step back. I scanned the room as if there were clues to be found regarding the scope of his party experience. One party? A few? Did he have a secret past full of alcohol, drugs, and debauchery? The obsessively tidy room around me screamed, *Impossible!* But then again, the compulsive way he made sure to keep the already well-worn carpet stain free could say something about why he preferred writing at home alone to getting wasted with me in a room full of strange people.

I sat down on that carpet, staring up at the back of his head. His ashy brown hair was cut neat on the sides. The top was messier, but it was hard to see from my angle. His head was down. His broad shoulders sagged. I studied him to see if something in his posture would reveal what he was clearly holding back. Because he let me talk so freely, I was realizing, I hadn't really learned anything about him. I told him all about me: like that I'd grown up in the area and was an only child. And my dad was in jail so my mom and I were super close, but I hated her latest boyfriend. He had even met the two of them at a number of *"family"* dinners and afterward, let me rant about the dirty hippie for hours. But he hadn't once mentioned his family or anything about his past.

So, I had to figure this one out blind. Maybe if I got him drunk, I could squeeze something more out of him. But first, there was the matter of getting him to the party.

And now that I knew he wasn't a party virgin, I would need to change my tactic.

"Look." I pulled out a joint and a lighter from my pocket. "I'm gonna party either way." He didn't turn around to see that my threat was serious. So I lit the joint, leaning back on my elbows. He caught a waft of the weed smell, and he finally spun around in his chair to look at me. I grinned, taking another pull. "So we can either go to the party together, or I can bring the party to you. I'm talking getting absolutely wrecked. It's not going to be pretty. Pills, pussy, probably puke. I've been known to go a little overboard at a party. And let me tell you, I'm not great at making it to the bathroom when I'm drunk."

I dangled the joint from my lip as he weighed the pros and cons in his head. He glanced up at the ceiling and sighed.

"Fine." He said it in the same mostly emotionless, yet slightly conflicted tone with which he had first accepted my friendship.

I cheered for my hard-fought victory anyway because it was very much a fight for me too. I jumped up and wrapped my arm around him, pulling him from the chair and positioning us side by side. He stiffened at my touch. I offered him the joint, but he shook his head. And we were off in the night.

I liked our friendship most when we were walking around campus together. Sometimes it was to get someplace—like the party I was leading us to that night—but sometimes, we just walked around aimlessly. I had a lot of energy, and he just liked the fresh air, so we'd go for walks. I'd talk, of course. He'd look at the ground, trying not to crack a smile and reveal he actually enjoyed my company.

What I really liked about walking with him was the way our gaits were so different from each other, yet, our steps always fell into the same rhythm. His walk was straight and consistent. One step at a time. He would press his hands deep into the pockets of his favorite army green jacket and put his head down, focused on the red brick of the St. John's pathways. I was more sporadic in my movements, charging forward or drifting back, sometimes walking circles around him with my hands out to balance myself. I also preferred to look up at the clouds or stars, but sometimes I just focused on him. Something about the sharpness of his jawline against his otherwise soft features intrigued me. Whenever I caught myself in his curious trance, usually while I was puffing on a cigarette, I'd have to muss up his hair. Or I'd wrap my arm around him because it made him tense up, reminding me that there *was* something messy about him. He was just good at hiding it.

"Compare and contrast me with parties," I challenged him. We were walking along the long diagonal path that shot toward the edge of campus, where the safety lights ended, and the city opened up. It was a balmy night, with a gentle pre-autumn breeze rustling through the leaves of trees holding desperately onto the last of their summer green. I hurried up ahead of him and began to walk backward so I could face him full on when he gave his answer. I wanted him to give it to me straight.

"A party is never self-conscious. Parties are the one place where people have the confidence to be fearless." He paused, bit his lip, lifted his head to look at me. "You're fearless all the time." He quickly shifted his eyes back to the ground, embarrassed. "But a party can easily get out of hand, and sometimes, people get hurt. You know how to control yourself. You're just doing it for fun, not trying to hurt anyone." He didn't seem so sure about the last part. It came out more like a wish than a fact. But I grasped onto it anyway, pocketing this rare expression of affection from him.

"You're like the end of the night," I returned, "when it's gotten quieter, but you're warm with the impressions the party has left on you and the drifting buzz of your drunkenness." I hummed at the pleasant thought of it. "That part… even though there are less people around, it doesn't feel as lonely. It's my favorite part."

I had fallen back beside him, our steps lining up.

"This night will end like that?" He looked at me, anticipation creeping into his voice, whether of fear or elation, I couldn't tell. "You think?"

"Most definitely," I reassured, trying to play into both possible sides of his expectation. "Don't you know you're riding along with the master of a good time?" I slung my arm around him, and when he tensed up, I smiled to myself. We were so different. We were just right.

The ancient brick of the historic East Coast buildings and the lush oak trees both absorbed sound, so we didn't hear the party until we were on the lawn of a house that spilled drunk college kids from every orifice.

I glanced over at him before we entered, trying to detect some sort of emotion leaking from his walls. He didn't look nervous like I might have expected if a bad experience was what had sworn him off of parties. But he didn't look excited either like he was secretly happy I had dragged him along. That hint of vague anticipation from earlier was gone. His face was stone, impenetrable. I couldn't tell if he was pushing the emotions so far down they struggled to surface or if they just weren't there at all. Both possibilities concerned me.

But not enough to suppress the pill I had popped, which was really kicking in at that point, and the party calling out to me. I led us forward.

Inside, the colonial-style wood floors were crowded with dirty sneakers attached to drunken legs. The living room was thick with bodies, pressed against each other under the dim yellow lighting cast through elegant stained-glass light fixtures. Everything about the party atmosphere contradicted the poise of the space. Next to the red brick of a grand wood-burning fireplace, a frat boy was doing a keg stand. Against the twisting mahogany banister that led up the stairs, stood a couple about as close to having sex as two could get with their clothes still on. On the granite countertop of a wide kitchen pass-through, a group of five raced to shotgun their beers. I was eager to become a part of the contradiction.

I turned back to him. His face had twisted into some semblance of a reaction, but I couldn't make it out in the murky lighting, with shadowed bodies swimming in my peripheral and in my increasingly impaired state. Whatever it was he felt, a drink would help him out.

I waved us ahead, pushing through the sea of people to the kitchen, to join in on the shot-gunning. Only, by the time I had finished my beer and poured a whiskey into a red solo cup, I realized he hadn't followed me. I did a 360, but the blurry faces of the people around me were all strangers.

That familiar feeling of loneliness started to bubble up from my chest, and I swallowed it down with my whiskey, not missing a beat as I immediately poured another one. And when I looked up from the bottle, there was a beautiful blonde running her manicured nail up and down my arm, pushing her shoulders back, so her boobs jutted out of her low-cut top. Before I knew it, we were the couple making out against the banister.

It was only when I paused our kiss to suggest we find a room that I remembered him, who I hadn't seen since we walked through the front door.

I felt suddenly desperate to find him, to know he was fairing okay in my world—which could be known to eat up unsuspecting victims like a Venus flytrap. I stood on my toes to look over her head at the bustling room, and despite the sheer number of bodies packed into the tight space, I found him easily, sitting on the windowsill seat of the huge front window. He was talking to a brunette who was looking at him with the same intrigued gaze I always found myself falling into.

There was also a desire there, the same desire my blonde— who hadn't given me her name—had for me, as she whispered, "Let's find a room," sensually in my ear. I grinned at her, but my eyes drifted back to him. I was curious to know how that conversation was going. Just like I had no clue about his experience with parties, I couldn't even guess what his experience was in the way of sex. He was a very introverted person, but he wasn't awkward in any way. He had a quiet confidence about him I could definitely see attracting a lot of girls.

The brunette he was talking to was clearly under that spell. She had her hand placed near his thigh, and she edged it slowly closer to him. She was leaning in, staring at his lips as he spoke. But he was acting oblivious to all of these signs.

"Um, hello?" My blonde waved her hand in front of my face.

"I think my best friend is about to get laid." I pointed to him.

She turned in that direction for a moment without really even looking and then came back to me. "So were you."

"No, but he's like, really reserved, you know?" I tried to explain. On the windowsill, he was edging away from the brunette's encroaching hand.

"Like he's a virgin?" Now she turned around to really study him.

"I'm not sure," I said shortly, insecure.

She scrunched her nose derisively. "You're best friends, and you don't know?"

My extended neck buckled, and my chin fell, a vexed puff of air escaping my lips. Her words stung, but I didn't want to linger in them and my own self-doubt. So I threw out the excuse, "He's quiet. I already told you," waving her off and refocusing my gaze on him.

The brunette had finally made the move to just outright place her hand on his knee, and I could see from all the way on the other side of the house how he stiffened—even more so than under my touch. Without thinking, I started to move toward them.

My blonde followed me. "Are we going to hook up or what?" We were weaving through the crowd to get to a place where I could eavesdrop on his conversation, but he wouldn't notice me.

"Yeah," I nodded. "Just let me listen in for a couple of minutes. We have all night."

She didn't look too sure, but she followed me anyway.

We stopped next to the green velvet couch, which I imagined by the end of the night would be covered with various stains. It was too good for this place—not the house, which matched its dignity, but the party, a total slob show.

I positioned my blonde strategically in front of me and then peeked past her to continue watching the interaction. I had to strain my ears from the subtle distance we had chosen, but I could just make out their voices.

"… not very creative myself," she was saying. "A major in physiology just means memorizing facts that have already been discovered. I can't fathom creating something from nothing. Where do you get your ideas?" Her eyes were bright, attentively waiting for his answer. Her hand was still resting on his knee, and she had begun to gently move her pointer finger back and forth seductively.

He either didn't realize what her body language meant, or he didn't care. Nothing about the way he sat or looked at her indicated any interest. It was actually the exact opposite. The more interest she showed in him, the more he looked like he wanted to escape.

He shifted uncomfortably in his seat but forced his voice flat and emotionless to respond. "I guess I usually write about my own experiences." He cleared his throat and rubbed nervously at his temple.

"I'd love to read your work sometime, get to know you better," she said innocently.

But I could see the way her words tightened every muscle in his body. His brick wall, fortified. His soft features went rigid, and he pushed himself back abruptly so that her hand fell limply off his knee.

"I need to refill my drink," he said suddenly. "I'll be right back."

He stood up and walked away, camouflaging himself from her in the crowd. He swept right past me and my blonde, but he was so determined to escape her probing he didn't even notice us.

"Well, he really missed an easy opportunity there." My blonde brushed off the situation. She took a play from the brunette and grazed her hand across my upper thigh. "Now can we find a room?"

"Just a sec." I spun around and did another scan of the room to find him and make sure he was all right. He was weaving through the drunk bodies, trying to make it for the break of people in the front hall. But apparently, I wasn't the only one following him because just as he reached the doors to the room, I saw the brunette in his pursuit.

I grabbed my blonde by the arm and dragged her down the same path he had taken so that once again, we were close enough to make out their conversation, but our spying wasn't apparent to him.

"Wait." The brunette placed her fingers delicately around his forearm, but it was like she had handcuffed him with the way he stopped cold. She released her grip immediately, having caught on to his touch aversion from their previous interaction, and took a step back, pausing to let him turn around. "Look, I'm sorry if I gave you the wrong impression back there, getting all personal. Your quietness—I guess I mistook it for sensitivity."

"It's all right," he muttered sheepishly.

"I just wanted to let you know, I don't need something serious. I'm fine with meaningless if that's what you prefer. I just think you're cute is all." She had her hands twisted innocently behind her back, but she leaned boldly toward him.

He didn't say anything to that although he seemed to be considering, and she took the opportunity to lean up and place a slightly cautious but still sensual kiss on his lips.

She pulled back to give him a chance to respond, and he did so by pressing her up against the wall—a little roughly, which surprised me from him—and returning her kiss.

They got pretty into it, but he tore away momentarily to double check, "Nothing serious?"

She nodded and took his hand, leading him up the staircase.

I turned to my blonde, my eyebrows high and mouth open in elation at what I had just witnessed. I had been so lost in their conversation that I was actually a bit startled to find her still beside me. She was there but looked right on the verge of giving up on me: her arms crossed, her toe tapping impatiently. She was definitely not as excited for him as I was.

"Why are you so invested in him?" she questioned. "It's weird."

"He's my best friend." I shrugged, not understanding what she found strange. As far as I understood it, friends were supposed to be invested in each other. That included rooting for them to get laid and extended all the way to knowing them intimately—which I felt like I had taken the first steps in tonight.

"Whatever. Are we gonna have sex?" Her arms were still crossed. I wrapped my hands around her popped hip and fell into her neck, sucking on it sloppily until she had loosened up and was giggling. Now that he was fully integrated into my world, I could focus on her. We moved our way down the hall and found our own room.

6

PANCAKES

———

I slipped my arms behind my head and sighed back into the soft ridges of the unfamiliar mattress, completely at ease and contented with the night's events. I had a beautiful woman whose bare skin, warm and damp from an after-sex glow, was draped across my own clammy chest, expelling short breaths of satisfaction. My state of intoxication had drifted into a pleasant, drowsy buzz that left my limbs warm and my eyes heavy. In another room, my best friend was likely in a similar position. I imagined later we would talk about it all in his dorm room like two gossiping schoolgirls, finally arriving at a closeness I had long desired between us.

I was ready to expedite that process.

"Are you good if we go find my friend and his girl, maybe get a bite to eat?" I proposed, sitting up gently so that she slid off my body. I pulled my ratty T-shirt over my head, looking back at her for an answer once I'd broken through the head hole.

"Sure." She shrugged, rolling over and beginning to collect her own clothes.

By the time we came out of the room, the party had slimmed, but those who were left were still going strong. There were plumes of smoke rising from a bong being passed around the green velvet couch. There was a series of make-out sessions draped along the deep auburn rug that ascended the staircase. There was a wildcard in a yellow suit drawing sharpie dicks on the cheeks of the lightweights, passed out on the hard wood among a slew of abandoned solo cups.

I took two pills out of my pocket and popped them into my mouth, pressing one past her lips with my tongue and swallowing the other for myself.

We began making out again. I cupped her hips, and she snaked her hand down my stomach. But just as I was about to push her back into the room for round two, forgetting momentarily my mission to find him, he came rushing up to us through the front door.

"Levi, I think we should head out." His voice was shaky, and he was looking around nervously.

He had read my mind, or I had read his. I turned to him with a grin, slapping a celebratory hand on his back. "What happened to that brunette you were with? We were thinking we'd all get out of here together."

He shook his head, ignoring me. "I was out getting some air, and I saw this guy, arms like trucks…" He was trying to find a way to elaborate, but the explanation was getting caught on the back of his teeth. He looked disgusted by the taste of it on his tongue. "I don't know. I just got a bad feeling about him. I think we should leave."

"Woah, why are you so freaked, man? It's been a great night. No need to worry." I slipped my arm up around his shoulder, which was already tense prior to my touch. My other hand was around my blonde's waist. "We'll get outta here. Just track down your girl, and I'll snag you a drink for the road to calm your nerves." His palpable fear couldn't stifle my own feelings of invincibility. In fact, it only worked to validate my notion that I truly understood him now. Plus, I was rising on an amphetamine wave, self-assured in the fact that I had a hot woman to my left and a best friend to my right. The world was in balance although the room was a bit spinny.

And it was that vague dizziness that had me dropping like a stone at the bottom of a lake when the truck-armed man he had been talking about stormed up to the three of us. He was a massive dude with football lineman shoulders and seriously monstrous arms. I'm talking arms that were eighteen-wheeler big; arms that bulged his moss-tinted skin, Frankenstein-like in their monstrosity. So I guess that was another reason I went down so hard when he punched me square in the face.

My blonde cried out, but she didn't drop to my side. Instead, she stepped toward Truck Arms. "What are you doing here?" she asked, although her tone indicated she wasn't actually surprised.

"What are *you* doing here with this fag?" Truck Arms spat, the intolerance bubbling up from the back of his throat, collecting in the saliva at the corners of his thin, villainous lips.

"You punched me because you think I'm gay?" I surmised from the hazy context clues. My mouth hung in disbelief as I tried to push myself up so I could beat the living homophobia out of him. But my head was thick from the impact of his fist, and standing was proving difficult. It felt like I'd been in a car crash, punch-drunk and sitting in the wreckage of the accident. I could feel snot, or maybe blood, running from my throbbing nose. I blinked hard against the yellow lights that were suddenly blinding, blending all the bodies above me into a smear of shadow.

Except for him. He was the one thing permeating my focus in the smudged scene. His back was pressed rigidly up against the wall. In his eyes, a terrified and childlike helplessness oscillated between me, lying on the ground in disarray, and Truck Arms, who had one of his meaty hands extended possessively toward my blonde.

"We broke up. I'm just having a good time," she was saying to the terrible truck of a man, her arms crossed objectively, but her stance open, toes pointed toward him.

"You're such a little slut." He lunged at her and grabbed harshly at her wrist.

I had made it slowly to my knees by then, but at the back-to-back bigotry—first homophobic, now sexist—I found a burst of energy to make it to my feet. I grabbed his bicep, my spindly fingers not even wrapping around half of the bulging thing, and tried to pull him off of her. My force didn't budge him, but my nuisance caused him to turn his full attention to me.

He yanked me by the throat, slamming me against the wall hard enough to shift the fancy gold frames hanging there. They continued to totter as he pummeled his right fist into my left cheek and then into my gut with a thump. My mouth was sticky with blood. I could feel it sliding down the back of my throat—where I'm sure a red imprint of his hand was making itself present beneath his clasp. He looked grossly satisfied as he wound up for a final blow.

Off to the side of my blackening peripheral, I caught a flash of his army green jacket, and I could just make out the terrified shape of him, his forlorn shoulders sagging. His eyes seemed caught in a distant horror, like a violent flashback assaulting him. Despite the fact that I was the one getting the shit beat out of me, I felt worse for him. I had absolutely no clue why he was so distressed, but I wanted nothing more than to make him feel safe, even though I was the one who had dragged him into this mess of a night in the first place.

So I gave him the stupidest smile I could—hoping to indicate something like, *I know this is nuts, but I appreciate you being here with me*—and a shrug. Then, I turned back to Truck Arms, closed my eyes, and lifted my chin to the sky, surrendering to what I had coming.

I expected to feel an impact and then wake up on the ground. But I opened my eyes and saw his green coat standing like a wall between Truck Arms and me. His shoulders were back in an unprecedented confidence, and he had his own strong hands on those monstrous arms. He was saying something to him. From the duet of a high-frequency ringing and the low drumbeat of my heart in my ears, I couldn't make out exactly what he said. I thought I could read "kill" and "love" off of his lips, but then again, my vision was screwy.

But whatever it was he said, it worked. Truck Arms looked confused, but he put his hands up in defeat and backed off. He took one more hungry look at me and a hateful glance at his blonde. Then, he just turned and walked right out of the house. His blonde ran after him.

And it was only then I realized the room had become silent. Every single eye—the bong crew, the staircase lovers, the yellow suit—was absorbed in our scene.

He seemed unaffected by the overwhelming attention as he slipped *his* arm over *my* shoulder.

"How about we get out of here?" he offered with a shaky sigh. But it wasn't of fear. Something had shifted in him. He seemed almost lighter, like the interaction with Truck Arms had somehow relieved him of whatever burden he had been carrying all this time in the pages of his journal. How the two things connected, though, I could not reasonably comprehend. One moment, he had been vulnerable as a child at the sight of those arms, and in the next, he had taken complete control over the spiraling situation. What had changed in that split second? And what was it that he had said to defuse the beating I had assumed inevitable?

"Well, what do you say, Levi?" he repeated since I hadn't responded. "Should we go get something to eat?"

Although the glaring mystery of him should have consumed my thoughts, I was still loaded, which meant the mention of food diverted my focus.

"Fuck yeah!" I smiled lazily, throwing my arm over his shoulder in return.

We circled over to the kitchen, where he got me some ice for my face and where I got myself another drink. With similar short attention spans to mine, the partygoers had returned to their previous drunken activities, but a few went out of their way to slap him on the back and congratulate him for standing up to *that asshole*. He had to fight to keep delight from spreading across his split lip—which I was just noticing.

"Shit, did he get you too?" I unthinkingly put my finger up to the bloody crack, and he winced. "Sorry," I pulled my hand back, feeling a twinge of regret.

"It's fine. It didn't hurt too bad." His head fell, and his gaze went momentarily faraway, his voice getting misty. "Nothing like what he did to you."

I paused, feeling guilty for having promised him a fun night and delivering him such a scare. He never let himself have fun. I thought *that*, at the very least, was what he could get out of our friendship since he had pushed so hard against it in the beginning. All I wanted was to see him smile. It was so rare.

I realized my eyes were on the ground, just like him, and I shook the guilt away, lifting myself up. I put on a fake gruff voice and flexed my arms downward to mock the faux hyper-masculinity we had just witnessed, grunting, "The bruises will just show the world what a man I am."

His chin lifted slightly, and the crack in his lip turned up into the tiniest grin. "Why don't you rub some dirt in it to really show them what you're packing?"

He punched me playfully in the arm, and I returned a couple of soft swings, keeping up the act, barking, "Fists can't penetrate me, neither can emotions," but it was hard to keep a straight face—he was smiling now too, fully—and we fell into each other, laughing.

I felt the ordeal of the party disappearing behind us as we broke out of the stuffy house into the open night. It was still warm, but a cool breeze helped release the drunken thickness clouding my head. The sky was wrought with bright stars, twinkling as if enlightened with an ultimate truth. But there was no moon, and so the weathered bricks beneath our feet were shrouded in the 4 a.m. blackness. He was looking down at them, his broken lip fixed in an appeased reflection.

I leaned sleepily on him as we headed back in the direction of campus.

"You like to look at clouds, but I don't ever see you looking at the night sky." I yawned.

"I've always thought it was too dark"—even though the sky was gleaming and it was his sightline that appeared hopeless—"but maybe I'll start." He turned his head, first to me, and then took a quick peek at the night sky, nodding. "Anyway, where do you want to go for food?"

"Breakfast is always good after a party."

So we changed our course for the twenty-four-hour diner a few blocks away. It was a classic run-down '60s café. Vinyl seating that stuck to your thighs in the summer and was worn from years of people scooting across the booths and children picking at the cushions. Marble tables marked by permanent syrup stains and silverware scratches etched into the speckled design. The iconic picture of Elvis in his tighty-whities staring you down while his music played over the colorful jukebox in the corner. And of course, the waitresses in their blush pink uniforms who popped bubblegum obnoxiously and rolled their eyes at whatever you ordered.

"Pancakes!" I announced to our waitress, whose eyes, on cue, jumped to the roofs of her lids and back down. In her defense, I was acting extremely messy.

"And two coffees," he chimed in responsibly, his eyebrows angled in apology to her, but his smirk indicating to me that he was still on my side.

"And another order of pancakes for my best friend, please," I blurted out before she pressed her worn order pad roughly closed and headed back to the kitchen in a huff.

"I didn't want pancakes," he said lightheartedly. The strain usually evident in his forehead was eased, and his general demeanor was clear instead of its usual disturbed murkiness. But the unfamiliarity of this contentment in him shot me back to the party, and the terror I had been unable to place, and the general black hole of understanding I felt whenever I tried to analyze his actions.

"They'll help sober us up," I reasoned, unconsciously peeling at the little paper ring banded around the silverware. I studied him subtly, now determined to piece the night's fragments together to finally reveal some complete picture. He tried to give me a head start.

"I'm not drunk," he admitted.

"What?" I gawked, somehow finding the picture even blurrier after his reveal. I looked around, confused, hoping to find that I wasn't alone in the shock of this revelation. But the diner was empty except for an old man at the counter with an unruly beard, who was trying to block us out with the pages of his newspaper, and the irritable waitress, who was tapping her toe toward the kitchen door, anxious to serve us our food so we would get out. I turned back to him. "You had a drink in your hand all night long!"

"It was just water. I don't drink." He shrugged, trying to be casual about it.

"Hmm." I sat back in the booth, biting my lip. I could feel my heavy eyes tearing up a bit. There was a distinct gnaw in my stomach, but it wasn't hunger for pancakes. It was the opposite of that warm end-of-the-night feeling I had described earlier. It was the cold, spiraling loneliness I usually felt at the height of a party—when the room is absolutely packed, and the faces are all strange, and I'm thinking about how I just might be drunk enough to throw up, but not one of them would comfort me if I did. They'd just look at me disgusted.

The feeling was overwhelming, and a wave of nausea passed over me. So I went for my usual remedy: I reached for another pill from the dwindling bag in my pocket and slipped it between my lips. I downed it with the coffee the waitress had just set down on the table beside our pancakes.

I watched the color drain from his face as I swallowed, his ease dissipating. But this time, I didn't even bother trying to work out why. I pulled a plate of pancakes over to me and started in, that momentary nausea shifting into a ravenous hunger.

"So what happened to the girl you were with? And what did you say to that monster truck of a man?'" I said through a full mouth, crumbs dropping down my chin. These were not the questions I wanted to ask. But I had submitted to the fact that I didn't have sense enough of who he was to form a question that would make me feel less estranged from him.

He didn't respond, and I looked up from my half-eaten plate to find a return of the weight on his back. He was slumped down in the booth, picking incessantly at a spot of dried syrup on the table. His pancakes were untouched although he was locked into a staring contest with their chocolate chip eyes.

"Are you all right?" I put my fork down, sobered by the rapid shift from the spirit he'd left the party with back to his everyday dejection.

"Yeah," he brushed me off, "I'm fine." To prove the obvious lie, he picked up his own fork and cut a chunk of the smile from his pancake. He navigated it to his mouth, chewing hard to obliterate it and swallowing as if it were sand. He couldn't hide how difficult it was for him to go in for another bite. But he did. And he went back again and again until it was gone.

I watched him while I sipped on my coffee. I didn't have an appetite for my own pancake anymore.

He pushed the plate far away from him when he finished and cast his eyes to the black-and-white checkered floor miserably.

"We're still friends. Right?" My voice was small. At the very least, I needed to know that his fear at the party and his current grief weren't because of me. I needed to know that he wasn't just another blurry partygoer, disgusted by me. "You don't hate me for dragging you into my mess?"

"Of course we're friends." He looked at me squarely, and I felt my heart swell. "It wasn't your fault."

We walked home silently under the stars. I felt the urge to put my arm around him as he walked with his head down and his hands thrust deeply into his pockets, but I didn't want him to stiffen. I wanted him to let go. Of whatever it was that was hurting him so deeply. He had protected me that night. I wanted to return the favor, but I just didn't know how.

Back in his room, I flopped onto his bed in an exhausted heap. He pulled out the covers from beneath me and brought them up to my waist—so they wouldn't cover my sweating arms but would still keep me comfortable in my drunken sleep. Then, he went to the bathroom.

I could have passed out, but instead, I stared at the sliver of light beneath the bathroom door and listened to the violent sounds of his pancake hitting the inner porcelain of the toilet. He claimed not to be drunk, so why was he throwing up?

I didn't want him to suffer, but I knew it would all have to come up for him to feel any better.

Once it did, he came out of the bathroom and sat at his desk in the dark, shoulders hunched.

"What *did* you say to that guy?" I whispered, but it sliced sharply through the thick room.

"I just told him it was time to move on," he said blankly, his shadow bent.

I didn't believe him. I remembered I had watched his lips form the shape of two specific words. I closed my eyes and tried to figure out the truth:

"There's no need to kill him over a girl. You're not gonna love jail."

"Kill the dramatics, man. So your girlfriend made love to someone else? Get over it."

"If you hurt someone I love again, I'll kill you."

There was no way for me to know for sure.

7

MOVING IN

———

The kitchen had never been so clean as the week after his mom had been put in the mental facility against her will. Charlie sat at the table and tried to focus on writing, but he kept getting distracted by the gleam of the spotless countertops in his peripheral.

The night before, after three brimming glasses of whiskey with their microwave dinners, his dad, in a drunk determination, had scrubbed down the entire apartment of its lifelong grime. He started in the bedroom, brushing the rumpled tissues on the nightstand into the wastebasket with a careless sweep of his forearm. That side of the bed was creased from where his mom had been unexpectedly plucked like a weed and disposed of quietly. His dad balled up the sheets and shoved them into Charlie's arms with their jar of laundry quarters.

While the downstairs washing machine spun his mom's scent out of the bedding, his dad continued on his cleaning rampage with the living room, tossing the empty bottles, cigarette stubs, and unfinished food molding on paper plates into a large, black trash bag.

He continued into the kitchen, sweeping crumbs and junk mail into the bag. He brought dishes, with leftovers dried like cement to their surfaces, to the sink and scrubbed at them viciously until each one shined, stacking them away in the previously empty cabinets. Then, while Charlie remade his parents' bed, his dad took up a shabby rag in one hand, a spray bottle of disinfectant in the other, and scrubbed the countertops of every stain.

Charlie thought he would have liked seeing the messy apartment of his childhood finally clean, but sitting at the table the next morning—his dad out the door early without explanation—he felt uncomfortable. It didn't seem like his home anymore. It was as if the past, and the people who moved around in it, had been erased. This was not just his dad's apartment or his, yet, his brother and mom were nowhere to be found in the newly polished space.

He tried to refocus his attention on the page, where he could immortalize the past—prevent his dad from discarding his memories in the same black trash bag he'd hefted out to the back dumpster at the end of the night. But as soon as the words started flowing from his pen, the front door opened. A woman he had never seen before shuffled in with his dad behind, a hand placed lovingly around her waist.

She was young, the skin of her thin face oddly smooth in contrast to the harsh folds in his dad's weathered hand. She seemed to be just a year or two older than his brother would have been but was trying to act much more mature. She wore an expensive-looking black velvet dress and carried an over-sized pink handbag with a gaudy logo that she held up in front of her torso. Yet, the immature features of her face held the truth. Her thin lips were smeared in a light, blush-colored lipstick and pasted in an apprehensive smile. Her taut cheeks held a natural blush of youthful insecurity. Her round, brown eyes were scanning the apartment nervously because even a deep clean couldn't fix its inherent shabbiness.

She set her purse on the table and put her hand on her stomach as she took a seat across from Charlie, smiling cautiously at him. Although the slimming dress tried to disguise it, Charlie could see her distended belly.

His dad sat beside her and resituated his hand on her stomach. They explained to Charlie that they had been seeing each other for seven months. They had met while his dad was gone on one of his business trips—which Charlie was old enough at ten to know had nothing to do with his job but was actually his dad staying in a hotel with other women in Chicago to get away from his mom. It was love at first sight, they said (she said, and he nodded along). Then, *this little miracle came along.* She beamed at his dad whose excited smile was not reflected in his hollow eyes. And so now that his mom *was away*—as his dad put it, instead of saying she was in a mental hospital—his girlfriend would be moving in so they could raise the baby together. She would be putting all of her stuff in their place. It was in a moving truck parked in front of the building, and Charlie would help his dad carry it all up. She would be sleeping on his mom's side of the bed. And the empty bedroom would be converted into a nursery for the new baby.

She looked expectantly at Charlie when they had explained it all, probably hoping he would jump up with excitement at the news, give her a hug, and call her *Mom.*

He stared blankly at her, his shoulders tight.

His dad did not expect any differently out of him. He instructed Charlie to help him carry her stuff upstairs, with little sympathy to the way he knew Charlie was coping with the news.

Charlie stood without objection, moving smoothly as if the stones in his stomach weren't burning hot flames, filling up his lungs with smoke and causing his eyes to water as he choked back tears.

She stood with them and made a big show to move to the door, as if to help them lug her junk upstairs, knowing full well that his dad would stop her.

"Baby, you just relax." He returned his hand to her waist and planted a gentle kiss on her forehead.

She smiled sweetly, blinking her big, innocent eyes up at him. Charlie looked down, trying to will away his tears and blow the smoke out of his ears, clearing any trace of emotion from his face. But he couldn't completely extinguish the embers still glowing in his stomach. On the way down the stairs, he thought about how his dad had called her *baby* instead of *bitch*; told her to relax when he was always screaming at his mom to get off her ass. And the way he kissed her on the forehead tenderly. He had never seen his parents kiss. He didn't recognize it as affection. It seemed more like a confirmation that things were changing.

His brother used to kiss him on the forehead every so often. It always seemed to happen before major controversies, when everything became different. Charlie had been the one to kiss his brother's forehead that last night when he tucked him in. That had been the start of a dramatic succession of changes.

His dad's girlfriend moving in was the latest on that chain. If not for anything but the fact that their apartment became a greenhouse after that day. When his dad threw open the door of the moving truck, it was a jungle of green foliage.

They carried potted plant after potted plant up the stairs and found a place for every single one in an apartment that had before been void of any green. Charlie had never noticed until that's all it became. Plants and décor. The few pieces of art his mom had on the wall—muted swashes of blues and purples that were calming for Charlie, like the unoffensive art in a waiting room—were taken down and tossed into the dumpster out back, replaced by paintings that fell into two categories: abstract portraits of the human anatomy and pictures of plants, because there clearly weren't enough of the real thing.

She also put throw pillows on the couch, so many there was hardly space for sitting, and all over his mom's bed, atop a new comforter. With her paintings, his mom's bedspread—which he had so carefully straightened across their bed the night before—went in the trash. It had been a faded red thing, loose threads hanging from the edges, a collection of permanent stains, and a worn corner she tended to clutch when she cried. She had spent so many hours beneath it, it almost seemed like a part of her. His dad discarded it. And his girlfriend replaced it with a brand new, brightly colored one of green leaves and cheerful pink flowers.

In the back of the truck, the very last thing they had to carry up was a crib. Charlie stared at it, out of breath, fire building again in his belly, smoke filling his lungs.

"Almost done." His dad sighed, setting down a beer he had been sipping on and wiping the sweat from his forehead, preparing to lift one of the crib's sides. He looked at Charlie to pick up the other side, but Charlie couldn't move, his back against the wall of the truck the only thing keeping him upright while he burned.

"Dad…" he sputtered.

His dad looked at him, not understanding. Not trying to understand. He was trying to start a new family since the last one had fallen apart on him. Charlie felt himself being left behind. He could see himself discarded as easily as his mom's comforter and his brother's memory—that black bag of trash at the bottom of a now-full dumpster.

"Not *his* room." It was a plea. It was Charlie grasping desperately at something to hold on to when all he had known his whole life was instability.

Though the entire situation demonstrated a lack of regard for the interests of Charlie, his dad finally looked at him with a bit of sympathy. He didn't go to console his son or apologize for the way he had barged all this change right into his already unstable situation without concern, but he did say, "How about we move you in there instead?"

So once they had the crib up the stairs, it was moving in part two as they packed up Charlie's things and brought them over to his brother's room—still and silent as it was. They mostly moved clothes because Charlie insisted on keeping his brother's room exactly the same. So it was Charlie's furniture that found its way out back with his mom's things. He didn't care, as long as his brother wasn't thrown out like he had been so many times.

He felt safe in this room, its furniture untouched.

Charlie could imagine his brother moving through the space, fuzzy with marijuana smoke: looking in the smeared mirror of the chipping, black dresser, trying to wipe the red from his eyes. Sitting at the desk beneath the yellow beam of his cheap lamp, sniffing up a line of white. Reading the poems Charlie had written for him, which he had hanging on the wall. Lying on top of the hunter green comforter, smoking a cigarette with the window open, and staring at the ceiling.

The entire room still had the vague scent of cigarette smoke. That night, Charlie breathed in deeply and tried to focus on his brother instead of the new sibling growing inside the strange woman sleeping on his mom's side of the bed.

That tactic only worked for a few days. Quickly, the room succumbed to Charlie's scent. He thought about taking up smoking himself to get it back, but he knew it wouldn't be the same. Plus, his dad's girlfriend was always going on about how bad cigarette smoke was for the baby. She used to smoke, she told him, but gave it up the minute she learned she was pregnant. Made his dad give it up too. And whenever they all went anywhere together, she turned up her nose at anyone with a cigarette between their fingers. She'd put her hands on her growing stomach and say, loudly enough for them to hear, "Kill yourself if you want with your *nasty* habits, but to risk the life of an unborn child? The nerve of some people!"

She would flip out if Charlie smoked in the room next to where her baby would sleep. She flipped out about every little thing. If his dad came home from work late, she accused him of cheating and cried. If he forgot to water one of her plants, she panicked that it meant he wouldn't be able to take care of a baby and cried. When Charlie's mom died, she cried for a week straight, going on and on about what a great woman she had been and what a loss they were all going through, even though she had never even met her.

Charlie's dad told him pregnant women could get a bit emotional, but he promised once the baby came, Charlie would see what a wonderful motherly figure she could really be.

She tried practicing the motherly role she was apparently born for on Charlie in the months leading up to her real baby's birth. She made him snacks after school every day and encouraged him to do his homework. She took him on outings to museums and parks. She came into his room while he was writing and tried to have heavy conversations *to get to know each other.* She did most of the talking. She told him how she had been in her second year of college when she got pregnant, but she dropped out because having a family had always been more important to her than anything else. She grew up as an only child in a rich home, and her parents hadn't been around much. She had been raised by a nanny. That's why, she said, she wanted to make sure she was the one who raised her child. That's why she wanted to be there for Charlie as a mother, *since he hadn't gotten that before.*

Charlie didn't say much to her like he was apt to do, and because of it, he knew she felt like he didn't like her. He didn't, but his silence wasn't indicative of it. Still, she doubled her efforts in a desperate attempt to win his words. She made her snacks more and more complex. She spent more money on more elaborate outings. She made her deep talks deeper and longer and more outrageous. Charlie was sure she fabricated half of the stories she told him to try and relate, but he didn't care enough to say anything.

One day she came into his room and finally let all that had built up come barreling out when he refused her mini quiches. "You're so cold to me, Charlie. So cruel! I've done nothing but shower you in all the love I know how and still, you won't say a word to me. Won't look up from that damn journal of yours for even a second to look me in the eye. Won't leave this room unless your dad forces you to. I know you're not used to someone showing you this kind of warmth, but I thought you would have appreciated it, not try to freeze me out." She had fallen onto the bed beside him, the tears pouring down her cheeks.

He wanted to say a lot to her then. He wanted to tell her that all her plants made his nose itch and his eyes water—that it felt a bit too much like the emotion of her moving in when he was around them. He wanted to say she was too loose with her tears and that made them less genuine: He knew what it looked like to cry real tears, to feel true despair, and hers were false. He wanted her to know he'd felt more love in his life than she could ever know because love didn't mean throwing money around, or baking fancy snacks, or having surface-level conversations about her childhood. Love was made in smiley-face pancakes. Love was found in cig-arette-scented hands that were always there to hold during big moves. It was seen in forehead kisses and blue fountain pens and looking up at the clouds. He hadn't looked up in a long time. Not for her. Not for anyone.

He glanced up now but only because she had fallen into a silence similar to his, and it caught him off guard.

She was looking down at her stomach, seven months large. She smiled at him. "Your little sister is kicking."

Charlie's eyes zeroed in on the stomach, trying to see for himself. She took his hand and placed it where he failed to see anything, but he felt it all right. His mouth fell open in awe. His sister was in there, alive and breathing. Charlie wanted to believe she wasn't actually kicking but reaching out her hand to try and touch Charlie. It was in that moment he realized he was going to have another hand to hold, to feel comforted by. It didn't mean the past was erased. It just meant the future was reaching out. He didn't have to be so lonely anymore.

He saw beyond the plants and the woman who had put them there for the first time. He forgot about his mom's com-forter splayed out in the city dump and his old room, which

was now painted pink. He was looking up from his journal
and seeing a little girl he would be an older brother to. He
would be the best brother he could be. He had seen exactly
what to do.

8

GIRLFRIEND

———

I'm not exactly clear on how it happened—because I hadn't considered myself in the market for commitment, and to be fair, I was pretty wrecked on the night in question—but I got a girlfriend. She strode up to me in a pair of outrageous stiletto boots and grabbed me by the crotch, her eyes locked directly on mine, her irises ablaze with a confidence that both scared and excited me. She bit my earlobe and told me exactly what she wanted. I gave it to her. Four times that night. And even more over the next three days when we locked ourselves inside her bedroom, away from the uncertainties of the outside world.

Everything within her four olive-green walls was assured: the contour of our bodies pressed against each other, the peaks of both our intimacy and our indulgence, the shape of the sunbeams traveling across her gold-accented furniture from the morning's rise to the evening's fall, all while we remained in her bed. Making love. Rambling about pasts buried and futures uncovered. Pressing pills between each other's lips with our tongues and holding each other in the haze of our cigarette smoke.

At the end of the whirlwind, when she finally told me I had to go, she also told me we were dating. I didn't mind. She told me she'd see me for dinner that night. I said, of course. And then I went straight to his dorm to tell him all about her.

"She's bold." He hadn't asked where I'd been all weekend when he came in from a run and found me sleeping in his bed. He had just handed me his bottle of water, and I started in. "Not just because those fire eyes are so sure, or because everything she says is definitive. She carries herself as if the world were hers for the taking. And it is. She works at the recycling plant and makes art from the things they can't recycle. Mostly she makes sculptures of plants. Isn't that fucking genius? Plants from trash! She showed me some of her work, and it's absolutely incredible. And she doesn't even do it for money or notoriety. She doesn't care if she gets recognized. It's all about fulfillment for her: artistic, spiritual, *sexual.*" I grinned slyly at him.

His face remained flat. He was being extra quiet that morning. He sat on the bed with me, listening, knees pulled up to his chest, sweat dripping down his forehead from the run. He looked tired, and I had never seen that from him even though I had also never seen him sleep.

I wanted to ask if he was okay—it almost slipped out—but I bit it back at the last second. I knew he would just deny any sort of problem and then immediately close off the small window of vulnerability he had unintentionally left open to me.

Instead, I decided to give him a little space to bury whatever was wearing him down. I offered to get us food while he showered. "Then we can go outside and eat."

He nodded at my plan and rose from the bed, straightening out the wrinkles his body had caused in the taut comforter. He drifted toward the bathroom door but turned around right as I began getting up, and self-consciously, I ran my hand across the bed where I'd been sitting.

But that's not what he had turned around for, head bobbing subtly in encouragement: "She sounds amazing, Levi. I can't wait to meet her."

Despite its weariness, his voice sounded genuine, round and full like a gleaming soap bubble. His approval floated across the room, bursting gently against me, and I glowed. I had two people I cared for and who cared for me. Now I only needed them to care for each other.

After his shower, when he had scrubbed away all traces of exhaustion from his face, we sat in the grass. He leaned up against the tree with his journal in his lap, writing unbothered like he always did, and I leaned back against my elbows, smoking a cigarette and taking in the beautiful day. The leaves on the trees had started to change, and there was a scattering of dead ones around us, but the air was warm with the uninterrupted glow of the sun—who I guess hadn't gotten the memo about the cold, dark winter we were barreling toward. I was glad about it. The weather matched my mood. I closed my eyes and let the rays meld with my own emanating glow. Every once in a while, I would chime in with something more about her:

Like how her hair was so dark brown, it was nearly black. But not quite black, still brown. It fell long and straight between her shoulder blades and was so dark I got lost in it.

Or how she didn't ever take her socks off. They were little gray socks that said *Hanes* in gold across the toes, and she kept them on the whole time. She'd get up to go to the bathroom, her whole beautiful naked body spotlighted by what sun was seeping in through the closed blinds, except for her feet. Her feet were wrapped up in those cute, gray socks. She told me it was because her toes were always cold.

And "God," I said to him, "the way she says my name. *Levi*. I can't even do it right. It makes my whole body warm. I'm telling you."

The sun peaked in the sky and then began its descent, and I began to get butterflies in my stomach just thinking about being back in her presence. I couldn't stop talking about her to him. I had shifted onto my stomach to face him. Leaves crunched and broke beneath me through the transition. I rested my chin in my palms, my feet kicking in the air as I daydreamed about her smooth skin against mine.

By this time, he had put down his journal and was watching the sun sink.

"Hey, you should come to dinner," I suggested, sitting up. The idea had come to me suddenly, but I thought it was brilliant.

He fought to tear his gaze from the dying sun. When he finally looked over at me, beaming at my own genius, he had to blink hard a few times to dispel the black spots that had formed.

"I don't think I should," he said uneasily, shaking his head in a small, rigid burst.

"You said you couldn't wait to meet her!" I challenged him lightheartedly, assuming it was just his opposition to interaction getting in the way. All he needed was a loving nudge. "And anyway, I told her all about you, and she felt the same! I'll just call her and tell her to whip up a little extra."

I didn't wait for him to object again. I pulled out my phone and dialed the number she had typed in that morning—her long, glossy nails causing each digit to make a satisfying click. She answered on the third ring and was thrilled for him to join us. She instructed me to bring a bottle of red wine and to be there at seven.

We tapped at the petite gold knocker on her door at 6:58. Although I was generally of the fashionably late sort, I was really trying to impress her. He was usually the one nagging me to make sure we were on time, but tonight, I had been rushing him. I had helped finish the buttons on the collared shirt I encouraged him to put on, and I had even licked my palm to flatten an out-of-place chunk of his hair. He cringed at my touch as always, but at the same time, he seemed a bit amused to see me trying so hard.

"You really like this girl, huh?" He smirked, but the words were soft with a pleasant surprise.

At that, I mussed the hair I had just fixed and shoved the bottle of wine into his hands, pushing us from the accustomed intimacy of his lamplit room into the distant chill of the shifting indigo twilight.

In the dull hall of her apartment, my fingertips tingled, and I was glad I had given the bottle of wine to him. I might've dropped it in my jittery nervousness. What kind of impression would that leave, an immense blot of red puddling on her doorstep because of me?

I chuckled away the vision of disaster as I heard the stride of her heels on the other side of the door. My two favorite people, in one room. The night would be perfect.

She answered our knock with a radiant smile, which was bright against her dark hair and the burgundy turtleneck dress that hugged every curve of her body. I had to hold myself off from jumping her right there in the hallway. But her attention was on him. She took the bottle of wine from his arms and shook his hand. "So nice to meet you! Levi made you into some sort of myth with the way he went on and on."

She ushered us in and finally gave me some attention, kissing me deeply and squeezing my ass with her right hand as she closed the door with her left.

"He did the same for you," he agreed as we made our way down the tight and dim front hall and turned into the offensive white lighting of the little kitchen. But even the harsh lights couldn't stifle her elegance.

"I guess we'll be a big disappointment to each other then." Even her close-mouthed grin radiated beauty. He had to be seeing it too, how her lustrous confidence filled the room. All the lights glowed warmer and brighter. The edges softened like in a drunken blur. But she was a crystal in the center, clear and gleaming like a chandelier.

She grabbed three glasses from the cheap, plywood cabinets, stained with ugly blotches of mustard brown grease from past tenants. Then, she led us out into the soft yellow mood lighting of the main living space, which reflected her tastes much better than the cramped hall or the dingy kitchen. Here, the overhead lights were permanently switched off and supplemented by a variety of antique lamps clearly collected from local thrift stores and garage sales. They gave the space its friendly appeal. As did the maroon couch, pushed up against the exposed brick wall, which looked comfortable and well-loved, with a recycled plant sculpture of her making on either side. The table and its set of chairs also looked used, but its elm wood somehow perfectly matched the grain of the flooring. For the occasion, she had draped a cream-colored, lace tablecloth on top.

He and I sat down across from each other while, next to me, she stood, working on popping the wine's cork. She tugged unsuccessfully at the cheap corkscrew she had twisted deep into the mouth of the stopped bottle.

"Let me help," I reached out, but she whipped the bottle out of my range.

"Not a chance." She grinned, turning her back to me, determined to succeed on her own. Finally, the cork came loose with a satisfying pop, "Aha…" but the force of her pull caused a splash of wine to escape and spread into a misshapen splotch on the tablecloth. "Oops."

He immediately fixated on the spot, and I flashed back to my vision in the hall, but she just shrugged, "Nothing a simple wash can't clean." She refocused our attention on the success of the open bottle by doing a little dance as she placed a glass in front of each of us and poured.

She got to his glass last, and I automatically put my hand over it for him. "Actually, he doesn't drink."

"Alcoholic father?" she assumed, setting down the bottle and taking a hearty sip from her own glass.

In an instant, panic spread across his face. The color drained from his cheeks. His bottom lip fell with a slight twitch. His eyebrows wrinkled up uneasily at the middle, popping the vein in his forehead, and his pupils narrowed. He was mortified.

But just as quickly, it all dissipated, and his face was flat and unrevealing once again. So quickly, she wouldn't have caught it—only me.

What she saw was him shrug casually.

She returned the gesture. "No big deal. You want water instead?"

"That'll be fine." His tone was controlled.

She took his glass and went into the kitchen, shouting back at us without turning that the spaghetti would be ready in five.

Meanwhile, I shot him a confused, desperate glare, which I meant to come across as an, *Is that true and you never told me?* But he avoided looking in my direction and didn't get the message. I was baffled she had found out more about him in two minutes than I had in the four months we had been friends.

I almost felt betrayed. By her, for stepping so effortlessly over the speed bump I perceived as a security wall and had spent months contemplating how to climb. And by him for lowering his defenses so quickly to her when he had actively shut me out since the beginning.

But as she came back in from the kitchen—the clawlike nails of her left hand curled around his filled water glass while she fearlessly balanced the full pot of spaghetti on her right palm—I thought, *this is why I already love her.* She set the glass in front of his lowered head without judgment and gave the pot a spin on the hot-pad, singing, "Ta-da!"

Of course he had opened up to her. She had a demeanor of unbridled easiness that made everyone around her immediately comfortable. And she was so intuitive, so empathic, that what little he had let his guard down was enough for her to deduce the reason he had it up in the first place. This was only further proof of how incredible she was. Not just good for me but for him.

I found myself captured in the same trance she had imposed over me from her first approach and through the blur of the weekend. I was mesmerized by the way her not-quite-black hair shone like her fire eyes in the dim light of that apartment. I was caught in her laugh, how it began like bells but with more glasses of wine became like a symphony, loud and messy and magnificent. I loved the way she interacted with him and his quiet. He had battened down in his defenses after the accidental breach. But that didn't stop her from taking him on. Not like an intruder, an imposing presence trampling carelessly over new terrain, but more like an explorer whose every delicate step respected the past that existed before them. I watched it all unfold, peacefully subdued in the drunkenness induced by half a bottle of red wine and her charm.

"Levi tells me you're a writer. You see yourself going anywhere with that?" Her nails tapped against the stem of her glass, their clink a flat pitter-patter that dropped onto the table.

"It's just for fun," played like an answering machine out of him, automatic. Like an *I'm good, how 'bout you?* in response to a *How are you?*—complete and utter bullshit we all accept because small talk isn't the time to get into it. To admit how irreparably broken you really are.

She snorted. "Fun, really?" She was the kind of person to answer *How are you?* with *Fucking terrible, let me tell you.* She said to him, "Tell me this: Do you not think you have the right to express your emotions publicly? Sadness, joy, whatever. You think you have to keep it to yourself?"

He halted in the incessant swirling of his fork, and the large clump of spaghetti that was beehived around the prongs began to unravel.

I froze too—a tail of spaghetti hanging from my lips, spreading sauce on my chin—and looked expectantly at him for an answer.

"I…" He squeezed nervously at his neck muscle, eyes shifting over the tablecloth, analyzing a workaround to her aggressively straightforward question. "I don't want to be a burden."

"And you think there's something about you that's inherently a burden on others." She proposed it as a deduction but sensing the immediate rigidity that cut through his whole body, she took a strategic step back, smiling softly. "I mean, we all do, right? Question our place in the world and our effect on each other? Usually late at night or after a couple of glasses." She tipped her wine so far forward that the bloody liquid nearly splashed onto the earlier stain but pulled it back at the last second to save the beautiful table runner more damage.

"I'm not sure," he said quietly.

"Not sure what?" she challenged.

"That we all question it, our place. Some people just seem… happy. Like they fit wherever they go." He really appeared to be pondering it. His muscles had softened in the distraction of her philosophical spin on the conversation.

"I definitely question it. All the time!" I chimed in, and he was genuinely surprised by that, swiftly exiting his inquisitive haze and turning his head sideways toward me. I shrugged and took a big gulp of my wine.

"So, what makes those people so different then—the ones who at least *seem* happy?" She leaned back in her chair, folding her arms smartly. "Is it love? Drugs? A genetic predisposition possibly?"

"Maybe it's a combination of everything?" I tried, seeing the way he was floundering at the questions, his lips opening and then closing like a fish. I wanted to save him.

"A ratio of love to loss," she built off of what I had said, taking my hand with a grin and squeezing it. I felt a swell up my arm as if she were inflating a blood pressure cuff with her grip, causing my heart to beat louder in my ears. "Winner is the one who gets out with minimal trauma and someone to love in the end."

"Is it luck, though, or do you deserve what you get?" he muttered, mostly to himself. But there were only three of us drifting in this black hole of existentialism, and we all heard it, resounding loudly off the cramped apartment walls we'd fallen with. Outside was a galaxy of stars, a haze, and that was the effect she had. I felt the same blur of the previous weekend smearing in my peripheral.

"Now there's a great question!" she encouraged, her spirits heightening. She sat up energetically, her back straight as if she were balancing philosophy books on her head. "How active do you have to be to get what you want out of life? What do you think?"

He pressed his lips so tightly together they fell in on themselves, leaving a thin line and two faint dimples that did not reflect any ounce of joy. Then, he emitted a tiny breath of courage and out of him spilled, "I think we're all just rolling endlessly down a hill."

She bit her bottom lip, failing in her attempt to suppress a wild grin, and nodded him on. "What do you mean by that?"

But immediately, he had zipped himself back up tightly against whatever it was that had opened him up. Locked, bolted, chained, sealed, and secured. He had flattened his face into an unaffected expression, his body fixed in a composed defense.

By then, the bottle of wine had been emptied. The room felt thick with it, and I felt sleepy, hardly able to follow their logic and the subsequent reason for his abrupt shutdown— big surprise.

She leaned forward, pressing her heat into him from across the table, but it avoided him, a fork in the road. Four determined prongs holding out, digging in. He stared at the red splotch of the spill from hours before.

She sighed, shaking her head ever so slightly in disappointment—so that only I caught it, not him—before downing the last drop of wine at the table from her glass. "You're just gonna stay rolling then? Not even gonna try to call out for help as you lose everything? What if someone else is falling down the same hill, and you can stop each other?"

Drunk, confused, wanting still for both of them to love each other as much as I loved them, I blurted out, "Nothing that's lost can't be created again."

———

That was essentially the end of the night.

We walked him to the door, and she shook his hand cordially. "It was nice to meet you. You upheld the myth."

"You exceeded it," he responded, mostly to me.

I made sure he was okay to walk back to campus alone, and he headed to his dorm while she and I went to her bed, popped a couple of pills, and had beautiful sex.

She was on her side, her back to me, and I was tracing circles around her sweat-stippled shoulder blades, staring up at the ceiling, when she said to me, "I don't really like him."

"What?" I pulled my hand away, momentarily unable to process her words. When it finally sank in, I sat up, more in disbelief than in anger—though the heat was building beneath my surface. "Why?"

"He's just so closed off." She had rolled onto her back, her chest open and pointed toward the sky. She was playing with the silky sheets between her fingers.

"I told you that. I'm still working on getting him to open up," I said defensively.

"But why bother, really? He seems to me like someone who just prefers to keep people at a distance. So let him!"

She acted so blasé about the idea of completely abandoning an entire friendship. Part of me wanted to tell her to fuck off. But her dark hair was spread across the pillowcase like a crown, and the light of the moon had snuck in, casting a glow across her face. She was stunning.

So, I just kept trying to defend him. "He writes things in his journal—personal stories—so he's not completely against expressing it."

"But has he ever let you read one of his stories?" She pushed herself up into a sitting position and leaned back against the white bars of her bed frame, pressing her boobs together as she crossed her arms.

"No." I hung my head sourly.

"Exactly, because he has that shit padlocked—diary-style, crammed into the dark abyss at the bottom of a sock drawer. You're not getting in." Her tone was almost mocking.

"Fuck you," it finally slipped out. She was expressing my own fears about him, and I was furious at her for it. What if he never loved me as much as I loved him? Never enough to share his joy and his sadness with me. Never enough to hold me through this endless fucking hill roll, leaving me to fall all alone.

My insecurity must've been all over my face. Her callous features softened, and she placed a gentle hand on my shoulder. "I'm sorry, Levi. I'm not trying to be a bitch. It's just… I'm an open book. You probably figured that out by now. And there's a reason. Both of my parents were super closed off, so I never knew what was going on until the rug was pulled out from under me. Like when they divorced. Or when my mom tried to drift off on an entire bottle of Prozac."

"God, I'm sorry." I brushed her hair behind her ear. Just another thing I hadn't known. I didn't know her either. Did I know anyone?

"It's okay," she purred in reassurance. "It just taught me not to waste my energy trying to understand people who don't want to be understood." As she said it, she resituated the piece of hair I had moved. "You don't have to try to break him open anymore. I'm here. I'm open. And I want you here with me." She placed a hand on my chest and leaned in, giving me a tender kiss.

Any lingering upset over the spat melted out of me. And a different heat rose. I pressed her back against the bed, and we went at it again.

Afterward, she fell asleep, and I worked back through our conversation to figure out what I was supposed to do. I definitely wasn't going to give up on him like she suggested. He meant too much to me, even if I didn't know him as well as I wanted to—maybe never would. And as closed off as he was, I still knew I meant something to him too.

Anyway, she hadn't really told me I had to ditch him completely. She just wanted to be alone with me, which was sweet.

So, my solution was to separate my time between her and him.

I didn't tell him what I was doing, though. The day after the dinner, he told me she was just as great as I had described, better even. *Perfect for me.*

It made me feel guilty for her and my bedroom discussion about him. He had only nice things to say about her, and none of it was bullshit. Which meant I had to bullshit him instead because I couldn't stand to hurt him. He already seemed to be going through something—his eyes were tired, just like the day before. But of course, he didn't say anything about it.

So I just told him I was happy they got along—vague enough—and tried not to bring her up when we hung out for fear he might ask when we were all getting together again.

But it was difficult to maintain both relationships without any overlap. I admit I spent way more time with her than him over the next few months. But it was new love, and it was exciting. I started sleeping in her bed every night instead of his. We would go to parties together, which meant I couldn't invite him. There were many periods where we spent days in her room—like the first weekend we met—drugged and making love, isolated from the rest of the world. Isolated from him.

I tried to make excuses for myself to keep from feeling guilty. Winter had arrived, and the weather was getting colder, so he and I couldn't hang out on the lawn like we usually did anyway. I always stopped by his dorm on the mornings she decided to go to work. And I tried to get to the classes we had together early enough to sit next to him— when I didn't skip them to be with her, which I was starting to do quite a bit.

He seemed unaffected by it all. Besides those few days when she and I first got together, where something had very clearly been bothering him, he was his normal, aloof self. I found him always writing. Speaking hardly, as he did. Yet, every time I saw him, he made sure to ask how she was doing.

She never asked about him.

Then, I didn't see him for two weeks. She had gotten her hands on some amphetamines, and, as had become our practice, we locked ourselves away and fell into our own world.

Only this time, it was the room that felt unsettled, not the outside. Our bodies didn't meld. I tried to fit to her curves, but she was all sharp edges—a lone cactus in a barren desert. The drugs weren't hitting right, and I found myself bottoming out and simultaneously failing to keep it up. There was no light. It was only ever night, and then night again, and night and night. But I never knew what time it really was.

She said my name, and it didn't do anything for me. I was hot, and I couldn't seem to find the motivation to take my socks off. It was so dark, as dark as her hair, and I felt lost—alone even.

I tried to open up to her about it, but she didn't listen. And even with her cuddled in my arms, snoring softly, I could feel the gnaw of loneliness returning. Sometimes I would drift off and jolt awake, expecting to find him, writing. Her desk was in the most shadowed corner of the room, unused. She had commissioned its surface for her disorganized collection of miscellaneous makeup products. When I looked over at it in the middle of the night, I could feel myself spiraling.

The pill bottle seemed endless.

On the last night of our bender, I realized I couldn't remember what he looked like when he smiled. He didn't do it much, but I had seen it a few times, and it should have been clear to me. What was clear was that I missed him. He was so far away. Or maybe it was me. I wanted to be in his bed, watching the rise and fall of his breaths instead of hers. But I couldn't move. The pills had me pinned to the bed. And I was afraid that I would never see his smile again.

———

Finally, I woke up to the sun. My lips were chapped, and I felt hardly myself, but I was there and coherent. She was there too, moving from the blinds she had violently pulled up at the window over to the closet to get dressed.

"I'm going to work today," she said shortly, her shoulder blades wound up tightly with burden and her squinted eyes flitting my way in annoyance. She threw my pants at me. "You should go to class."

My head was pulsing, my body shaky and weak. The olive walls made me nauseated, and her collection of white furniture made me feel unclean. I tossed my pants off the side of the bed and rolled over, closing my eyes.

She ripped the covers off my naked body, exposing me to the icy air.

"What the fuck?" I jumped up, fully awake.

"It's time for you to get out of my place. Do something with your day. Catch up on some schoolwork. Hang out with a friend. I don't care." She zipped up her pants and went over to the desk to start on her makeup.

I stood there naked, staring at her, shivering. I couldn't figure out how she decided when to reject reality and when it was time to go back, but she always seemed so sure. She was confident picking up the scattered pieces on her own. Didn't need any help. It was something I had once admired. Now, I felt abandoned.

"You don't care?"

"I don't care," she repeated, lining her eyes in black. I could see them in the reflection of the mirror, and they were cold.

"You cared enough in the beginning to tell me who you didn't want me hanging out with," I said, bitterly.

"You're an adult, Levi. You get to choose who you spend your time with." Her voice was a shard of glass. "In fact, you get to make all your own choices although it seems like you'd much rather drag along in my wake." Even though there was evident acrimony in her words, she didn't bother to turn around. She just kept painting on her face—which appeared unfamiliar somehow, despite all the times I had studied it while she slept. She was distant, I realized then, and not because she wasn't open, but because she was wholly independent. I was a drain on her pursuit of fulfillment. She didn't need me anymore. Maybe never had.

He needed me. And I needed him. He may have kept himself closed when it came to his past, but I still felt close to him because he had always been open to my needs. He listened to me. And just by being there, I listened to his needs too. That was until I had chosen her over him.

"Apparently, I chose wrong," I muttered.

She capped her eyeliner pencil and dropped it on the dresser, where it hit with a harsh clatter. She still didn't turn but was glaring at me through the mirror.

"Go to him then," she said, her voice coarse. "But he's never going to let you in."

I shook my head, trying to ignore the fear creeping back in that she was right. I quickly put on my clothes as she went back to her makeup.

"He really liked you." I stopped at the door on my way out, looking back at her, almost hoping she would stop me—tell me she needed me, fight to keep me forever in the whirlwind that was our relationship. "Said you were perfect for me."

She was laying mascara on her lashes heavily. "Guess he was wrong."

I found myself back in the hallway of her apartment building—fingertips tingling, red puddling—like it had all never happened. But instead of him beside me, I was alone. It was quiet except for the buzz of the cheap lights, which pinched at my headache, and I wasn't sure what exactly had just happened. I also wasn't sure what to do next.

So, I decided I'd go to class. It was a class he and I had together. And even though I felt terrible physically, there was nothing I wanted more than to walk into the room and see his face, front row, pointed down at his journal. I hurried away from her apartment toward him.

9

LOCKED DOOR

I stood outside the classroom door—a different dingy hallway, my head pounding just the same. Bodies glided past me, engrossed in their own lives, their own conversations, their own dramas. And in that way, I felt almost invisible.

But at the same time, I felt myself like a blaring red emergency light spinning and flashing its disturbance in an otherwise sophisticated space. There were dress shoes against the polished wood. There were glossy flyers pasted to the bulletin boards announcing poetry readings, charity nights, literature clubs. There was the musty smell of the aged building—the bricks it was built of, the books it was holding, the academics it was raising. And then there was me: rumpled T-shirt and jeans holding two weeks' worth of drug and sex sweat, with crusted hair strands stuck to my sweaty forehead and bloodshot eyes.

So in both ways, I was out of place.

The only thing that kept me from turning around and booking it back to her apartment, begging for her forgiveness so I could hide in the messy safety of her stash of pills, was the thought of him in the front row. Bent over his journal, pen gliding across the page, he could restore my sense of belonging in an instant.

Only when I did step over the threshold, his usual seat was empty. I scanned the rows and rows of English majors, their individualistic appearances blending into a strange mass. He was nowhere among them.

"I'm happy to see you're alive, Levi," the professor said from behind her desk, pulling out a disarray of papers from her tote. "I was starting to think I might be receiving a funeral invitation for you in place of a midterm."

"Nope, alive and well." I glanced over the room one more time and at the clock, two minutes from the start of class. I rubbed at the back of my clammy neck, feeling a sense of disorientation, and walked over to the side of her desk. "Although I assume my grade is just about buried?"

My eyes kept instinctually shifting between her long gray braid, already beginning to unravel, and his empty seat. She had a deep concern set in the lines around her eyes.

"I'm happy to help you if you're willing to put in the work." Her voice was coarse from a clear pack-a-day cigarette habit that probably spanned back to her own undergraduate years, but her tone was comforting. The caring, bohemian quality about her reminded me of my mother. "Same goes for your partner in crime. You two need to start showing up, though."

"What do you mean?" My head turned back to his empty seat among a full room, the clock (a minute out), and the door still open but vacant.

"He hasn't been in class since last week. I figured the two of you were ditching together." She shrugged, nonchalant about it. But didn't she know he never missed class? It didn't matter how late we had stayed at a party the night before or how I begged him to ditch with me. He never skipped. Just like he always did his homework and turned in essays on time. He was neurotic like that.

Something had to be wrong.

"Levi, go ahead and take your seat. We can talk more after class." Her voice was just a buzz in my head, swarming. The space around his unoccupied chair swirled into a hurricane of dull colors.

I turned abruptly from her desk and ran for the door. She might've called after me, but I didn't hear. My breaths were heavy, and my heart was pounding as I sprinted across campus. My sneakers crunched through the sporadic piles of browned snow left over from some storm I had completely missed while locked away with her on our bender. The barren trees waved their grayed arms at me in frustration. The hot cloud escaping my lips flew back past my cheeks like the steam of a train at full speed, but still, the tips of my ears felt encased in cubes of ice.

Entering his hall should've been like a hug from the wheezing vents spewing heat, but when I flew inside, it was more like a punch in the gut. I didn't falter, however, continuing my pace to his door.

It was the one thing that had been open to me from the beginning—the last time I had run being the morning I burst into his room and begged for his friendship. Even then, as he was shut tight, his door had been unlocked.

I fidgeted with the handle, up and down up and down. But it was locked.

I began banging on the door and heard nothing in return. I called out to him. "Open up!" I begged desperately. I was in a full panic. I thought about busting it down, but I knew I'd get into real trouble for the damage.

So, I went down to the front desk and concocted a lie, said my friend was in the hospital but needed something from his room. The girl had one earbud in and was smacking her gum obnoxiously. She was unamused by my story, but frankly, didn't give a shit either way and gave me a copy of the key without opposition.

I hurried back upstairs and fiddled with the lock until finally, it clicked. I opened the door to find him sitting at his desk, writing like he always was. He didn't even look up at me.

"What the fuck? Why didn't you open the door?" I almost laughed. I was so incredulous. It felt like a prank, how terrified I'd been. I didn't even know what I had expected to find on the other side of his door when I turned the key, but I had been out of my mind with the expectation it would be something gruesome. Only to find him in a position so familiar to me it had become what I thought of at night to lull me into gentle dreams.

I walked over to him, pissed but also relieved.

He didn't reply to me, and I glanced down at his journal. The page was blank. And it was the last one between the covers. The rest of the pages were crumpled and scattered around the room, which I only then noticed was a complete mess. His rumpled clothes were scattered across the expanse of carpet with the rejected notebook pages; his comforter too, strewn off the bed, only holding on by the tucked-in portion of his gray sheets.

"Are you okay?" I touched his shoulder, another onslaught of concern consuming me. These slight but significant shifts in our universe—the bolted lock, the disheveled dorm—racked me with Twilight-Zone levels of disorientation. He didn't even shift at my touch. He just calmly turned to me, and I was able to see how pale his face was, like a spotlighted actor in a black-and-white picture on a snowy box TV. He looked like he hadn't eaten or slept in days.

"I don't know what to do," he said vaguely.

His tone had reached unprecedented levels of emotionless, even for him. It extended far beyond his usual brick-wall way of speaking. The words came out like Novocain, thick and numb. Meanwhile, I could feel fireworks popping off in my stomach but tried to stifle the worry leaking into my voice. "About what?"

"I wanted to write a happy story. Just one happy story. But I can't. I *fucking* can't." The layers upon layers of brick he had mortared into place began to break down as he spoke, apathy revealing upset revealing turmoil revealing hysteria. And finally, he slammed his fist on the desk, his voice shaking violently. "I tried, but I can't."

His eyes were welling with tears. My own went wide. It was something I had never seen from him, and I didn't know how to react. All I could do was keep my hand firm on his shoulder and say, "It's okay."

He shook his head, rejecting it.

"It's okay," I repeated myself, not confident that it was but injecting a stern reassurance into the proclamation anyway.

Only then he was crying, full globs of viscous tears pouring down his red-flushed cheeks.

"My dad is dead," he sobbed, barely discernible. He bent over the desk, and his tears drowned the blank page below him.

For a moment, I stood frozen, shocked by his tears, by his show of emotion, and by the news of his father, whose existence I had only first heard of at the dinner months ago. But shock wore off fast in place of instinctive condolence, and I picked my best friend up into my arms and held him while he cried.

The bounce of his sobbing shoulders up and down in my embrace was illusory. I had a moment where I questioned whether all of this was just a hallucination in the bender my girlfriend and I must've still been on. I felt almost outside of myself—as if I was stuck to the ceiling, tripping balls and cackling at the outlandish scene transpiring below me in a myriad of colors.

But no, the blotchy, red skin of his arms was radiating very real heat into my own, stippled with goosebumps. It spread a warmth through my body, and if it wasn't the result of such a tragic scenario, I might've enjoyed the feeling, reveled in it even. But my stomach was gutted with the outpouring of grief racking his fragile body. I wanted my hug to be enough to alleviate his pain like the two Ibuprofen he always set out for my hangover headaches. I knew it couldn't. So I just tried to stay solid for him, concrete, unwavering.

He stayed in the strength of my arms until his eyes had run dry. He sniffled the wet evidence of his break from the tip of his nose and tried to tug away from my grasp, apologizing. But I held on tightly, and he was too feeble.

"You don't need to apologize, ever," I whispered firmly in his ear.

Then, I lifted him up. I walked him over to the bed, cleared off the crumpled pages of scribbled blue ink, and helped him in. I crawled in beside him and righted the neglected covers on top of us. We both stared up at the light streams on the ceiling without a word. I was starting to notice just how sick I felt from two straight weeks of being high, and I think he was grappling with all that he had shared after months of keeping me at a distance.

Finally, he came to terms with what he had given me and decided to give me more. "A couple of months ago, I got a call from him. He told me that he had had a heart attack. I don't know why he called me. We hadn't talked since I left. He said he was fine, said it was nothing. It bothered me for a few days, but I got over it. If he said he was fine, I believed him. But I got a call last week, saying he had passed away from heart failure." He paused. Whispered, "I'm all alone."

I turned onto my side and hugged him, held him. Now that he had regained himself, he stiffened at my touch, but eventually, he gave in, softening in my arms.

"The funeral is next week," he said quietly. "I hate funerals."

"Do you want me to go with you?" I offered almost before he had finished his sentence. I have to admit, more than wanting to be there for him as a friend—which I absolutely did—I couldn't ignore the blaring thought that a funeral would blow his secret past wide open. I would finally learn something about his family, about his childhood, about him in general. I couldn't pass up the opportunity, hungry as I had been for that information from the very beginning.

He didn't say anything in response, but as little as I was perpetually being reminded that I knew, I did recognize the assent in his silence.

I held him for a bit longer, but out of the window, the winter sky was already starting to darken. He felt thin and fragile in my arms, and I was scared to stay there long enough for the shadows to creep in across the ceiling. I stood up and instructed him to shower—it was apparent he hadn't in a few days—while I got us something to eat. He wanted to object, seemed afraid to be alone with himself again, but he didn't. And even though I felt bad for the fear I saw in his eyes, I knew what I was doing would be the best thing for him.

When I got back to the room with chicken strips and fries from the dining hall, I could still hear the shower running behind the bathroom door. I set down the to-go boxes on the floor and fell beside them. I was feeling awful. Part of me wanted to blame her. If I wasn't with her, I might have been there when he got the news. If I wasn't with her, he wouldn't have had to be alone with it for a week. If I wasn't with her, I wouldn't be so desperate for a couple of pills. I had always had it under control before her. Now, there was something inside me—unsatisfied, hungry—and it scared me. My hands were shaking, and I blamed her.

The shower had been running for a while, I realized. I knocked on the door with my shaking hand, calling softly for him. And no response. I felt the same unbounded panic as earlier explode in my chest.

I burst in with my shoulder, scanning the shoebox space wildly for carnage. I just found him sitting quietly on the floor outside the shower, still dressed, letting the water run. He glanced up at me, empty. I felt empty too.

I collapsed down beside him, aching all over with exhaustion.

"You don't look great," I told him tiredly. My eyes drifted over the shell of him as if I were facing myself in a fogged mirror, not recognizing the sunken eyes staring back. It was disturbing to see him so wrecked, but at the same time, I felt helpless to do anything, too disconnected from my own image, surely just as broken. "A shower would help," I suggested half-heartedly.

"You don't look so good yourself," he countered, confirming my suspicions. I hadn't had the chance to see the effect the months I'd lost with her had on my body, my face. With all the drugs and sex and nights spent locked in her room, it had been a whirlwind. There hadn't been a moment to stop and view how I had changed. Until it had come to an abrupt end that morning—a lifetime ago.

"I'm fine," I lied, trying to rub the protruding bags from beneath my eyes.

"That's usually my line." He ran his finger dejectedly through the grout lines between the tiles. "But I can't bother with that lie right now."

"I think I'm feeling withdrawal," I admitted unexpectedly. But I didn't take it back once it was out there. I joined him, running my finger through the grout, trying to find the lines opposite of those he was tracing. Inevitably, we ended up running into each other. I took the opportunity to grab his hand. "We could just stay here and be not fine for a bit."

He let me keep his hand, and we rested them against the cool tile of the floor. "Okay."

———

I felt sick for a few days after that—tired, sore, shaky. He took care of me. He felt empty for weeks—spacey, unresponsive, broken. I took care of him. He told me he was afraid that because he had no one to tie him to this earth, he would float away. I told him I felt like a shadow of myself and was starting to believe I would sink into the dirt.

Alone, we were falling apart. But that meant we were closer to each other than ever. I had unlocked a door that was previously closed to me: vulnerability. It began in his dorm room with the tears and followed us all the way to his father's funeral and back. We returned with an unspoken intimacy between us—a confidence in our friendship. In that way only, we were mended.

And so, eventually, he was able to write his one happy
story.

10

ONE HAPPY STORY

———

Charlie's mom was having one of her rare good days. She had risen from her pillow that morning and floated to the window to throw open the blinds. She had run a brush through her hair and put on a long skirt patterned with strawberries the color of her rose-tinted skin.

Charlie's dad was in town for once and enjoying his wife's pleasant mood. He had even kissed her on the cheek and complimented the dewy scent of her perfume before they left the apartment.

And Charlie, age four, was in the back seat of the car, moving his hopeful blue eyes between the two of them with a half-smile on his lips.

They were on the way to the rehabilitation center to pick up his brother, ninety days sober.

It was a beautiful day.

"Excited to see him, Charlie?" His mom turned around in her seat, her red lips fixed into a warm smile. Along with the sunlight that entered through the peeling tint of the car window and fell in his lap, that smile spread a glow from Charlie's fingertips to his cheeks.

He didn't say anything because he never did say much, but he rested his head back, contented, and bit back the other side of his budding smile.

"Do you think he even remembers him?" Charlie could see his dad's eyes in the rearview mirror, passing briefly over him before directing the question toward his mom, whose response was, *Of course.*

Because he never said much, his dad assumed he didn't pick up on most things. But he did. He knew his brother was in a place called "rehab" for his "addiction," and when they picked him up, he would be "clean." And from all that, Charlie gathered his brother would be more like the loving brother from his earliest memories and not the scary brother from his more recent ones.

He also recognized it would be one of his mom's good days because he knew what a bad day looked like. The knotted hair impressed into her pillowcase. The curtains drawn, casting the stuffy room into shadow. The same pair of unwashed pajamas bitter with sweat. Her whole face, gray.

This wasn't one of those days.

And he knew there was a chance his dad's pleasantness could turn sour once they met up with his brother because often when the two of them got together, there was a lot of yelling. His dad's face could twist with rage just by the sway of his brother's body, and then it was all over for anyone with ears nearby.

But Charlie hoped since his brother was finally "clean"—which was what his dad was usually yelling about—there would be no need to yell.

So, feeling soothed in all this, and with the gentle hum of their aging minivan, Charlie kept quiet. He drew his gaze from the road ahead to the window beside him, where the sun was shuddering through a family of trees, and patiently awaited their arrival.

What he knew most of all was that his brother would smell like cigarettes, and he couldn't wait to be in his arms.

They pulled into the parking lot of a low, square building made of ashy bricks with hardly any windows. It reminded Charlie of the public library and the sort of gentle exhale he felt every time he sat down in one of the scratchy, tweed chairs. He'd tilt his elbows up to rest on the wooden arms and melt into the seat with a picture book, happy.

He was thrilled to find the exact same sort of chairs—in a murky blue instead of the mossy green of the library—when they entered through the automatic doors. They surprised Charlie with their sudden whoosh but delighted him just the same with how smoothly they glided closed behind his family.

At the front desk, a cheerful man with a bald head, a big belly, and a welcoming smile greeted them. Charlie had a hard time seeing him as they approached the counter because the extended edge towered over the top of Charlie's messy brown hair. But he could see just above the man's chest, where he had on a wooden necklace shaped like a circle with one line down the middle and two shooting off the sides.

The man's voice was so low it was almost sing-songy, which made everything he said sound comforting. He handed Charlie's mom and dad a clipboard of paperwork and a pen, and he reached all the way over the counter to hand Charlie a blue raspberry lollipop from his own *secret stash*.

The three of them fell into the relief of the chairs, and Charlie sucked on his lollipop while his parents worked on the forms.

"It'll be so good to have him home," his dad commented over the scratch of the pen against paper.

"And to see him doing better," his mom nodded, looping her arm through his dad's and resting her cheek on his shoulder to look over the paperwork.

Charlie had his eyes locked on the swinging black door through which people in stark white uniforms, same as the front desk man, kept pushing in and out of, their white tennis shoes chirping like birds against the shining floor as they moved. The speckled white tiles were polished spotless and reflected the glistening fluorescents above them. The entire space felt clean and full of air. Charlie pulled in a large breath of its freshness, and as he exhaled, the door swung out again.

Revealing his brother, also clean. Charlie bolted over to him, the lollipop ping-ponging between his inner cheeks, and bounded up into his arms. He buried his nose into his brother's green jacket. The raspberry flavor of his lollipop had nothing on that sweet scent of his brother.

"How's it hanging, Charlie boy?" It was something only his brother called him and was something he loved. His brother also kissed him on the forehead, and this was the first time Charlie associated the gesture with a change: his brother, no longer faraway.

Their parents approached shyly behind Charlie. His brother looked up at them and set Charlie down.

"How are you?" their dad asked, a hint of mistrust in his voice. The two of them had stopped enough of a distance away to indicate their wariness.

"I'm really good, Dad. I think it's going to stick this time. I really do." He looked at Charlie when he said it and nodded for reassurance. Charlie gazed up in admiration, a blue ring around his lips and his now empty lollipop stick hanging from the bottom one like a cigarette. He believed his brother wholeheartedly.

It also convinced their parents. Their mom broke into the void between them and gave him a long hug.

"That's good to hear," their dad said, also giving him a hug. It was shorter but just as deep, and his usually rigid features softened in relief.

And then it all seemed really good—and it seemed like that really good would stick this time, just like his brother said it would.

"How about we go get something to eat?" their mom suggested, one hand rubbing up and down her older son's back and the other mussing Charlie's already disheveled hair.

"Sounds great," his brother said, taking Charlie's hand.

As they walked out of the sliding doors, the lollipop man waved pleasantly. The *really good* would stick this time, Charlie knew.

———

Charlie's dad let his brother pick where they ate. His brother made the decision while looking at Charlie.

Soon they were pulling open the fancy silver door handles of a breakfast diner, which Charlie had never been to before that day. When Charlie saw a tray full of smiley-face pancakes pass them while they waited to be seated, he was convinced that his brother had chosen this place on purpose. Usually reserved for tough nights, his brother knew a chocolate chip smile was a guaranteed way to make Charlie's day better. On an already great day like this one, the pancakes just pushed everything to perfection.

Their shoes squelched against the sticky checkers of the floor pattern as they followed the waiter to a weathered booth, which was hurriedly being wiped down by a busboy with a blackened rag. It still held all of its cheerful neon from the '60s era it was modeled after, but if you looked closely enough, you could see that there was a considerable amount of wear: the cushions were fraying at their edges, the table was streaked with cloudy lines from the busboy's dirty dishwater, and even the framed picture of the Chevy on the wall hung a little crooked.

Still, the upbeat four slid in without complaint and ordered a round of smiles. Plus coffee for the adults and a chocolate milk for Charlie.

While they sipped on their drinks and waited for pancakes, the conversation picked up where it had left off at the rehab center.

"So what do you think is different this time?" their dad asked, looking for a hole, a way to deflate the perfect day.

Charlie's brother wouldn't let it fall apart. "I want to stay clean this time. That's the biggest thing. If an addict doesn't care to stop, it doesn't matter what you do—doesn't matter how many days you lock him away—as soon as he gets the chance, he'll keep using." He was looking at the floor. Charlie was looking right at him. "I never really wanted to get clean before."

"So why this time?" their dad repeated, leaning forward.

"It gets tiring." He drew his eyes back up, glancing first at the skylight above them and then landing on their dad. "I was exhausted when I went in. And the withdrawal? I didn't think I'd make it out the other side. I just decided it wasn't worth it."

"That's great, honey," their mom said, her close-lipped grin revealing a set of endangered dimples illuminated over the more familiar lines in her face—from frowning and worrying. Still, she peeled nervously at the paper ring around her silverware, and when that was in pieces, she began folding the straw wrapper into a tiny square.

Their dad wasn't done with the interrogation. He was still poking the cracks of the perfect, fragile day to see what it could withstand. "But what about when you start to feel strong again? When you get further away from the pain of withdrawal and convince yourself it wasn't as bad as you remember? How will you stay clean when you get tired of sobriety?"

"I'm gonna go to meetings, get a sponsor, do the steps." His brother's face blazed with determination. "Like I said, I want to stay clean this time, so I paid attention. And while I was inside, I figured out a lot about myself—about who I really am. It was something I had been trying to suppress by getting high. But I'm ready to stop hating myself. I'm ready to accept the fact that I'm—" he took a deep breath, preparing for the reveal, but just then, the waiter approached the table with a tray full of smiles and began passing them around.

With a chocolate smile staring him down, their dad decided to pull back. But he shared a look with his eldest son that Charlie picked up on, which said that they would return to this conversation later. Charlie's brother nodded.

But for now, they all ate their pancakes and enjoyed the happiness as it settled in their stomachs, unfamiliar and warm but also fleeting.

———

When they had each cleared their plates, they rose together, Charlie's hand finding its way securely into his brother's, and exited to the mild afternoon sunshine. They all agreed it was too nice outside to head straight home, to close the book on their pleasant day. So, they took a detour to the park.

They walked on the path around the pond like the image of a perfect family, talking about the strange way the waiter had pronounced their last name and laughing at a stray goose who trailed behind them, quacking every time their dad tried to say anything. When they got to the hill—where later, Charlie would find stories in the clouds—his brother suggested they roll down it together and see who could make it to the bottom first.

Charlie lost, but only because he had slowed himself on the way down to enjoy the feeling of the world as it spun past him. The blue of the sky melted into the green grass and created a blur of colors as he turned and turned. Charlie thought it might have been scary, that blur, because he had no control over it. Usually, he hated feeling helpless against the mess around him, which he felt a lot at home. But as he rolled—dirt kicking up in his wake and dusting his clothes— he only felt good. It was fun. Even the dizziness he felt lying at the bottom.

His brother collected him in his arms, and they both laughed back into the grass. The world began to resettle into its dull order: grass below him and sky above. And Charlie found himself already missing the blur. Not just the joy it brought but also the way it made everything that was bad, hidden in the true picture, fade.

"Is addiction like rolling down a hill?" Charlie asked his brother later as they sat on the swings. Their family had made their way over to the playground at Charlie's request. Their mom and dad had found a bench. She rested her head on his chest like a pillow, and he had his fingers interlocked with hers. The sun was moving toward the horizon behind them, and so Charlie had to squint to see them, their figures mostly shadowed.

His brother was beside him, rocking himself gently forward and back. He had pushed Charlie for a while, who had giggled, "Higher, I want to go higher!" but now they just sat there peacefully. Charlie's legs couldn't reach the ground and they dangled listlessly in the air.

"I guess it is a little bit," his brother said curiously, seeming to convince himself more and more of the truth behind Charlie's question by the end of his own sentence.

"So it feels good," Charlie concluded. "Why is it so bad then?"

"At first, it does feel good." His brother bit his lip. "You feel a big rush and everything around you looks new and wonderful. You think you never want it to end. But this hill is actually an endless hill, and it stops being so fun really quick. Instead of coming to the bottom you just keep spiraling and spiraling. You start going so fast you no longer recognize where you are. And you get so dizzy you feel sick. But even if you try to stop yourself, since the hill is endless, you're always just one slip away from falling again."

"So you might fall again?" Charlie's lip quivered and he rubbed anxiously at the back of his head.

His brother looked past the swing's chain at him. His eyes were like a lake—clear but watery, yet, calm.

"I might," he said honestly. "But I'm going to try my best not to, for you." His brother stood up, kissed his forehead, and circled behind him so that Charlie couldn't see his face. He could just feel his hands on his back every time he swung backward and shot forward with more speed. A bit of the blur began to return.

"How?" Charlie asked, having to raise his voice to hear himself over the whir of wind in his ears.

"I'm going to be honest."

———

The sky was starting to turn purple by the time they left the park. Their dad bought everyone an ice cream cone from a vendor before they headed home. The car ride was quiet with contentment.

As Charlie stepped over the threshold of their apartment, the last one working on his dripping ice cream, he looked around to see if anything was different—feeling like maybe it should have been. But the blinds were all drawn on the already dimming sky, blackening the entire place like a cave. It was as messy as they had left it: bills, bottles, and stains all over the carpet.

Their dad turned on the clouded bulb that hung over the kitchen table and threw the keys down with a clank. Their mom swung the front door closed, having to lean into it with all her weight to hear it click shut in its uneven frame.

His brother took a deep breath in. "I never got to finish my thought at the diner. I need to tell you guys something important. I'm—"

Just then, Charlie's weepy strawberry cone slipped from his little kid grasp and splattered face down on the carpet. Charlie froze in terror at the sight of puddling red. He glanced up to see his mom's shoulders sag dejectedly and his dad's eyebrows angle down in a boiling rage. Here it was, the yelling he had been anticipating all day. Only, directed at him.

But as always, his brother protected him by taking the weight on himself. His fists were clenched tightly and thrust slightly behind his hips, causing his chest to jut out with a forced confidence, seemingly prepared to take on what was coming.

"I'm gay," he blurted out. His breaths were short and choppy, his stance faltering a little as he looked around nervously at the room's reaction—which was a stunned silence. He pressed on with a little less assurance. "I'm gay. And in order to move forward in my recovery, I needed to tell you all that."

Charlie had no idea what that meant, but from the relief that visibly spread through his brother's body once he had gotten it out—the release of his clenched jaw, the loosening of his tight limbs—he was sure it was a good thing.

But then, their dad started screaming. It was slow at first, having to funnel its way through the hole he'd been prodding for all day. It was just, "No, you're not," and, "Not my son." But soon, the edges of the hole began to cave in, and then their dad's anger erupted out in full force. The veins in his neck popped. His face was purple, and spittle flew from his vicious tongue.

Meanwhile, their mom had drained of all presence, her face left ashen and empty. A sob began to well up in the form of a low moan at the back of her throat and burst out into a wail of rushing tears. She fell back against the wall, her sagging shoulders bouncing up and down as she whimpered.

Charlie moved his eyes to the floor and locked onto the retched ice cream cone, the catalyst to the end of an almost perfect day. Instead, it ended up a mess like all the days before it.

Charlie looked back up at his brother, who had been pushed into a corner by their dad's accusing finger. His lip was quivering, and Charlie thought about what he had said at the park: *always just one slip away from falling.*

"Get out of my house!" their dad roared, which was how these yelling matches usually ended.

Except, his brother usually replied with, "Gladly," his eyes red and faraway.

There was a different sort of farawayness in his eyes this time as they blurred with tears—more like he was being forced out of himself instead of choosing to drift off.

"Please, Dad," he croaked.

Charlie silently begged alongside his brother, although physically, he was rooted in place. He was still confused by what was happening. All he knew was that familiar helplessness creeping up in his chest.

"Get out," their dad said through gritted teeth.

His brother dropped his chin to his chest—the position he had assumed earlier to roll down the hill. And when he looked back up, his expression had changed from turmoil to complete ease. His shoulders went slack; his strained temples released. He thrust his hands carelessly into his jacket pockets. And he walked right past Charlie out of the apartment.

His parents retreated to their room, his mom dragging her feet and his dad slamming the door behind both of them.

Charlie hurried after his brother.

He hadn't gotten far. He was just outside the apartment building, wiping tears from his eyes with the back of his hand and smoking a cigarette. Charlie felt his eyes becoming wet too, thinking about how he had finally gotten back the cigarette-scented hands he loved to hold, and just like that, they would be gone again.

He grabbed for a hand and wrapped it around himself, burying his face into the side of his brother's leg.

"What does gay mean?" he asked. "Are you not clean anymore?" Charlie knew a lot of things a four-year-old shouldn't have to know, but there was still so much he didn't understand.

"I'm clean right now, Charlie boy." His brother sucked desperately on the cigarette. He rubbed Charlie's back. "I just love in a way some people don't understand."

"How do you love?" Charlie inquired innocently. The only source he had to draw from on the subject of love was from his brother, who he believed loved him excellently. Whenever Charlie was sad or scared, his brother did whatever it took to make him feel better. All the sticky emotion that seemed to float aimlessly around his insides welled up into a warm-chest feeling when he thought about his brother's hugs. He couldn't see a better way to love someone.

"I love boys instead of girls," his brother explained simply, blowing out smoke and rubbing angrily at the greasy skin above his eyebrow with the thumb of the same hand clutching the burning cigarette.

Charlie shook his head. "What's wrong with that? I love boys. I love you."

"I love you too, Charlie boy." His brother put out his half-smoked cigarette abruptly on the bricks of the apartment and tossed the butt onto the sidewalk. "I gotta go."

"Don't," Charlie begged, his emotions welling but in a terrible way, churning around his stomach with the ice cream, causing a dull ache. His cheeks were getting all hot, and his eyes stung with the forming tears. His arms were clamped around his brother's scrawny thigh, holding on for dear life as though he would plummet if he let go. "You're clean. You don't have to leave. You don't have to fall. Just stay with me."

"I love you," his brother said again, removing his fastened arms without difficulty. He eased Charlie back a step and kissed him on the forehead. "Now go on back upstairs."

"Are you coming with me?" Charlie whined, clenching his fists and stamping his feet against the concrete like a toddler on the verge of throwing a tantrum. He wasn't that type of kid—had never been—but the frustration he felt then, the helplessness, was almost enough to send him over the edge. It wasn't fair, not one bit. His brother was clean, so he shouldn't have to leave. There shouldn't have been any yelling or crying. The perfect day shouldn't have been ruined. It made him want to throw himself on the ground in fitful protest.

But his brother's calm demeanor was enough to dispel the urge from Charlie's thoughts, leaving him just numb and heavy. "Go on," he repeated.

Charlie started to shake his head, refuse again, but his brother's eyes were fully present, deadly serious, and hell-bent on heaving himself back down the hill. So Charlie turned quickly, unable to stand it—that look in his eyes far worse than any farawayness—and ran, hot streams flooding down his cheeks.

He bounded up the stairwell, flashed down the hall, and burst through the door, past the ice cream, into his brother's room. He climbed on top of the bed to look out the window at the dark street corner below—illuminated only by one dull orange lamp. He was just in time to watch the shadow of his brother disappear into the night.

Charlie crawled off the bed and pressed himself into the corner, holding his knees and staring straight ahead.

"I'm all alone," he whispered. The empty room didn't bother to disagree.

11

ROAD TRIP

———

"We have to get going if we're gonna make it by tonight." I stepped out from behind the wall, which veiled the bathroom door, the flush of the toilet surging from behind me.

He was sitting sideways at the end of the bed, his curved back leaning against the white cinder block behind him, his knees pulled tightly up to his broad chest, staring blankly forward. He looked so young, so fragile, so sad. I hated seeing him like that. He was too unaffected to be sad, too strong-willed to be fragile, too sensible to appear like a child frightened by the monsters under his bed. Yet, the brick wall that had made him so solid as long as I'd known him seemed to be crumbling at the news of his father's death.

Seeing him like that from across the room—my hands trembling as if frightened just the same—there was a part of me that wanted to help him rebuild the wall. Yes, I had been working to tear it down from the beginning but watching him break was so difficult.

Especially when I was at my own breaking point. I had spent most of the week in the bathroom, losing my guts out of my ass, and in his bed, trying to suppress the moan of my aching limbs. The whole time, I thought of the blissful cocoon a single pill would wrap me in. Which only amplified my suffering.

I had almost shattered that morning when I was in my room packing and found a forgotten Ziplock of white powder in the pocket of a crumpled-up pair of jeans. I could feel all of my blood racing straight to my brain, causing my temples to pulse and sending out morse code beacons of pain that begged, *Do it.*

It was only at the thought of his wall withering away— folding the suit he would bury his father in—that I found the will to shove the baggie deep in my pocket and rush to his bathroom to flush it away.

As the toilet's water tank settled in the background, I saw that withering wall in him and knew at the same time, it would be good for him to keep that wall down, to open up. And selfishly, I wanted him to share the pieces of himself with me that he had been keeping beneath brick for so long. If there was ever a chance to find out something about my best friend's mysterious past, it was this weekend, staying in his childhood home, attending his father's funeral.

"Are you ready?" I asked softly, moving away from the bathroom and toward his bed.

He nodded, but he didn't give any indication he was going to stand up. I stuck out my hand, and he looked at it for a moment as if he didn't know what it meant. Then, he accepted it, nodding again once he was on his feet to thank me. He made an attempt to let go of my hand, but I held onto it tightly for another moment. "I'm here," I said. "I'm not going anywhere."

"I know," he said, but I wasn't sure if he meant it. I would have to keep reminding him.

We started off on the road. I was behind the wheel, and he rode shotgun, which was strange for us even though it was my car. He didn't have a car of his own, but he was usually found driving mine while I was intoxicated in the passenger seat.

Today, I was sober, the last of my drugs dissolving into the city's sewage system. This trip was an experiment to see if I had really lost my handle on things or if I'd just gotten a bit too deep. But based on how I'd felt the last week and the current headache pulsing behind my eyes, I was starting to think maybe my casual relationship with drugs had become more serious than I thought.

And we had just set off, not even out of Annapolis, thirteen hours still to go before we reached Rockford. I'd have to find a way to push through. I wasn't going to make him drive, even if he offered.

I turned down the music, turned up the AC, and started in on testing the limits of his dismantled wall to distract myself.

"So this is where you grew up. Right? Same house and everything?" I started simple, yes or no.

"Mmhmm," I barely caught over the thrum of the engine and whir of the road whizzing past us. He was resting his chin on his fist, staring out the window.

"Was Rockford a good place to grow up?" I drummed my fingers on the wheel, trying to make my questioning seem more casual. I knew he wouldn't surrender the information I was looking for easily—especially if I took a straightforward route of questioning. I'd have to maneuver him like one of the convoluted canonical texts from our English courses, featuring a slew of wrinkly, white dudes trying to sound smart enough to earn their unbounded privilege. My plan was to pose strategic questions and close read his vague answers for deeper meaning. Unfortunately, it is quite difficult to perform collegiate levels of analysis when your left eye is twitching painfully, and the book you're trying to read is blank.

My question yielded no response from him.

"What made you decide to come all the way to St. John's?" I tried instead, eliminating the possibility for him to answer with a yes or no.

His nose stayed pressed to the window. "Wanted to get away."

"So then, not a good place to grow up," I deduced out loud, hoping he would fill in the picture a little more for me. Plenty of people *want to get away* after high school for reasons as innocent as looking for a new adventure or taking the leap to move to their dream city. But most people *want to get away* from *something* or *someone*. I would generally consider my own childhood pretty happy, and I ended up at a college not ten minutes from my house. I had to assume his reasons for leaving aligned with *most people*, and there was a lot more proof behind that assumption than the four words he had just given me.

"It's not about the location," he said, turning his head slightly back, his eyes over his shoulder, a touch of frustration creeping up behind his words.

But I had gotten something concrete: It was a case of *someone*. Which meant I couldn't give up now despite his palpable discomfort.

"What's it about then?" I pressed. The road switchbacked, first harshly left and then right, the endless expanse of empty forest on either side trapping us in the weight of my question. The false air trickling from the vents could not disrupt the thick air between us. My question ballooned.

But, like a magician, he exited through the floorboards. "Can we talk about something else?"

"Sure," I said calmly, confident I could use my own form of misdirection to empty his pockets. "Who all's gonna be at the funeral?"

"I don't know," he remained firm.

"Your mom?" I volleyed.

He shot me down, shaking his head. I bit the inside of my bottom lip, scrunching up my nose at his masterful ability to cause a traffic jam in a conversation seemingly speeding with momentum.

I laid my foot down harder on the gas as the car whined up a hill. "Any siblings?"

I held my breath at the thoughtful pause that followed.

"An older brother," he said abruptly, as if getting a great weight off his chest, "and a younger sister." His eyes were glued to the white line passing by outside his window, his dejected words tumbling out and becoming a distant speck in the review mirror: "But they won't be there."

I turned my head toward him, angling my chin up and my eyebrows down but keeping my sightline vaguely on the road. Such little information, yet, it was huge. Two siblings I had never heard a single word about. Not even a mention, an accidental slip of the tongue: nothing.

I quickly wiped my face of its concern, not wanting him to pump the brakes on the speedometer steadily rising.

"Why can't they make it?" I took my eyes off the road then and looked directly at the back of his head.

He could feel my gaze, his shoulders tensing, and he stared harder out the window. The glass might have shattered under the severity with which he stared. "I don't want to get into it now." His words were tight, a coil of charged wire at the very top of his barrier, meant to electrocute anyone who had made it that high.

I didn't care if I was shocked. "Tell me about your father then."

"Levi." He whipped his head away from the window so fast I feared an oncoming explosion, but instead, he just looked at me with a sad expression, shaking his head *no* almost imperceptibly and biting his lip.

"It's a long drive…" I backed off from the attack and moved to the defensive. "We have to talk about something."

No response. I glanced back over and found him once again looking out the window.

"How about you tell me a story?" I suggested, the distraction of interrogating him wearing off and my nerves beginning to shake, the pulse of my head intensifying.

"About what?" His voice was sullen. It was clear that he didn't think the idea was worth anything. But he also didn't outright reject it.

"Come on. You're always writing. Tell me one of those." I swallowed hard, my voice dry, and glanced over at him with a look of desperation.

He shifted his head away from the passing white line— not looking at me, but at his lap—considering. From what I could tell from my profile view, a look of hesitant resignation rippled over his face: the tight *O* of his pursed lips spreading out through his softening features and expanding to his falling limbs.

He breathed out gently and lifted his head.

———

There was a boy, he said, age eighteen, who had just gotten out of rehab, had just had a lovely day with his family, and had just told his father he was gay. And his father had kicked him out for it. And even though the boy had been kicked out before for being on drugs, he was clean this time, so it was more painful. And he left the house with the idea that he wouldn't be clean much longer.

And that boy had a younger brother who was only four and didn't understand as much as he thought he did. He ran after his brother. He asked what it meant to be gay. He asked if his brother was still clean. His brother just kissed him on the forehead and walked off into the night.

Back upstairs, he saw his father was smoking on the balcony. The younger brother, he didn't speak a lot. He was just a quiet kid. But that night, he found the words when he went out to the balcony and begged his father to let his brother stay. He said many things that night. He said his brother was clean. He said being gay didn't mean his brother was suddenly dirty. He said he was gay too. He said he loved boys. He said he loved his brother. He said he loved his father. He said he wished his father was gay so he could love them back.

His father had put out his cigarette. He knew he had made a mistake. He loved his sons; he really did, despite it all.

So the two of them went off into the night to find the older brother.

They drove for hours, down the dark and scary streets the older brother had wandered all alone. The younger brother was not afraid. His eyes were glued to the window, searching for the shadow of his brother. There were lots of shadows that night.

The shadow that turned out to be him was lying in the park atop a large hill, like he might be looking at the stars. Except he was unconscious with a needle sticking out of his arm.

His father picked him up as if to tuck him into bed but rushed to the car with his other son running behind and drove them to the hospital. The whole time his cheeks were streams, and he kept saying he loved the both of them no matter what.

And in the waiting room, his father held the younger brother's hand and told him over and over again that he loved him. It was the only night he ever admitted such a thing.

———

His body had curled in on itself while he was telling the story: back hunched, chest creased, neck bent parallel to his seated thighs. Each word came out clinically as if he were reciting the periodic table of elements to me and not a key component of his own familial makeup.

I misinterpreted it at first. I thought he might be trying to tell me he was an addict and that he was gay. But then it became quite evident that he was the younger, not the older brother of the story.

And I didn't know what to say about that. I could've come up with something clever if he were gay to let him know in a lighthearted way that it didn't make a difference to me. And we could have bonded if he was an addict. Maybe I could have asked him for some tips.

But he was only an observer in the story. Just a kid when he had to endure such trauma—it broke my heart. What could I say about that?

Yet, I had asked for it. I had pressed and pressed him to give me a piece of his past. I thought I could be a comfort. Why did I think that? Here it was, right in front of me, and I couldn't even look at it. My stomach flipped with the shame of my cowardice.

And he was looking at me—no longer out the window or at his lap—but directly at me, waiting for some sort of reaction. It was my turn to keep my eyes locked on the road.

I watched the gaps in the road's center line shoot past my driver-side tire in a disappearing act. Which gave me the idea to escape through the trapdoor he had used earlier in the form of a subject change.

"Maybe," I breathed my uneasiness out, "you'd like to hear a story from me?"

I lifted an eyebrow his way, hoping he wouldn't be angry. The tension that had built up in his body with the telling of his story seemed to fall away, a soft smile of relief spreading onto his lips. "Sure."

"Um, it's about my dad, if that's okay."

He nodded me on.

"I've told you before that my dad's in prison. Right? But he wasn't really around much even before he got locked up. He would just show up randomly every once in a while, talking about sticking around, but he'd be gone a few days later. I wasn't ever one to wallow in it. He was just a restless man, and I understood that. So I always enjoyed him when he was around, and I never really got angry when it was cut short."

I rubbed subtly at the visible pulse that had started up at my temple, hoping he didn't notice. "Anyway, the last time he came, when I was ten and about a week before his arrest, he seemed all apologetic about it. Maybe he knew he was about to be bagged—I don't know. But he kept going on and on, saying, *God, I missed so much,* or, *Oh, I wasn't there for you. I'm a deadbeat*—shit like that. Everywhere we went: the bowling alley, the mall, ice cream shop, fucking everywhere. Finally, I just got sick of it. *Dad, I'm fine,* I told him. We had just finished a couple rounds of paintball, and he was driving me back to my mom's place. And despite how he had been harping on about the way he'd screwed me over, he said, *I know you are, Levi. Being gone like I was, I couldn't teach you much, but I did one thing for you. I made you strong by not being there. You're strong, kid.*"

My eyes were getting watery, and I gave a sort of cough-laugh to shrug off the tears. "He dropped me off after that and drove away, and I haven't seen him since. He's serving thirty out in New Mexico for drug trafficking. And I know what he said, well, it's kind of a cop-out on his part. But I don't know. It meant something to me."

I looked at him to see what he was getting out of my story. He seemed to be taking in each word.

I proceeded delicately. "I don't really know anything about your dad or what it was like for you growing up. But I do know you're the strongest fucking person I know. So whether he was there for you when you were young or not, I know you're going to move forward from this weekend even stronger."

"Thanks," he mumbled, putting his head down, uncomfortable with my compliment.

"That said," I continued, "just because you're a strong person doesn't mean you have to be so strong all the time. You're allowed to break. After my dad went to jail, and I realized who he truly was—that I had never known him and never would—I fell apart. Not long after, I started experimenting with some soft shit—alcohol, weed. And I was so fucking ashamed of myself for not being strong like he said I was. It took me a long time to realize there is strength in allowing yourself to express your emotions."

The car was quiet, but it was a comfortable silence. I had given my spiel, and even though he didn't say anything, I could tell he was grateful to have heard it. We drove on then, lighter. We listened to music and talked about the sort of things we normally did. I was starting to feel a little better—a little more in control.

———

We arrived in Rockford around 11 p.m.

The first surprise to me about his childhood home was that it wasn't a house. We pulled up to an apartment building. And a run-down one at that. The outside itself was falling apart at the seams—chipped paint, boarded windows, and a general lack of care. The inside was worse, with its stained and torn carpet, flickering lights, and cold atmosphere. It was clear this deterioration wasn't recent either. He looked unfazed as we climbed the concrete stairwell, indicating to me this was indeed the place he had grown up—nothing changed.

The second surprise got both of us, though. When he opened up the door to his father's apartment, we were met with a sea of glass: empty bottles absolutely everywhere. They clanked against each other as the door shifted them from their comfortable pattern like a jigsaw on the carpet. There was other trash too, and miscellaneous items that had accumulated in piles—bills, last notices, and the like—but most jarring was the bottles. It was hard to believe one man could have collected so many, let alone drank every one dry.

He was frozen at the sight, his jaw dangling. I put my hand on his back to comfort him, but he gathered himself quickly and shifted away from my touch.

"Hmm," he murmured as if it were a curious sight but nothing sad, and he immediately bent down to start picking them up.

"We don't have to do this tonight." I bent down beside him, my voice soft, trying to be sympathetic to how he must feel, seeing his childhood home in such a state.

There was no reply but the clink of bottles against each other as he collected them in the crooks of his arms.

I shook my head, a bit irritated that he was actively ignoring what I had said to him earlier about forfeiting his act of interminable strength.

I grabbed his elbow forcefully and made him stop to look at me. "It's been a long day. And we have to be up early tomorrow for the funeral. Let's just go to bed. We have all weekend to clean and pack up this apartment."

He looked ready to grab another bottle, but I maintained stern eye contact and instead, he dropped all the bottles in his arms back onto the floor. Their crash was deafening.

"You're right," he said sensibly, although not as if he believed it. "I think I'll sleep in my parents' bed. You can have my brother's room, the one at the end of the hall."

He didn't say anything else, just walked through the bottles and shut himself behind the door across from the kitchen.

"Sleep well," I said after him. Then, I locked the front door and took a real survey of the place. It was small for a family of five. Living room with just enough space for a two-cushion couch, coffee table, and a small TV situated on an upside-down crate. Kitchen, about the same size, with old, worn-down appliances and a circle table in the middle, leaving barely enough room to navigate the limited counter space. Then the hall, where I walked past the room he had shut himself into. There was a bathroom, closet-sized on the right, no pictures on the wall, and two doors at the end. I poked my head into the one on the left. The walls were a faded pink shade. There was a baby changing station but no stuffed animals and no little girl clothes. Really nothing else but a few scattered bottles—not nearly as many as the rest of the place—and at the center of the room, a crib in pieces, as if destroyed with a bat.

I closed that door, holding my breath. I didn't understand.

I turned to the room he had told me to sleep in and entered it like a sanctuary. It looked like a normal room. Tan walls, double bed on a frame, nightstand with a lamp, a desk, and a dresser. I saw myself in the mirror of that dresser. I looked frightened. I couldn't tell if it was because of everything I'd seen or the way the bottles all over the place made my heart beat.

I lay down in the bed, but I couldn't sleep. I just kept thinking about how there had to be bottles somewhere that weren't empty. The thought consumed me, and I was just about to get up to look when I heard an unmistakable clank outside the door.

I imagined he wasn't sleeping either and had gotten up to start cleaning. I got out of bed, thinking I would probably fail to convince him a second time, and I'd have to join him in cleaning with this itch at the back of my head. But when I went out, he wasn't in the living room.

He was on the balcony, sitting in the single lawn chair, looking off into the night.

I joined him, taking a seat on the ground and leaning my back up against the railing. He was holding an unlit cigarette between his fingers, just fiddling with it.

"You smoke now?" I teased him, knowing he didn't.

"Nah, I just like the smell on my fingers." He offered it to me. "Want it?"

I took it gratefully, grabbed a lighter from the table beside him, and sucked in greedily. It wasn't going to get me high, but it was something. The cloud I blew out was especially full because the air was sharp with cold; his empty exhales across from me were also visible. I rubbed harshly at the arm yielding the cigarette and took another pull.

"I'm afraid I've lost my control," I admitted to him.

"You couldn't have." He scratched the back of his head, looking at the ground just past me, down three stories. "We never had any control to begin with. You, me. Anyone."

"What I mean…"

"I know." He nodded. And then he shook his head. "But I think you're fine."

I flicked the stub of my cigarette through the bars and didn't wait to see the sparks of it hitting the concrete below before prompting him to hand me another one. I puffed away at it once it was lit. "How do you know?"

He considered it for a moment, choosing his words carefully.

"You've always reminded me of my brother. The way you take the world by storm, the way you admire the stars, and how your love can feel so stable even though you're constantly trying to liquify anything solid. And just like him, I think you prefer to see the world spinning instead of straight. But somewhere inside that desire to be high lies the only difference I can see between you and him." He had gained momentum as he spoke and was looking directly at me, speaking confidently, like he was giving me something from his very core—something he knew undoubtedly to be true. "You enjoy life on its own. You just think it's fun to get high and that when you are, it only enhances everything. Right?"

I nodded, watching his bottom lip bob with each syllable, hanging onto every word. I had never heard him say so many at one time. I had none of my own, but he had a few more.

"He did it to suppress life. Never for fun." He had picked up the last unlit cigarette from the pack and was playing with it between his fingers. "It was necessary for him."

I moved from watching his lips to watching that cigarette. I wanted it. And I rubbed hard at my forehead. "It seems like…" I swallowed, "it's starting to feel a bit necessary."

He stood up from the lawn chair and flicked the full cigarette over the balcony with my butts. Then, he turned around and sat down on the ground beside me.

"I think you just need to take a step back. You'll be fine." He put a hand on my knee. His fingers were icicles against my exposed skin. Yet, the tingling that spread from his handprint through my body spurred an unexpected warmth in my stomach—like I'd just slurped a whole bowl of steaming soup. It was the ultimate comfort: this physical closeness paired with his verbal reassurance.

I sighed into it like a blanket, looking up at the stars, which were starting to fade as the sky lightened. I could hear the morning birds already beginning to chirp.

"We're going to be exhausted at the funeral." I laughed, running my fist across the bags of my eyes.

"Should we stay up until it's time to go?" He grabbed for the railing and pulled himself up to overlook the place where he'd grown up, becoming lighter with the sky. It was the view of a sorry attempt at a city. Neglected buildings of no higher than five stories, empty lots with faded For Sale signs, the road crumbling in on itself every few feet. I imagined him young, trying to look out between the bars and see a bright future for himself. Only seeing smog. My eyes began to mist.

"Brew some coffee." I moved myself to the lawn chair and sniffed my emotion harshly in through my nose.

He brought out two mugs and a kitchen chair, and we sat sipping our drinks and talking lightly as the sun rose to our left. Just as it peeked over the horizon, we went inside to dress in our black for the funeral.

12

ANOTHER FUNERAL

———

All the words he had found in the dark of night on the balcony fell away on the car ride to the cemetery as he resorted back to his usual quiet self. I didn't push him because I could tell he was just trying to focus on his breath, focus on getting through this day.

I'm sick of funerals, I remember him saying. He looked sick. Physically sick. His body curved in on itself like the misshapen lumps of a deteriorating statue: rigid, pale, with sunken dark lines running like cracks beneath his eyes.

As I parked and turned off the car, I thought I might have to pull another motivating story out of my ass to get him to move. But he had opened and closed the passenger-side door before I could even open my mouth, buttoned up his suit jacket, and waited patiently for me.

I got out wordlessly and followed him through the front gates of the cemetery. It was a nice space: calm and quiet, with green grass and an appropriate scatter of trees already budding new flowers of the coming spring. You could feel the shifting season in the air, the sunlight warm even though there was still a bit of a winter nip around the edges. The funeral site, set up with white chairs and a pre-dug hole, was on top of a hill. There was no one there but the priest, the casket, and us.

"Will anyone else be coming?" the priest whispered to him, ten minutes after the service was set to start.

"No, you can begin," he said stoically.

My throat went tight, glancing back at the three rows of empty seats. As the priest started in, his tired reassurances that *God needed another angel* and that his dad was *in a better place* were like wisps of thin candle smoke in the meager breeze. There were not enough living, breathing bodies there to absorb the clichéd homily and render it comforting. Instead, it felt cheap and flimsy, disintegrating upon impact against the plastic chairs. I glanced at him in my peripheral throughout the service, his posture unnaturally straight, making him look especially heavy but also solid in contrast to the shallowness of everything else. I rubbed my sweaty palms on my thighs and tried to mimic that air of stability, but the rows at my back sucked the life out of me. Their hollowness dug in and scooped out my spine, leaving me slumped wretchedly in my own seat.

"I told them not to set up so many chairs," he said after the service had ended, once the priest had finished with his verses, and he had thrown a handful of dirt over his lowered father. We stood a little distance away from the grave and watched the funeral home pack up those somber folding chairs while the groundsmen filled in the hole. I still felt the ghost of their hollow inhabitance in my chest. "Guess I should have been more specific."

"The responsibility of planning this thing fell on you?" I hadn't known that. He had either made the arrangements whenever I was in the bathroom or immediately after he got the call because I hadn't seen him planning anything.

"Who else?" He glanced over one shoulder and then the other, his lips pressed together tightly in a way that could be interpreted as sarcasm, but I felt more closely resembled disappointment.

I pulled at a bit of skin poking up from my chapped bottom lip with my teeth and crossed my arm over my chest to massage anxiously at my tight shoulder. "Your mom? Your siblings? I know they couldn't make it, but they could have at least helped out."

He squinted at the men with the shovels, the steady movement they made from dirt pile to hole. Dirt pile to hole. It was nearly full.

"Let's walk around for a bit," he suggested, turning away from the men. "We'll come back when they're done." He started in the opposite direction, each step of his dress shoe sharp against the ground, never lingering long enough to absorb the tension of his weight. I hurried after him.

We wandered aimlessly—or so it felt to me—through the rows of headstones instead of following the set path. I had never been to a cemetery, but in my mind, I had always imagined them to be creepy all hours of the day—the sort of misty Halloween scene of the movies. But with the sunshine drifting down on our necks and the spongy grass bouncing back from the impact of our soles, the graves seemed almost like an art installation. Instead of screen-printed Campbell's Soup Cans, we had headstone sculptures that reflected our culture in a different way. We live, we eat, we die. Maybe we find love along the way. A lot of the headstones had inscriptions that read, *In loving memory.*

Below the name of the one we stopped in front of, it just said, *Mother*. The date of death was nearly eleven years ago. He had been ten.

These facts passed through me like a vague wave of nausea on their way to my brain. It was there that the pieces of this headstone connected into a clear and harrowing picture of his reality: orphaned at twenty. My mouth filled with thick, sour saliva that I nearly choked on, and my thoughts immediately jumped to my own mom, who I couldn't stand to live without. My eyes grew misty even at the thought.

While I had been working through my imagined grief, he had gotten down onto his hands and knees to calmly pick at the weeds, which appeared as if they had been growing uninterrupted since that day.

"God, I'm so sorry. I had no idea." I shook my head of the made-up mourning I'd concocted and refocused on his actual mourning, my heart feeling just as heavy. But I didn't know the right thing to say to bring him comfort. I considered bending down to put my hand on his back or to help him with the weeds, but my legs were stiff, my neck locked down on the headstone I had just considered art. Now I saw that there was a vacant human life buried beneath. I inhaled sharply as this realization twisted its petite blade in my lungs.

"Of course you didn't know. I didn't tell you." He stacked the weeds in a neat pile.

"How?" I hesitated, not sure I wanted to ask.

But he had already answered. "She had a lot of mental health problems. Struggled with depression my whole life." He took a beat. "She killed herself."

"I don't know what to say," I finally admitted. I felt awful. I had pressed for this sort of information the entire trip, for our entire friendship, really. And every time he handed me another brick in his wall—and I could tell it was so hard for him to do—I had no proper response to what I found behind the gaping hole.

"You don't have to say anything." He gave up on the weed picking and sat back, just looking at the headstone. I fell down beside him, my arm brushing his. He didn't retreat but leaned into it. "You came here with me. And I'm so grateful for your friendship. I know it's been pretty one-sided—"

"It hasn't," I interjected, hoping to alleviate what little grief I had a hand in. It was the only thing I could think of in the otherwise floundering position I found myself. He had been slowly sinking beneath the water this whole time. Finally, he had waved his arms for help, and here I was, trying to pull him into my boat. Only to realize I'd sprung my own leak. The water was pooling, and we were both drowning. My head was pounding, and I wanted to cry.

I clutched the blades of grass beneath me, trying to ground myself. "You're there for me. You listen." The well of my emotions left my voice blunt and tight.

"But I don't offer anything. You tell me everything. And I give you nothing in return." He was picking meticulously at the grass blades with his thumb and forefinger, not looking at me. Each one he plucked let off a subtle snap. "I know you're curious."

"I'm curious, yes," I admitted, my shoulders lifting in concession, "because I care about you. You're my best friend, and I want to know you better. But you don't have to tell me anything you don't want to. I understand it's painful. And I get plenty from our friendship already." I placed my hand on his back, the tension of his muscles this time releasing at my touch. Or maybe the relief my statement brought him.

His face softened as he turned it to me. "It's painful," he agreed. "But I still want you to know."

I turned up the corners of my mouth into a gentle smile. Although I could feel a cold sweat stippling my lower spine from the headstone we were resting against, the heat of his chest angled toward me flushed my body with a warm affection.

His mouth remained a straight line despite his softened exterior.

"I'm going to tell you a few more painful things today," he said. He stood up, and my hand fell to the ground, the warmth dispersing. I pulled out another weed and tossed it in his pile. Then, I pressed myself up, and we kept walking.

He stopped us at another headstone, this one so small. No weeds at all. And fresh flowers at the base. The date of death read just seven months after that of his mother. And the date of birth was only six months before the date of death.

"My younger sister," he explained.

The knife twisted again, its blade growing. My eyes watered. *What all had he been through?* My mouth opened to say something empathetic, but nothing came, and I closed it, shaking my head. I wanted to know how it happened, and at the same time, I didn't. I tried to imagine him at eleven, dealing with the death of his mother and his younger sister at the same time. I imagined him shutting down, not allowing himself to break. I wanted to let him know he could cry. I wanted to catch that young boy before he could build a brick wall around himself, give him a hug, and tell him he didn't need to shut everyone out.

It was too late. I blinked away my own tears and glanced at him, dry-eyed. He turned from the headstone before emotion could even threaten him. He nodded me on, and again, we walked.

The final grave was his brother's. I knew it before we even arrived. And etched into the stone below his name was con-firmation: *Brother.* Just twenty-two years old. And he had been eight when it happened.

He sat down beside it like an old friend—like we had previously been sitting. He leaned his temple against it, ran his finger across the word I had used to identify it. It didn't matter that I was there. It was clear he did this every time.

"I used to visit him a lot. But after my mom and my sis-ter, I couldn't stand to come here anymore." His voice was deadened, and he gazed ahead longingly.

But he quickly shook himself from his trance and looked up at me. My eyes were hot and blurry, wet lines running down my cheeks.

"You're crying." It wasn't a question. Just an observation.

"Your whole family," I choked. I was more baffled than anything, my tears almost automatic in their release. The scope of his loss was too large for me to absorb. I was a mea-sly paper towel against a flood of casualty. I couldn't even fully take in the grief he had faced, let alone do anything to wipe the lasting stains of that trauma away. I looked at him mournfully. And then I made an observation of my own: "You're *not* crying."

"I've cried plenty." His face was stone—it was statue, it was art. His fingers hovered over the inscription.

I shook my head. "No," I sat down beside him again, but this time, I wrapped my arms fully around his heavy shoul-der, "you haven't."

He tried to fight it. I could feel him flexing the muscles of his back and arms, trying to harden, trying to make himself stronger than stone, trying to emanate impenetrable brick wall, but he couldn't this time. Not at this grave.

He wilted in my arms and finally let his tears fall.

"I'm all alone," he whispered into my chest.

"No," I objected again. Not him. And not me. Not when we had each other. Yes, I had felt the gnaw of my loneliness begin to return, lying numbly in her bed, the drugs lowering the floorboards and raising the ceilings until I felt impossibly desolate. And even when I returned to his bed, felt the comfort of his presence and his sheets, my gut twisted in deprivation from the pills I craved, and it felt the exact same way. But being there with him, feeling his own loneliness soak my shirt, I knew we had each other. I had him to save me. I'd felt that from the beginning. And he had me.

But he didn't see it, his eyes pressed tightly closed. "It started here, with him," he bawled, finger still grazing the carvings, "and now everybody's gone."

"You have me," I reassured. "I'm here. I'm not going anywhere." I had said it at the beginning of our trip, and I now meant it even more. Problem or not, I was going to stay clean because he needed me to. He needed me to be a brother to him, but one who wasn't at risk of going under for being high.

And this was what I would use as my motivation to do it: him crying in my arms. I think having me at his brother's grave meant something more to him than he'd expected. He hadn't shed any tears since he first told me about his dad. And even that hadn't felt long enough to account for how deep his grief clearly ran—hadn't truly seemed complete. This was the cathartic cry I imagined had been building up for years. He let his tears run their full course, and I held him through them all.

As they began to subside, he lifted himself from my hug and lay back on the ground, looking at the sky. I joined him.

"I wish you could have met him." His words were thick with the stuffiness of his nose, but they also cracked at the edges, his throat raw from the vulnerable display.

"Me too." I paused, hoping not to be insensitive. "Did it happen that night you were telling me about in the car?"

"No."

"Was it the story that washed away in the rain on the day we met?" I glanced over at him.

He nodded.

I looked back up. "There are no clouds today," I observed.

"That's all right." He flicked the last remnants of his tears from the corners of his eyes and sat up. "I bet the grounds-men have finished. You wanna go?" He stood and extended a hand to me.

I took it, and we headed back in the direction of his father's grave, but not before he ran his fingers one more time over *Brother*.

———————

As we approached the hill, he slowed, and I did the same. There was a couple standing above the freshly patted-down pile of dirt. The man was tall, well-built, and rich too by the looks of his suit. She was young—significantly younger than him—with disproportionately large boobs to her thin face, explained by a bulging stomach that appeared when she noticed us and turned.

She smiled widely, recognition spreading across her caked face, and waved, taking the man's hand in hers and power walking toward us.

"Oh my goodness!" she squealed once she had cut the distance between us. "Look at you. You're an adult!"

"Good to see you," he muttered. His head was down, his hands shoved deep in his pockets. The vulnerability I had seen open throughout the day was zipped up tightly.

She tried not to let her smile break at his obvious discomfort. "Come here." She pulled him into a hug. "I was so sorry to hear."

He nodded, pulling away and taking a step closer to me.

"And I'm so sorry we missed the service! Our nanny was running behind this morning, and then we had to stop by—"

"I saw the flowers," he cut her off, not wanting to hear more. But then I could see one of her words catching at the back of his own throat, leaving a sour taste on his tongue that twisted his face as he repeated it: "Nanny?"

"Oh, yes! So rude of me. This is my husband." She pulled him forward toward us by the hand. He shook it stiffly. I did too, though I still hadn't been introduced. "We have four little ones at home. Beautiful, rambunctious boys." She looked lovingly at her husband, squeezing his hand. He looked indifferent, even sneaking a glance at his expensive gold watch. "And we actually just found out yesterday," she placed her hands on the bump that had thrown me off, "twin girls." She beamed.

He was at a loss for words, so I covered for him. "Congrats." I shoved my hand out, and she shook it with a confused smile as if she were just noticing my presence. "I'm Levi. A friend from college."

"College. Wow. It really has been a long time, huh?" Her eyes joined his on the ground. Softly, almost shyly, she asked, "How are you doing?"

He finally looked up, shaking off his shock. "I'm good. Yeah." Everyone knew it was bullshit. "So nice of you to come. But we've actually got to get going. Have to clean out the apartment and get all his things in order."

"Oh, all right." She was disappointed. "You should stop by for dinner before you head back to school." She nudged her husband, who dug out a business card from his pocket and held it out carelessly.

"Yeah, definitely." He shoved it deep in his pocket. "Good to see you."

He hurried us in the opposite direction. I could feel her eyes after us. I wondered if she knew he wouldn't call.

"Who was that?" I asked on the ride home.

He didn't respond, and I didn't press. He had given me so much in the past two days, I couldn't ask for more, as curious as I was about the odd interaction.

It was a silent ride back to the apartment. And silent still but for the clank of glasses when we arrived and started throwing bottle after bottle into big, black trash bags.

He spoke for the first time since the cemetery after we had tossed the last bottle and the floor was clear—a three-hour job it ended up being. We could actually see what the place looked like. And what he said was, "He doesn't have a single plant. Not one living thing."

"He has a lot of empty pots, though," I noted.

"Yeah, because they're all dead. He killed them." Bitterness bit at the outskirts of his tone, which was otherwise framed as a stating of the obvious.

I didn't understand, but still, I tried to reconcile. I could see the anger building up in him—which was just as rare a display as the earlier tears. "Some people just don't have a green thumb, I guess." I shrugged.

But it did nothing to calm the buildup that suddenly over-flowed and came out in action. He grabbed one of the empty pots, stormed outside with it, and chucked it over the balcony rail. It shattered down below, and I ran over to see the dirt that had spilled out from the broken pieces.

"What was that?" I emitted an uneasy chuckle, caught off guard by the impulsive act. Normally I would've been fully amused, especially if I had a couple of drinks in me and was feeling rowdy. But because of his evidently sensitive emotional state and the stressors materializing like triggered landmines over the last two days—plus the fact I was sober as hell—I couldn't help but feel mostly concerned. I turned to him, prepared to talk him down from this outburst, but he had already bolted back inside to grab another pot, which found its way over the edge with the first.

"What are you doing?" I followed him inside as he grabbed two more, one in each arm.

He ignored me, marching right back outside and letting them fly one at a time.

"Stop!" I yelled, moving in front of the door to block his way back in.

"Move."

"No." I crossed my arms defiantly, my feet planted shoul-der-width like a disapproving authority figure reprimanding a disobedient child. "Why are you smashing all the pots?"

"I hate plants. Why does it matter?" He tried to push past me, but I stayed firm.

"Is this about that woman at the cemetery?"

He didn't say anything. He crossed his arms and glared at me, trying to appear hateful, but it didn't suit him, and I could already see the facade cracking.

"Who was she?" I inquired gently.

He sighed, the momentary lapse of anger slipping out of him. He crumpled into the lawn chair.

"She has a big, healthy family. And my dad's dead. So it's me. I knew it was." His forehead fell into the palms of his hands, his body hunched in the same dejected curve as the morning.

I moved around the front of the chair to face him and sat down at his feet.

"She's my sister's mom." He looked at me. And then back at his lap. "She lost her, same as me. But look at her now. So clearly, I'm the problem."

"You're not." I placed both my hands on his knees, trying to be as emotive as possible so he could see just how absurd his statement was. But he was so far off in his own self-deprecating headspace, he hardly registered my touch.

"My dad kills plants, and I kill anyone close to me," he murmured faintly. "It's in the genes. Better get away while you still can." His eyes refocused, his wandering thoughts returning to the balcony, and he saw the way my wheels were turning, trying to come up with something consoling to say. "You don't have to give another pep talk. I'm not going to cry."

"Well, I'm out of pep talks," I said glumly, defeated by my incompetency at being there for him, finally being put out in the air. "How 'bout a smoke instead?"

"Sure." He went inside and was back in seconds with a full pack. I took no time lighting one up and breathing in deeply. Then, I offered it to him—a habit. I quickly realized who I was offering it to and began to take it back, but he snatched it from between my fingers and took a pull. He didn't cough like I expected. He blew the smoke out expertly and went back for another hit.

I furrowed my brow at him. "You don't really think it's you. Do you? The reason they're gone? Death is random."

"Really? Cause it looks like a pattern to me." He phrased the statement like an amusing piece of irony, even though the tone of his voice was harsh and cold. The *Really?* had gotten caught on the sharp edges of his throat and came out constrained like someone had him in a chokehold.

My bottom lip quivered up at him, my eyes going bleary.

"I'm kidding. Of course I know death's random." He tried to write off my sympathy—or as I'm sure he viewed it, pity—with a scoff. I could see right through the lie in the way his left knuckles had gone white at how hard he clutched his fist, four little lines of blood probably appearing where his fingernails were digging into his palm. In the other hand, he was nursing the cigarette between his trembling fingers, not seeming as if he'd offer it back to me. So I pulled another one out of the pack and lit it up as he reconciled his lie with an, "I'm just angry."

"At pots of dirt?" I attempted a joke instead of challenging his deceit. I just didn't have it in me.

He took another deep inhale, shaking his head. "That woman, when she moved in, she brought a shit-ton of plants. And I absolutely *hated* them. They covered up the home I'd always known. A place that didn't belong to her, but to *my* mom, and my brother, and me." He exhaled smoke out his nose. "When my sister came, that's when I started to love all the green. Those plants brought life to such a dark space." He flicked away the cigarette butt. "But of course, they wilted. It was so stupid of me to think it would last. Dirt. That's all I have. Fucking piles and piles of dirt."

I stood up silently and handed him the rest of my cigarette. Then, I walked inside.

I didn't have anything helpful to say. I hadn't had any-thing helpful to say all weekend. But who was I to be dolling out sage advice anyway? And I finally realized that's not what he needed from me.

I grabbed two pots and walked back out, handing him one. He raised a brow.

I shrugged. "It looked fun."

So we spent the night throwing every pot of dirt in that apartment off the balcony.

PART II

13

SISTER

—

After his mom died, Charlie kept almost exclusively to the balcony. He pressed himself as far into the corner as he could, positioned his knees just far enough from his chest that he could rest his journal there, and wrote. It was the dead of winter in Rockford. He wore a sweater but no gloves, and his fingers—their tips turning blue—curled numbly around his fountain pen, which made the physical motion more difficult but the writing easier overall. His mind was also numb. He watched the words appear behind the cloud of his hot breath in the freezing air. He surrendered his control.

His dad's girlfriend poked her head out from the sliding glass door, but not to try and coax him into the apartment's warmth—she'd long given up on that.

"Come carry up the plants I bought," she instructed.

Charlie closed his journal and stood up without objection. As he followed her inside, he was hit with a thick barrier of heat which felt suffocating against the skin of his deadened face.

She sat down at the table, sweating, out of breath, and cradling a bulging stomach.

He didn't ask her where the new plants would go, every flat surface in the apartment already overwhelmed by green. He didn't ask her if she really should be driving herself around at eight months pregnant. He definitely didn't ask if she knew when his dad would be back.

But that's what she asked him: "How long do your dad's business trips usually last? We're closing in on seven days!"

She hadn't figured out what a business trip meant yet, and Charlie wasn't going to be the one to tell her. Even though he didn't care for her all that much—with her subtle digs at his mom and her unwarranted attempts to nurture him—he still didn't want to rain on her anticipation of a perfect family. He knew what it was to have that picture torn to pieces.

So he just shrugged in her direction as he slipped on his boots and donned a beanie.

"You should have been wearing that on the balcony," she pointed out as another one of her half-hearted shots at being motherly.

He shrugged again and headed out the front door.

By the time he got to her car, tiny snowflakes had begun to fall. Just a few. Flakes that could fit on the tip of a needle; flakes that disappeared as soon as they hit the concrete.

Charlie could feel the numbness from the balcony building up in his chest, expanding like a bubble and filling him with a resounding hollowness. He was so alone, even the snowflakes didn't bother to stick around.

He had been trying so hard to cement a wall of bricks around his grief in the weeks since the funeral. He didn't want to burden his dad's girlfriend with his mourning and doubted she would be helpful anyway. And he didn't trust his dad to console him—not after the realization he had come to about his role in the losses they had suffered.

But Charlie was tired of the detached feeling resulting from his suppression. He could feel the grief starting to seep out of his cracks, puddling, and he wanted to express it. To be exposed.

He took off his hat and tossed it aside. He took off his sweater. He took off his shoes and his socks. He lay down on the concrete and let the flakes fall over him, disintegrating the moment they made contact with his skin. He was freezing, but still, they evaporated against him. Gone, with no more than a tiny smear of water as their trace.

"What if it's me?" he whispered out loud, his throat welling with all his collecting sorrow. It was the first time he had considered any possibility beyond his dad being the one to blame. What would it mean for him if it was true?

Suddenly overwhelmed, Charlie shook the emotion away and sat up. That inkling of guilt, blooming like a thundering wail in his chest, left him too exposed. He put his layers back on and grabbed the plants from her car.

"I'm due in two weeks," his dad's girlfriend said as soon as he walked back in the door. "He needs to come home."

Charlie set the plants on the table in front of her and sat down beside her, his body tingling. He rubbed his deadened hands together slowly, trying to reintroduce sensation, and stared forward vacantly, hardly hearing her ramblings.

"Doesn't his company know he's about to have a baby? They should be offering him leave, not sending him away for a week. Right? And right after a funeral too!" She stood up with a grunt and picked up one of the pots. "Where should these go?" She started to wander around, searching for an opening that didn't exist. The counter space was consumed with a mess of leaves. Charlie had decided immediately he preferred the familiar dirtiness of his childhood over the literal dirt brimming each of the terracotta pots she brought along with her.

He watched her ponder the plant dilemma, experimenting with a few failed locations. His cheeks were starting to flush as his exterior warmed, but his bones were still frozen, and the contrast sent a chill up his spine. He needed to shiver but fought against it, forcing himself to remain unaffected.

She was still talking to herself about his dad. ". . . I mean, I get it. He's had two children already. The thrill is gone. But he could at least be excited for me. This is all I've ever wanted, and he's acting like it's no big deal. Leaving for business trips at the height of my pregnancy? He should be here serving me hot tea—decaf, of course—and rubbing my feet and answering to my craving for peanut butter and marshmallow sandwiches. Hard to do those things all the way from Chicago… Aha!" Somehow, she had found a place for the plant in her hands. Charlie was almost stunned into expression. She slipped the pot perfectly between two others, and the sound of them rubbing against each other was excruciating.

And then she came back to the kitchen for the second one—no way she could do it again.

"Did your mom ever tell you anything about how your dad acted when she was pregnant with you?" she asked Charlie as she scooped up the second plant in her arms.

He was shaking his head when suddenly, the plant slipped from her grasp. Almost in slow motion, it toppled head over heels through the air, its leaves shuttering fearfully with each revolution. Charlie could see her pink-manicured nails shoot up to cover her over-glossed lips, forming a dramatic O as she watched it tumble.

The pot made an impressive cracking sound against the kitchen tile as it shattered into terracotta shards, dirt spreading everywhere.

Charlie could no longer contain his face in stoic composure. His eyebrows shot up, and his chin dropped as he stared at the floor, mesmerized by the wreckage. It was a grand spill. The floor had a dent from the impact and was probably permanently stained. Yet, Charlie was thrilled. He wanted to see it again. And again, and again. He wanted to take every plant in that place and smash it fantastically. There was an impulse inside him that he might have really acted on. But he didn't get the chance. She was also looking down, mouth open, not at the pile of dirt but a puddle of water at her feet.

"My water just broke," she squeaked.

Charlie hardly heard her. The impulse was boiling up inside him, heating his cheeks to a fiery red and obstructing his ears with its loud bubbling.

"Charlie!" she yelled, breaking him from the spell. "I'm in labor!"

He finally tore his attention from the wreckage and saw what a panic she was in. The chaos that had been swelling inside of him was subdued by the ensuing chaos around him.

"Oh my god. Oh my god! It's too early. I'm not due for two weeks. He's not even here. Oh my god. How am I going to get to the hospital? Oh my god."

Charlie calmly went for the phone to call an ambulance, stepping over the mess with a tinge of remorse at the missed opportunity. Dutifully, he got her a coat and a pair of boots.

"Call your dad. Get him here." She was hysterical as he led her down the stairwell and out to the front of the building to wait for the ambulance. He brought the phone with him and kept trying to dial his dad, but there was no answer. He left a few messages. On the third, she snatched the phone from his hands and screamed into the receiver, "I'm in labor. Where the fuck are you? I'll kill you if you miss the birth of our child." She thrust the phone back to Charlie as she keeled over, clutching her stomach.

He kept trying. Even as the ambulance came and picked them both up, he sat beside an EMT and dialed over and over again.

"Looks like he might not make it. It might be up to you on this one, little man," the EMT said as they were pulling into the hospital.

A bunch of nurses ran up to the ambulance and helped the EMTs pull the gurney from the back. Charlie followed as they led her through the halls, questioning the EMT and her. "How far apart are the contractions? Three minutes? Dilation? Nine, already? Ma'am, how long have you been feeling contractions?"

"I guess since last night?" She held her stomach and groaned. "At seven months, I was having Braxton Hicks contractions. I figured it was just that. I'm not due for another two weeks." She glanced uncertainly at Charlie, her face awash with fear. He stared back, blank-faced, neither concerned nor comforting.

"Take her straight to the delivery room," one of the nurses instructed. She pulled Charlie away from the gurney. "Will you be going in with your mom?"

Charlie didn't correct the nurse. And he didn't hesitate. He knew he couldn't leave her all alone, abandoned and afraid. She didn't deserve that.

He nodded firmly and hurried after the gurney.

———

Two hours later, he was holding his little sister in his arms.

Her skin was delicate—soft and pink—and her sleeping smile was beautifully unburdened. Charlie's heart swelled as he cradled her against his chest, able to feel the steady rhythm of her breathing. Whatever apathy had frozen over him in the span of two funerals was melted by the life of this little girl. He felt tears welling in his bottom lashes, and he allowed them to fall, absorbing into her pink blanket. He wanted to protect her. He loved her. And in the warmth of her touch, that love felt like enough to keep her safe.

His dad didn't get to meet her until she was four days old. He received all the messages a few hours after she was swaddled in pink and sleeping behind glass, and he called back while Charlie stood watching over her. But by then, a big snowstorm had blown into Chicago, and the roads were too bad to risk the drive.

When he finally made it home, the real storm had just begun.

A familiar pattern of angry shouting rolled in, just like Charlie remembered growing up. But instead of the fight being confined to the bedroom like it had usually been with his parents, this war was apartment-wide, and Charlie had to close himself behind the baby's bedroom door to try and escape it. *Try*, but with little success. Their arguments were penetrating. She would be sobbing about how distant he had been, how little he cared about the baby and about her: *Couldn't he see she was struggling?* He would berate her for being hysterical. She'd throw the fact of him missing the birth in his face, among other things she threw. He would call her a *psychotic bitch*. And back and forth they went, ever-escalating in volume.

The neighbors complained, and his sister couldn't sleep.

Charlie wanted to pretend he was impenetrable as he held the phone between his ear and his shoulder, trying to console the neighbors enough to ward off their police threats while bouncing his sister in his arms to try and console her constant tears.

She hadn't stopped crying since they had crossed over the apartment's threshold. Charlie had watched his dad's girlfriend bounce the baby on her knee, hold her to her shoulder and dance around the living room, even whip her boob out of her shirt to try and coax it into her mouth. Nothing could calm her terrified wail. After three hours of fruitless attempts, her mom—hair knotted and frizzy, wild eyes sunken into already forming bags, braless breasts sagging beneath a spit-up-soaked T-shirt—muttered something about it not being like she thought it would before dumping the inconsolable baby in her crib and retreating to the bedroom.

Charlie slipped into the baby's room after the master bedroom door had closed. It was his old bedroom, but it looked unfamiliar now that the windowless walls were a bright pink—although they looked brown in the dim lighting cast by the weak glow of the dinky butterfly lamp.

He stood over the crib, and his heart broke at the pain pervading his sister's small, delicate features. Charlie understood why she was so scared. One minute, she had been held safely inside her mother, and then everything had changed so quickly without her control. But he didn't know how to help her.

Because he wasn't impenetrable. In fact, he had never felt more vulnerable in his life, staring into her big, sad eyes, already wise to the misfortune of life in this home. He wanted to rebuild his walls around the both of them to keep them safe. He wanted to be the strong older brother he had seen in his own. But he was afraid. He didn't know how his brother had done it—protected him as much as he did. Even if Charlie were to lay himself down in front of the crack in the door to absorb the sound, the sorrow would still leak from beneath it, reaching into the crib with its devastating hands.

Charlie held out his own hand, begging his sister to take it instead of the sorrow. And she did. Her soft, little fingers wrapped around his weathered index, grasping tightly. Immediately, her crying ceased, and her big, wet eyes looked up at him gratefully. Then, she dragged his finger to her nose and held it there, breathing in deeply and sighing with relief. He wondered then if all older brothers had a comforting scent and it hadn't been the cigarettes all along.

He let her hold his finger until she drifted off to sleep. And even after, as he watched her calm breathing and came up with every single reason he loved her.

She loved him too. Even after the storm of his dad and her mom's raging fight fell into a period of feigned peace— meaning he was mostly out of the house, and she had taken up residence almost exclusively in bed—Charlie was still the only one who could calm his sister's tears just by giving her his hand to hold.

She held his finger up to her nose every single time, and those big, wet eyes would look up at him, mesmerized. And he would hold his breath, looking back at her, their love resounding.

At night, he would read her stories while she held his finger. He started by checking them out at the library every day after school, but eventually, he began writing his own. These weren't the usual sort of stories he wrote. He created these ones especially for her, and so they always had a happy ending. And unlike his everyday writing, these stories were all make-believe. They had to be. That's not how he normally liked to think. He preferred to lock on to tragedy, analyzing it from every angle until he felt numb to it, an outsider in his own memories. But she loved the cheerful tales he made up for her, giggling often and squeezing his finger, so he made them as outlandish and fantastical as he could.

The worst was when he had to take his finger away from her before she had drifted off to sleep. The peace behind her eyes would dissipate, and she would start to whimper. So, he came up with the idea to get her a little stuffed bear to hold when she couldn't hold him. He slept with it for three nights so it would smell just like him. She was thrilled when he gave it to her. As soon as her hands were on it, she brought it to her nose and found the tag to stick her fingers through.

That's how he left her on the last night when he kissed her forehead—bear pressed desperately to her nose, drifting off with a peaceful murmur.

He should've known. It was always the same: A lull in the night that felt like the last line in a perfect drawing but turned out to be the picture-ruining stroke. The tear he had wiped from his mom's cheek, tucked into her arms the night before his dad carted her off. The shoulder of his brother he had shaken, opposite the arm holding his hand, the night before the paramedics had carted him off. And this, a kiss on his sister's forehead as she clutched his toy bear with her tiny hands.

———

In the morning, he found her cold and blue.

Charlie had seen death before, and he still didn't know how to take it. And this was even harder to see than his mom in the casket or his brother on the bed. It was impossible. It took whatever had been left of his feeble walls and obliterated them. Then, it obliterated him into nothing but hot liquid, which drained away, down his legs, and out onto the floor. Himself was no longer inside himself. He was nothing but a puddle on her fuzzy pink rug. He tried to make a sound, but without himself, it was nothing but a puff of air. He tried to move, but as an empty shell, he had no control over his hollow limbs. His chest fell in an attempt at breath, and met nothing behind. Muscle, gone. Lungs, gone. Heart. Gone.

He felt frozen in time so that the subtle spin of the earth on its axis was enough to knock him on his ass. And he just stayed there, waiting.

It was about an hour before her mom came in. The inhuman shriek that fell from her lips at the sight of her baby was deafening.

She collapsed onto the bars of the crib, wailing, her face a deep red and all tears. She called an ambulance, hysterical. The paramedics arrived and took them away.

Charlie stayed where he was, unmoving.

Until he heard the soft sound of the front door shutting. At that, Charlie crawled on his hands and knees to the door and cracked it slightly so he could peek out. Her mom had walked in with their dad behind—he was the one who had shut the door so quietly. It was only the two of them.

She went straight to their room. Her face was ashen and empty. Her limbs hung low and heavily as if she were carrying barbells. Her whole body sagged with the weight, and she looked nothing of the young, bright woman who had entered the apartment just months before. Charlie had thought then that she was trying to act far older than she looked. Now, she had aged years, but the trauma left her quivering like a child.

His dad didn't follow her to provide comfort but grabbed a bottle of whiskey from the kitchen and a pack of cigarettes from one of the drawers and went out to the balcony.

Charlie opened the door completely, balancing his body against the doorframe. He realized then how suffocated he had been in the room. He felt cool air fill his lungs for the first time that day. He wished he could breathe in enough cold to make it snow inside him. He wanted to feel something, but he was numb all over again.

He shut the suffocation behind him by closing the door, and he pushed himself up with everything he had left. Then, he went to the balcony.

"She's gone," his dad said as soon as Charlie had slid the door open. He was already deep into the bottle, and his words slurred.

Charlie stood so still. He was afraid the frigid night breeze would just blow him away, so he focused on becoming an inanimate piece of the balcony.

"They all leave me," his dad moaned to himself—Charlie wasn't there. But those words brought him back to life with a harrowing realization. It was one he had almost arrived at just before his sister's birth.

"You're not even around," Charlie exhaled his revelation through chapped lips.

His dad must have interpreted the statement as Charlie casting blame because he reacted with a heavy backhand across his cheek. His thick, round knuckles pianoed into Charlie's still-soft, babyish skin, impressing heavily into him the anguish behind the long-repressed action. The force of it dropped Charlie to the ground. Stunned, he instinctively lifted his hand to the feverish handprint created by the slap, although he couldn't feel the pain of it.

His dad immediately recoiled, falling backward onto his chair, his face twisting in grief as he began to weep. He bowed over, dropping his head into his hands, shaking with his sobs.

Charlie shifted into a seated position against the railing and pulled his knees up to his chest. He was not angry at his dad like he had been since the funeral. He knew he deserved to get slapped. Because what his dad had taken as an insult was actually Charlie understanding for the first time that *he* was the reason everyone in their lives left. His dad wasn't around enough to be the cause. It was him. He had tucked each of them into bed the night before their successive departures. He had whispered his love through the air, and then they were taken. Somehow his affection was the mark of death.

He couldn't go through it again. He wouldn't. He would close himself off completely, lock away whatever was left of his capacity for connection before he allowed someone else to fall.

Most at risk, his dad, who had raised his head momentarily with red and watery eyes and looked at Charlie regretfully.

"I'm sorry, Dad," Charlie apologized in advance, fighting the quiver in his voice—swallowing it and using it as a sealer in his wall.

"You're gonna leave too. Aren't you?" his dad sniffed.

"Yes." He had to.

Charlie didn't mean that night, or the next day, or really anytime soon. But he knew he would have to leave eventually, and he would never look back. He believed it was best he distance himself, just in case the wall didn't work. He couldn't protect his brother, or his mom, or even his sister, as much as he had tried. But he would protect his dad. He was all Charlie had left.

14

STARGAZING

———

The first Friday night we were back from Rockford, we both decided we shouldn't go to a party. He was still dealing with his loss, and I was still trying my hand at sobriety. But that didn't mean I was going to let us sit in his room all night and mope. I needed something to keep my craving mind occupied. And more importantly, I had made a promise to myself to be the ridiculous and wild friend he needed from me.

But, I'll admit it, it was easier for me to be wild and ridiculous with a little something in me. I was feeling uninspired.

"What do *you* want to do?" I tried to inject genuine investment into my voice to disguise the fact that I was putting the responsibility on him to deflect my own shortcomings.

"I already told you,"—he wasn't at his desk writing but in bed, facing the wall—"I just want to stay in."

I sat on his floor, looking up at the muscles of his back rise and fall beneath his white, long-john shirt, his broad shoulders hunching in. I felt tired and defeated.

"What's something you've always wanted to do on a Friday night, but I dragged you to a party instead?" I tried a different angle, fighting to keep the weariness out of my tone.

"Have a quiet night alone in my room." He rolled toward me and sat up. The bags beneath his eyes were heavy and marked with subtle lines at the corners from strain. The skin between his eyebrows was shiny with the grease of a long day, and in general, his skin had a dull complexion. I wondered if I looked just as close as him to the end of my rope. "How about you?"

"What have I always wanted to do?" I played dumb.

"No," he said, pensive, "don't you ever just want a quiet night in your own room?"

"I get too lonely." I stood up from the floor and sat down next to him on the bed, putting my arm around him and brushing off his question. "What's something you wanted to do on a Friday night when you were a kid but never could?"

"Go to a beach," he said automatically. As if it weren't something he'd ever consciously thought about but had always been something itching at the back of his mind.

"Great idea!" I hopped up from the bed, feeling a slight jolt of energy. "Let's go." I started for the door.

"It's 10 p.m. It's dark and cold out." He didn't move from his seat, the left half of his face shadowed, but still, his grimace was quite apparent.

"I'll make sure to keep close for warmth and safety." I motioned him on. He tried to break me with the cross of his arms and a defiant eyebrow raise, which normally would be powerless against my determination, but tonight, almost made me question if I really wanted to go walking around in the cold. But I held strong long enough for him to admit defeat and rise to follow me.

We walked through the night like so many others, but it felt strange being sober and headed in the opposite direction of all the best party houses. The night was calm. No distant sound of trashy music and drunk students. Just crickets, the wind, and our footsteps against the brick.

Things were quiet between us. He was walking his usual way—hands in pocket, head down—only, I realized I had adopted the same stride. I pulled my hands quickly from my hoodie pocket and tried to loosen up. My eyes were heavy. I fought a yawn.

I shook out the knots in my slumped shoulders and rubbed my hand down my face to try and wake myself up. Then, I hurried ahead of him like I normally did, and to prove a point to myself, I pasted on a dilapidated grin and began walking backward. "Compare and contrast me with a beach."

"How can I if I've never been to the beach?" His chin did not lift, even a centimeter.

I was taken aback. "Wait, you've never been to a beach?"

"Yeah, that's what you asked me. Isn't it?" A twinge of uncertainty percolated into the otherwise dry question.

"I asked what you never did on a Friday night. I didn't know that meant you'd never been ever." I had slowed up in my surprise, and we were back to being side by side. But he had quickened his pace. "We live pretty close to one."

"Yeah, I didn't know. I haven't explored much off campus." He tried to push his fists even deeper into his jacket pockets, his shoulders narrowing self-consciously. The streetlights were sparse, and we were in a dark expanse between two. I had to squint to make out his obscured features, and still, I could not get a read off of him.

"You're always going on runs. Where do you run?" I pouted my bottom lip, trying to calculate what wasn't adding up in my erring mind.

"Around the area," he said with a note of defensiveness. "I've seen the water, obviously. I've been to the harbor. I just haven't been to a beach, with sand and swimming and all that."

We broke out of the residential area, and the claustrophobic maze of houses cut off at an expansive river of murky water. There was a lookout point to the left of the spanning bridge. We ended up against the rail. I pointed thoughtlessly toward the speck that was our destination across the way, but I couldn't let go of what he had said and kept the conversation fixated on it.

"You grew up just an hour or so outside of Chicago," I fought. To what, prove he was lying? "They have beaches. You never went to one of those?" My tongue slapped unhinged against the back of my teeth, the unintentional antagonism of my interrogation hardly registering until it was too late.

He slumped onto a deteriorating wooden bench behind us, its gold plaque gleaming in the quaint light of the bridge's vintage lampposts. I couldn't quite make out the name of whatever rich benefactor had donated a penny of his wealth to the pathetic seat. He looked just as distressed as the slats he sat on. "My dad went to Chicago when he wanted to get away and pretend he didn't have a family. He never took us along."

I felt instantly shitty. Since the funeral, I had tried to tread cautiously around what all I had learned about his past. I actively monitored my facial expressions to make sure I didn't catch myself staring at him sympathetically. I knew he wouldn't want me to look at him any differently. But I did. And I usually kept it on my mind during our conversations to avoid saying anything potentially triggering or insensitive. But of course I had slipped up. Just because I was sober didn't make me any less of the mess I had always been. Fucking up was inevitable for me. I just hated how now that I had all but forced him to open up to me, my mess would affect him.

I fell dejected onto the battered bench beside him, unable to come up with any sort of optimistic response. The defeat felt amplified by the twitch pulsing in my wrist and the glob of need welling in my throat. I wanted to give up trying, honestly. Stop trying to be helpful, stop trying to be sensitive, and most importantly, stop trying to be sober. It was all worthless.

I stuck my hands back into my pocket and positioned my head toward my feet.

"Why don't you do it?" he asked.

"Do what?" I glanced over at him.

"Compare me with the beach." He smiled, a beacon in the nearly moonless night. His eyes were on me, and his hands were up, chest open, challenging me to read him.

I considered the proposition with a hum, but it didn't take long for the affection to come tumbling out of me excitedly: "Well, it takes years and a million waves to wear you down from stone to sand. You're deep and mysterious, but beneath the surface is something beautiful. And there are dark places no one has ever been able to explore, maybe never will, and that's okay because standing on the shore, just getting my toes wet, is enough for me."

He looked back down, embarrassed. But the subtle grin on his lips made me think he appreciated what I said, and that flushed a warmth through my veins like the injection of an intoxicating concoction. I went all fuzzy around the edges, and my heart was fluttering as if morphing from caterpillar to butterfly. It was a familiar feeling, but at the same time, it was not quite like anything I had felt before. I was confused by it and, self-conscious, I tried to snuff it out by blurting out jokingly, "You're also fucking hot and make women so wet."

He smacked me in the arm, laughing. "And you are a beach."

I sighed, feeling the moment lighten. "I do try." I stood up and bowed. He rose too and pushed me playfully. Then, we started across the bridge, the cross-breeze aerating any remains of the strange sentiment that had overtaken me.

When we arrived on the other side, the parking lot was empty, and when we got down to the sand, there was no one else around. It was past midnight. There was only the sound of the water gently lapping onto the shore.

After scanning the ramshackle beach—pebbles, twigs, and cigarette butts disrupting the meager amount of sand—I turned to him to get his impression. He was staring at the sky.

"It's not the *best* beach." I felt suddenly insecure. "Maryland isn't exactly known for its beaches."

"It's great." He nodded to reassure me. Then, he focused his attention on the ground, drawing his toe through the sand.

"Take off your shoes," I ordered, hopping on one foot as I tugged at my dingy Converse.

He stepped on the heel of each sneaker with the other foot to remove them. When both were off, he balled his socks, stuffing them inside, and then wiggled his free toes. He basked in the sensation for a moment. "You think I'm like sand?" he asked.

I tossed my own shoes haphazardly aside, their frayed laces flopping through the air.

"Definitely." My toes wriggled beneath the cold, damp earth. I had the desire to sink chest-deep into it—imagined him descending beside me. First his shoulders, his lips, and then the tips of his hair. We'd hold hands the entire time, and together, we'd feel our toes popping out the other side. At that point, we would let go and dive down into it, coming out face up, wiping sand from our eyes to find a sunny day. There, I'd still be erratic but needing no assistance—filled with energy and there for him perfectly at all times. His shoulders would be back, his chest open, so I could see directly inside, and there'd be no more mysteries between us. We'd make love to the earth, and a whole slew of girls, and then finally, to each other. We'd make an ocean of love and drown in it. And none of it would matter too much. It wouldn't mean anything more than a wink. We'd chalk it up to impulse, and why not? If we could get away from this life, if it was just us beneath the sand, why not finally be happy?

"What do we do now?" he asked, breaking my fantasy.

I exhaled. I could see my breath. "Collect driftwood for a fire."

We walked around the shore, reaching down for twigs and sticks. I could only see his bent shadow behind me, but I knew he was smiling.

We made a pile, and I lit it, along with a cigarette. Then, I began to undress.

"What are you doing?" he asked.

"Now, we're skinny dipping." I handed him the cigarette, pleased by the amused confusion that had spread across his face as he held it between his upturned thumb and pointer finger. I gave him a staunch salute as if I were a Navy sailor about to board a sinking ship, and then I bolted for the water. As it consumed me—toes, calves, knees, thighs—I felt a tingling not dissimilar to the way my heart had skipped back on the other side of the bridge. My breath caught at the sensation, unexpected and piercing.

When I looked back, waist-deep in freezing darkness, I saw the glowing cigarette end at his lips. He took a deep pull and tossed the rest of it into the fire, beginning to get undressed himself. I plunged myself beneath the water.

"Fuck," he said from beside me when I came up for air. "We're gonna freeze to death."

"That's what the fire is for." I grinned wildly.

His teeth chattered; his arms were crossed, hands rubbing at his biceps to keep the deadened nerves alive. "Imagine someone finding us floating down the river."

"How blue we would be."

I began floating on my back, canvasing the array of stars above us. My ears clogged up with water, and I could only hear the thick sound of nothing. I glanced in his direction and saw just the top of his head skimming the surface, the rest of him beneath the water.

I couldn't tell why I was feeling like this. I thought it might be because I still wanted something to drink and was beginning to get delirious with that desire. It could have been because of the cold or love. Or maybe things were just different now that I had seen his home and the gravestones of his family. Our relationship had evolved.

He came up, dripping and rubbing his eyes. I had to dunk myself again. I blew all my feelings out in bubbles. Then, I floated back up. "Let's get the fuck out. It's freezing." I was shivering.

We splashed all over the place, running out of the water and up onto the sand, where we threw back on our clothes and huddled close to our fire.

He was laughing as he shivered. His amusement came out shaky. It was the first time I had seen him laugh so freely. I laughed along at the novelty and because I thought it was beautiful. Our laughs echoed off the empty beach and drifted into the night like paper lanterns with secrets scrawled across the insides.

I felt warm after that, and I sat back, satisfied. "You were looking up at the stars earlier," I noted. "I thought the night sky was too dark for you?"

"I'd have thought you were too drunk to remember a thing like that." He gave me a sly side smile even though the corners of his eyes were low in a distant sorrow.

"I remember everything," I volleyed back, my words hollow.

"What a curse." His chin was tilted down to the fire so that the bottom of his face glowed a jubilant orange, but above his nose was shrouded in the sky's indigo. As always, his expression was difficult to decipher, but I understood what he was doing just by nature of knowing him.

"You're avoiding my question," I accused and then held my breath for the answer. His response felt significant somehow.

"The sky and I have a complicated relationship."

At first, I didn't say anything, hoping that he'd elaborate. He didn't. "Fine, and why is that?" I caved.

He bit his lip, not wanting to tell me. But we had evolved, and he knew he should. But he did it like I had a gun to his temple, voice strained and body stiff. "I've always been accustomed to looking at the ground, even as a kid. And he saw that—my brother did—and he was always reminding me to look up for inspiration. That's why I started writing. And when I look up at the stars, all I can think about is the image I have of him looking up in that same way on the night he died: in awe. I looked up, and I saw it too, for a moment. And then he took it all away from me."

"So why'd you look tonight?" I whispered out like a breath, my lips hardly moving.

"I wanted to see him, even if it hurt."

I let the back of my head fall against the sand. I heard him do the same. We sat there silently awhile, both trying to find his brother in the sky. I wanted to ask his brother how to go about being enough for the boy beside me, who I cared for so deeply. I knew it was impossible, and still, I searched the stars for an answer.

The result was the beginning of a headache pulsing at my temples. It might have been from straining my eyes so pointedly, but also, I'd been getting these headaches almost every night, from full days of fighting off intrusive thoughts about him and parties. Just the thought of a full kitchen island of bottles, a baggie of coke, and someone's house key passed around in a backroom made my mouth dry.

I broke our silence with an admission: "I think I'm done being sober for now."

"Okay," he said although I wanted him to tell me *no*, "but if it's because you don't think you can keep it up, I hope you haven't forgotten your own strength."

"No, nothing like that," I brushed him off. "I just figured it's time to try again. I feel fine."

I feel like you're lying, I wanted him to say to me, but he said, "That's good to hear."

"And you?" I countered. "How do you feel? You know, I haven't seen you write a word all week. And I haven't known you to go more than a couple of hours without jotting down at least a few words in that notebook of yours, if not a novel."

"Maybe I'm trying the same as you," he deflected.

"Finally coming to terms with your addiction? I'm proud of you." I turned on my side so he could see my grin.

It encouraged the truth from him: "Usually, I'm writing to try and make sense of the memories that bombard me out of nowhere. The funeral brought up a lot—too many. I'm feeling a bit overwhelmed right now."

"Just start with something small," I suggested softly, wanting to give him genuine, useful advice at least once. To tell him what exactly he needed and to make myself more deserving of him.

He whispered into the sky, "It all feels big."

"Don't give it that power." I felt like I had all the answers for him now that I had decided to give up my sobriety. I guess that's what happens when you learn something crucial about yourself—like that you're useless without a drink or that you have feelings for your best friend. Suddenly, everything becomes clear.

We talked for hours back and forth past a dying fire. At one point, we collected more wood to regrow its flame. And then, we kept talking—about lighthearted topics like the upcoming season of our favorite TV show, the rumors of our professor's apparently outrageous sex life, and the superlative assignments of all the English department students (me, most likely to wake up in a different country with no memory of how I got there; and him, most likely to hold out in a police interrogation as a witness in whatever crime I was being accused of).

Eventually, he fell asleep, and I watched him closely as the sky began to lighten. It was the first I had ever seen it; I had come to believe he never did. But here he was before me, eyes closed, breathing steadily. It wasn't a deep sleep, and he didn't look peaceful per se, but he did look softened. I moved my eyes between the image of him and the embers of the now-dead fire, and they lulled me into a dream, unburdened.

15

VISITING HOME

———

He nudged me awake for the sunrise. With only about two hours of sleep under my belt, I wanted to groan an objection and drift back off into my pleasant dream—the fine details vague in my half-awake state, but something to do with a big house, a king-sized mattress in the master bedroom, and someone beside me I loved. But I peeked one eye open and saw the delicate pink haze of the skyline giving way to the blazing orange of the sun, and I pushed myself from the sand to sit up with him, watching the day begin. My body ached from the hard ground, but his glowing face in my peripheral eased the tension in my back. That, and the decision I had come to last night—to abandon sobriety. The headache I had woken up to for weeks was absent that morning; just the thought of the drink I'd have later set my mind free.

Once the sky was fully blue, we threw sand over the remains of our fire and started back to his dorm. We were both quiet with the tired satisfaction of our night.

But not two minutes after I crawled into his bed face first for a fat nap, and he had taken post at his desk, I jolted up with the remembrance of a dinner my mom had invited me to for that night. She had some *big news* to share is what she had told me over the phone earlier in the week. And I had agreed to come.

Now the groan came long and dramatic, a deep dread settling in my chest. I loved my mom to death. She was a single mother, and I was an only child, so we had leaned on each other when I was growing up. We were incredibly close. But I couldn't stand her latest boyfriend. He was half my mom's age, just five years older than me, and a total hippie. He had convinced my mom to go vegan, and now all they did together was meditate and have mindfuck sex that they weren't afraid to bring up in great detail around me.

"What?" he asked to my groan. He wiped at his nose with a tissue and then used the other side to clean the sheen of oil from his forehead. His under eyes sagged a bit from lack of sleep. I'm sure I looked the same.

I flipped over and propped my back against the wall. I could see little bits of sand in his tousled hair, and I concealed a grin. "My mom invited *us* to a dinner tonight."

It was not the complete truth. She hadn't specifically invited him. But I needed backup against the hippie, and she wouldn't mind. She absolutely loved him—thought he was the best friend I had ever had and expressed that to him every single time. I knew he liked hearing it too, and he liked coming along even if he would never actively admit it. Though we were far from a normal family, my mom was very loving, and I could tell it made him warm to be around her.

But he was immediately skeptical, crossing his arms over his chest, half in cold and half in distrust. "She *actually* invited me? It's not a family thing you're bringing me along to without her knowing?"

I had lied to him plenty of times to get him to come. What was one more? "Of course she invited you. She loves when you come along. You're part of the family."

Despite my track record, he continued to believe me. Maybe because half the time, I was telling the truth and she really had invited him. And maybe the rest of the time, when he had to face her surprise at finding him on the doorstep beside me, it was still worth it. He would never impose himself. But I knew he appreciated me imposing for him. Even if he gave me a punch in the arm every time the invitation turned out to be a lie.

When we arrived that night, it was no different. My mom opened the door and pasted on an overly big smile beneath wide eyes—a failure to conceal her surprise, even though she probably should have come to expect it by now just like him. He deflated for a second. His shoulders had already been a bit heavy, skin pasty as we approached the door, in expectation of this exact reaction. Yet, he was still disappointed to realize she hadn't invited him. But she reeled him back by ushering us in enthusiastically, "So good to see you! Come in. Come in!" and pulling him into an earnest hug.

She held him a bit longer tonight, and she said quietly into his ear, "I was so sorry to hear about your father."

He nodded a thank you once she released him, but he looked a little less restored by her hug than usual.

I stepped over the threshold behind him into the remnants of my childhood home. The bones were still the same.

There was the plush carpet, a despicable shade of '70s brown that perpetually looked dirty. It probably was dirty from a young, mud-soaked me wandering in from outside without bothering to take my sneakers off. But also, it had looked that way from the beginning. There were the sagging cushions of the same couch, its dingy plaid upholstery worn down in the space I planted my butt every afternoon in high school to smoke a joint and veg out in front of the same hunking box TV. There were still stacks upon stacks of rock 'n' roll records—the music I'd been raised on—scattered across every surface, with matching posters as proof of concerts my mom had attended in her twenties.

But there was also new art hanging on the walls. Lots of intricately detailed mandala renderings of trees and flowers. Hindu gods and goddesses in grand headpieces, with bands twisting around their many blue arms. And not because the hippie was Hindu, because there were also plenty of Buddhist symbols hanging around to confuse the message. There was a large, gold Buddha statue sitting atop the front console, surrounded by a number of tea candles with contradicting scents. There were candles everywhere, and they stank up the entire house with the musty smell I had come to associate with the hippie.

My mom either didn't notice or chose to ignore my disgust at the poor taste—not to mention cultural appropriation—of the hippie's choice in decor. She wrapped me up in a bear hug and went through all the motherly pleasantries like, "You look tired. Are you getting enough sleep?" and "You know a little meditation can do wonders before bed to clear that whirring college brain of yours."

"Good to see you too, Mom," I muttered the typical mix of faux-embarrassed gratitude that comes with being loved so well by a parent.

She pulled me back in and gave me a fat kiss on the forehead. "My beautiful, sarcastic creation. I cherish you."

He liked to look down at his feet during these intimate moments. And she noticed that just the same as me, so she always tried to keep them short.

"Come to the kitchen, you two," she chirped gaily. "Dinner's just about ready."

"Ah yes, tofu and wild mushrooms. I'm salivating." I delivered the joke to him when her back was turned, and he responded by punching me in the arm like I'd been waiting for.

Her boyfriend, the hippie, was in the kitchen, in flowy pants and with no socks, his ponytail sweaty from standing over the stove. His ridiculous influence over my home had centralized in the kitchen. Sure, the appliances hadn't changed, but no longer were the cabinets full of fruit roll-ups and potato chips like when I was growing up. The fridge, covered in grainy coming-of-age photos of me held up by state magnets my mom had collected in her hitchhiking days, was full of health-conscious, vegan food from the pretentious organic-only grocery store. Not a single off-brand, sugary soda in sight.

"Hello, friend," the hippie always greeted me with, even though we weren't friends, and I had made that abundantly clear to him with an arsenal of snide comments I brought out each time we were together.

"Yeah," I breezed past him without a glance and opened the fridge. "Mom, where's all your beer?" Although there was no soda, I could always count on my mom having an array of alcoholic options. Thankfully, hippies were still more than down for intoxication.

"We don't have any right now. We've got some homemade kombucha, though."

I groaned dramatically—*the one thing I had been looking forward to that night.* I slammed the fridge door, and a few of the photos teetered beneath their magnets.

"How about tea?" the hippie offered, trying to be friendly to me. He was always trying to be horribly friendly so that one day his *Hello, friend* might not be a load of bullshit. But I had no interest. Especially now that I had found out I'd have to experience the night sober.

"I'll just have water." I dejectedly grabbed myself a glass. The hippie's shoulders slumped over the stove at another failed attempt.

From the kitchen table where his green-jacket-clad shoulders had quietly slipped into a seat, he called to the hippie in a gravelly voice, "I'll take some tea." The hippie perked right back up. I made eye contact with him so he would know how displeased I was that he had undermined my attempts to tear the hippie down. He just shrugged, and I knew it was his revenge for lying about the invite.

I sat down at the table beside him with my water, and the hippie brought him and my mom mugs of tea. The hippie poured a glass of kombucha for himself and then brought the pot of mush he had been slaving over to the table.

"Tofu stir-fry," he said, quite pleased with himself.

"Looks sublime, lover." My mom leaned over to kiss him inappropriately.

I gagged twice as I scooped a heaping pile of steaming tofu onto my plate.

"Wait," the hippie pulled away from my mom, her slobber forming a ring around his lips, and he held his hand up to stop me. "Let us have a moment of silent reflection before we eat." He and my mom closed their eyes and let their chins drop as if praying. Which was a hilarious sight to me because my mother was a raging atheist. I couldn't stifle a chuckle.

They ignored me and went on with their silent reflection. But once their heads were raised, the hippie felt the need to comment. "Silent reflection may seem a bit silly or 'lame'"—he held up air quotes, and all that was missing was an, *as the kids would say,* even though he was only twenty-six—"but it is actually a very powerful way to improve ourselves as human beings."

"I save up all my reflections for when I feel a big shit coming on." I stabbed at the tofu with my fork.

"Levi!" my mom criticized, only because the hippie was visibly hurt by my words. I could see the laugh she was swallowing. "Enough about our differences." She looked at the hippie for that one, letting him know it was time to shut up. "Tell me all about what is going on in the life of my beautiful, albeit crude, son. How is school?"

"My grades are shit this semester." I shrugged into my plate. "And it's pretty much a lost cause at this point."

"A big letter stamp on your forehead is no mark of success or happiness. I'm asking how are you enjoying yourself? Do you still find pleasure in your classes? Are you fulfilled?" she asked. The hippie was nodding along beside her as if he was truly interested. I rolled my eyes, but I could see in the seat next to me, the recently orphaned him was wishing he had someone to care about not just his academic life, but his happiness.

I had to answer seriously because of him. "I don't know what I'm passionate about. But I do enjoy my classes, so I guess I'm happy where I'm at right now."

"That's good to hear. It takes some people their whole lives to realize what they truly want out of life. There's no rush to find it. As long as you can find happiness in the present, you're doing just fine." She squeezed my hand, and I have to admit, I felt warm. She may have become a hippie out of left field, but she was still my mom, and I loved her for it. "How about you?" She looked across the table at him, making sure that she spread the love around. "Are you doing all right? I know how it hurts to lose a father. When I lost mine, I felt so alone and confused." Instinctually, her thin fingers slid onto the table, reaching out, and the hippie took up her marooned hand.

"Mom…" I tried to stop her, shaking my head.

"We weren't very close." He moved the tofu around his plate, his face a subtle tint of green. I couldn't tell if it was the tofu making him nauseated, or just the conversation, centering on him and his grief.

"Still," my mom continued, ignoring my signals, "it can be hard to wrap your mind around death. It took me years to find a way to cope. And it only came once I accepted in death comes peace. I just hope you know that and can find peace for yourself like your father has now found."

He set his fork down and was motionless, looking at his lap. He appeared pale and possibly on the verge of tears.

I tried to divert the attention away from him because that was the only way I knew how to help.

"Mom, enough about that. You had big news?" I shoved a bit of tofu past my lips to further divert the scene and chewed uneasily at it while I spoke. "That's what this whole dinner is about anyway. Right?"

She looked at me like she had forgotten my presence entirely in the delivery of her wisdom. "Yes, but that's for later. Can't we just have a conversation first?"

"I'd say we've had a good bit of conversation: school, passion, death, bathroom habits." I checked on his expression to see if my rambling was doing any good. He was completely spaced out, and I couldn't let my mom notice, or she'd go into total concerned mom-mode. I continued eccentrically: "Plus, I've been on the edge of my seat all week waiting to hear this news! You can't leave me hanging any longer."

"Ah, my beautiful, flippant son." She smiled at me. I knew that meant I had won her over. "Fine, the big news then." She leaned into the hippie and put a hand on top of his. He purred creepily at her touch and beamed at her as if she were the artistic magnum opus of mother nature herself. My mom's free hand hovered in slow motion through the air, finally coming to rest on her stomach. "We're pregnant."

My mouth fell open, but I had to close it quickly to keep the few bites of tofu I had struggled through from coming back up. I swallowed hard and then let my jaw hang once again. "What?"

"We've got a little baby girl on the way." My mom was glowing with joy. And the hippie too, who I noticed then had a bit of tofu stuck in between his two front teeth. I felt like punching those teeth right out of his mouth just so I didn't have to look at that disgusting bit of food. He was disgusting. And his child was growing inside my mom.

I shuddered. I had to force myself to look away from the hippie so I didn't gag, and I turned instead to the chair next to me. It was then I noticed how the color had completely drained from his face.

"Are you okay?" I whispered from the corner of my lip.

He tried to shake himself out of it. "Yeah," he said to me, and then to my mom, "Sorry, I just… congratulations! That's wonderful news. I'm—I'm gonna use the restroom real quick." He pushed back in his chair and hurried off down the hall.

"Is he all right?" my mom asked, already prepping her comforting embrace as her motherly instincts engaged.

I glanced in the direction he had run off toward, not sure. But I threw out an excuse to my mom for him, knowing it's what he'd want: "He's just struggling with his own family issues, I'm sure." Then, I redirected the conversation back to the unwanted news. "When did you find out?"

She put her concern for him on the maternal back burner as her new-baby excitement came back with full force. "A week and a half ago."

"And you already know it's a girl?" I scrunched my nose skeptically, wanting to debunk the whole thing somehow. "How far along are you?"

She parted the center slit in her long, floral shirt to reveal a prominent bump. "Seven months."

"Oh my god!" My eyes bulged at the sight. I could feel the veins in my temple pulsing as my mind swam with the news. God, I needed a drink. "You're fifty-two, Mom. How the hell did this happen? And how did you not know about it until two weeks ago?"

"You're right. I'm fifty-two! I thought I was just going through menopause. Imagine my surprise when I go into the doctor for a routine check, and they tell me I'm going to be giving birth in eight weeks!" She and the hippie chuckled at each other like a sitcom couple brushing off an ironic but inconsequential mishap on screen as the laugh track plays.

But I wasn't laughing. Far from it.

"And months ago when you started noticing a growing baby bump, that didn't clue you in?" My shock had turned into anger. I didn't want my mom to be pregnant with that dirty hippie's kid. I'd already been angry enough when she first brought him into my home—the place I was meant to feel most safe, just her and me at the kitchen table, devouring a bucket of chicken while she slipped me sips of her beer. She was supposed to be the one person I never had to worry about ignoring or overlooking me. It had always just been us. I could tell her anything. I had wanted to find a moment tonight to talk with her alone about what I'd been feeling between him and me. I knew she'd be understanding, and there'd be some good advice buried beneath all the bohemian jargon.

But all that was out the window. Not only had I lost her completely to the hippie, but now they were starting their own little hippie cult, from which I was excluded. I didn't want to be a part of it anyway. And I definitely didn't want a little sister who was twenty years younger than me. I just wanted my mom back.

"I figured the menopause was affecting my weight." She shrugged casually. Too damn casually. "Gaining weight happens much faster when you get older."

"God, Mom! What the hell?" I shook my head in disgust. "You're fifty-two, and you're having a child with someone half your age. You do realize you'll be seventy by the time this kid graduates high school?"

"I understand this was not the news you were expecting, Levi, but there's no need to get mean." My mom's tone was completely calm, and she looked at me with love despite how juvenile I was acting. She was still that tending mother I needed—still had an exclusive place for me in her heart underneath all that "free love" bullshit. I immediately felt guilty for my cutting criticisms. "This pregnancy has given me a new lease on life. I know it's uncommon to have a child at this age, but I couldn't be happier. I hope you can see my happiness and be happy for me, even if it's not necessarily what you want."

"I'm sorry, Mom." My anger didn't dissolve, but the guilt just rang out louder. "You caught me off guard. If you're happy about it, I'm happy for you… for both of you," I included the hippie with gritted teeth, but looking at his arm around my mother's shoulder, the anger I had suppressed bubbled anew. And a dark mass of loneliness started swelling in my gut.

"Thanks, Levi." She stood up and pulled me into a hug, but it didn't feel as warm as it had at the beginning of the night. It was no longer mine. "You're going to be such a wonderful older brother."

I pulled away, motioning toward the direction of the bathroom. "I better go check on him."

"Bring him back quickly. We bought a vegan cake to celebrate, and I've been itching to get at it!"

"The idea of vegan cake alone will be enough to get him racing back here, I'm sure." I rolled my eyes and wandered down the hall.

I knocked softly on the door and let myself in when I heard a "Mmm," on the other side. He was shivering in a wretched ball on the floor, resting his cheek on the side of the tub.

"Jesus, are you okay?" I asked, my eyes bugging, caught off guard by the fragility of his appearance. I closed the door behind me and sat down on the tub beside his head.

"Yeah, I just started to feel a bit sick back there."

"You sure it had nothing to do with my mom's news?" I prodded, knowingly—a self-assured performance at my newfound understanding of his past.

Or my believed understanding anyway, because he shook his head and then placed it back against the tub. "I'm just a bit cold, is all."

I had to suppress my visible disappointment at once again being foiled trying to prove myself in our friendship. I channeled the defeat into concern as I touched my hand to his forehead. "You're burning up!" I was then genuinely worried. His eyes were closed; the sheen of sweat I had noticed that morning had returned in full effect. "It's probably from sleeping outside last night, after swimming in freezing water. God, I'm sorry."

"I'm fine," he tried although he couldn't hide the fact that he had the flu behind a wall like everything else.

"I'll go tell my mom we have to go." I stood up from the tub.

"No!" he objected with all the energy he could muster. "I'll catch the bus back to campus. She wanted to celebrate her news with you."

"You can't ride the bus like this." I almost laughed at him. "She'll understand."

He looked miserable, but he didn't have the will to fight me. So I left the restroom and let my mom know what was going on.

"Oh, poor baby. Forget going back to campus. I'll care for him here!" The motherly instincts that had been threatening all night were fully activated, flashing and whirring behind her maternal framework.

But I shot her down right away. "Mom, you're pregnant. You can't be around someone with the flu."

"Fuck that!" she said defiantly. "He needs someone to care for him."

I needed that too, but there hadn't been a chance to tell her.

"I have to agree with Levi, lover," the hippie chimed in. He placed a hand on her lower back and the mechanical stiffness that had built up in her spine visibly released.

I fought an eye roll. "Mom, I'll take him straight to the health center on campus. They'll take care of him."

"Fine," she surrendered unhappily, "but you fascists aren't going to keep me from giving that precious boy a hug on the way out."

And she did. She hugged the draining life out of him, and he pretended to be uncomfortable for a moment but quickly wilted into her arms. She had to pass him off to me, and I helped him out to the car, buckling him in and circling around to the driver's seat.

"I'm sorry I ruined your family's special moment." His eyes were closed, and the side of his face was squashed up against the window. His words came off delirious.

"You didn't ruin anything," I tried to reassure him as I turned the key to start the engine.

He didn't hear me. His ears were probably ringing. "Me and family are impossible. I just destroy it."

"Stop it. That's not true," I fought, even though it felt like I was sliding down an endless hill, grasping at loose dirt but unable to stop myself or him, tumbling beside me. Once again, I saw that scarce vulnerability in him, and I didn't know how to help. Just like at his father's funeral, I didn't feel like enough. I couldn't help him because I couldn't even help myself. I wasn't strong.

"Don't introduce me to your sister." Now his head was up, his eyes open, and he was looking at me directly to convey the seriousness of his message. "Don't do it."

"Jeez, you must be pushing 103." My face twisted with worry as he let his head fall back against the window. I disregarded everything he had said. "Don't worry. We're almost to the health center."

He sat back up. "Just take me to my room. I'm fine."

"You've got the flu. You need to at least see someone. If they send you back to your room, fine. But they need to check you out first." I tried to be firm, to feign confidence as the starless night whirred past our windows, all-consuming. My headlights were the only break in what yesterday was an adventurous unknown but tonight felt like a spiraling black hole.

"I'm fine," he whined into the void.

I pressed my foot down a little further on the gas to try and break out from the oppressive shroud that seemed to lay over the top of my car, denting the roof in on us both.

But even when we got to the school's health center, and I slammed the car door behind me, trying to gulp in a fresh breath, I still felt impressed upon by an invisible weight. I had to drag myself to the other side of the car for him. And then I had to drag the both of us from the parking spot across the street, up the stairs leading to the front door. He fought me the whole way with what little energy he had, repeating over and over how he was fine.

He wasn't fine. They took his temperature, and he was at 103.4. The nurse saw that number and looked nervous. It was serious enough for her to attach an IV drip to his arm and tell me he needed to stay overnight. He threw out another objection, but after I shot it down, he was too tired to try again.

The nurse wouldn't let me stay, so I told him I'd be back in the morning to check on him.

Instead of a normal goodbye, he just repeated, "I'm fine."

I didn't believe it. I had never believed it for him. Now I didn't even believe it for myself.

16

SICK

———

Charlie, age seven, knocked timidly on his parents' bedroom door, a grimace plaguing his pale face as he clutched the right side of his tender stomach.

There was no response from the other side, so Charlie turned the knob softly and peeked his head in. All the blinds were pulled shut, blocking out the early morning light. The room was shadowed and stuffy. One side of the shabby queen bed was perfectly made, having gone days without being slept in. The other side was rumpled and messy, and there was a lump of a body hiding beneath, facing away from the door.

Charlie shuffled his way around the bed, each step shooting a sharp pain through his belly, and stopped in front of his mom, letting out a shaky breath. Her hair was tangled and spread out across her pillow like a spider web. A sheen of grease coated the skin on her forehead and near her mouth, but her pink lips were dry and cracking. Her eyes were open, but she didn't shift them up to look at Charlie when his body obstructed her gaze—she just continued staring forward through him.

"Mom, I don't feel good." He stifled the whine trembling from his stirring gut and stated the fact as composed as he could.

"Oh really?" she mumbled, not really hearing. No hint of concern entered her flat expression.

"My stomach hurts. I don't think I can go to school." He swallowed hard at the tangy spit collecting in the back of his throat. He wanted to crawl into his mom's arms so she could gently wipe away the hair sticking with sweat to his forehead and tell him it would all pass. He was trying not to shiver, thinking about her warm hug.

She finally glanced up at his green-tinted cheeks but apparently didn't find his feeble image convincing because she pulled the comforter higher up to her chin and moved her eyes back down.

"Are you trying to skip? Going to start being absent like your brother and father." She said it like an accusation.

Charlie shook his head vigorously, but that made him more nauseated, so he quickly stopped. His dad had been on a business trip going on three weeks now. And his brother had relapsed only a few days out from his most recent rehab stay and so was out of the house. It had been quiet, and Charlie almost missed the commotion. He spent most of his time alone in his brother's room, writing at his desk, hoping to hear the front door open.

His mom rolled over laboriously, turning her back on Charlie.

He swallowed hard once again. "I'll go to school, Mom. I'm feeling a little better," he lied.

He waited momentarily for a response but got none, so he shuffled back out of the room, making sure to close the door without a sound.

He stuffed himself into a heavy jacket, even though it was sunny outside, to stifle his chill, and walked uneasily to the bus stop. He stood further off from the other kids than he normally did and focused hard on staying upright even though his legs felt wobbly and weak. He collapsed into the first open bus seat and pressed his head against the window, closing his eyes for the duration of the bumpy ride.

By the time he had settled into his chair in his second-grade classroom, he felt much worse than he had when he asked his mom to stay home. Sweat dripped down the back of his neck, but he couldn't take off his winter coat, or else he would visibly be shivering. The whole room was spinning, and his stomach was roiling. He tried to lay his head down on the desk to help the nausea pass, but his teacher scolded him.

When he lifted his head again, he knew he was going to throw up, so he asked to go to the bathroom. He walked calmly there but vomited violently as soon as his face was over the toilet bowl.

When he went to the sink to rinse the bitterness from his tongue, he saw himself in the mirror—smeared with grubby little fingerprints—and thought about how visible his distress appeared to him. But nobody saw it. He thought about his mom that morning, who had looked directly at him and assumed he was faking. Her sickness announced itself to everyone through her misty eyes and the way her body sagged. His dad's anger was the same: loud, physical, obvious. And the farawayness of his brother—Charlie could instantly detect when he wasn't clean. But none of them ever saw how Charlie was feeling. Not his family, not the classmates who spoke to him on occasion, not even his teachers.

And, he decided then, nobody would. He didn't want to be a burden. Another reason for his mom to be sad, his dad to be angry, and his brother to be faraway.

So he wiped the look of strain from his face and went back to class.

He managed to make it to lunch without losing his stomach all over his desk but spent the whole time in the bathroom, heaving. When the bell rang to indicate the end of recess, though he felt more horrible than he had ever felt in his life, he pulled himself together again and went back to class. By holding his stomach gently and through sheer willpower, he made it to the end of the day without throwing up again. He had felt it coming at one point and had asked to go to the bathroom, but his teacher said since he had been once that day already, he couldn't go again until tomorrow. So he swallowed hard and held it in.

When the end-of-day bell finally rang, he hurried back to the bathroom and let his stomach contents—what was left of them—erupt.

A janitor found him an hour after school had gotten out, curled up on the speckled bathroom floor, clutching his stomach, eyes squeezed shut, vomit on his chin. He called an ambulance and then Charlie's home—where there was no answer.

The janitor rode with Charlie to the hospital and stayed with him until his mom finally listened to the multiple messages two hours later and showed up. Her hair was in its same disheveled state as the morning, and she was still in her silk pajama top, tucked haphazardly into a long skirt.

She was just in time for the news from the doctor that Charlie had appendicitis and would need immediate surgery. A bunch of nurses flooded in and began shifting the devices he was connected to, lifting up the handles on the sides of his bed and wheeling it toward the door.

In the background, his mom was bawling. "Don't leave me."

Charlie could see flashes of her red pajama top between the bustle of the nurses in muted blue scrubs. Her cheeks were the same color as that top, thick globs of tears running down them. She turned to the doctor and pointed an accusatory finger in his face. "Don't let my poor baby die. I won't be able to live if I lose him."

"Ma'am, he'll be fine." The doctor's tone was clinical, detached. The face behind his glasses was as impersonal as his mom's had been that morning. "It's a standard procedure. Nothing to worry about."

Charlie took one last glance back at his mom before his bed was out the door. He didn't feel comforted by her dramatic show of concern like he might have thought when she was blank-faced in bed. He just felt a violent and raging war inside his stomach. And fear, as a crowd of masks gathered over him, backlit by a harsh overhead light. He wanted a hand to hold, but there was no one there for him.

But they held a mask all his own to his lips, and suddenly he felt wonderful and sleepy. The room spun gently, and before he went under, he thought maybe this was the feeling his brother was after with the pills and why he kept going back.

When he woke up, he had forgotten all about that thought. His mind was foggy and slow. But he was coherent enough to realize that someone was squeezing his hand. His first thought was his mom. But as his blurry vision cleared, he found his brother standing over him.

"Welcome back from the brink, Charlie boy."

At the same time Charlie remembered the surgery and noticed the intense pain below his belly button, he felt an intense relief that his brother was back, which dissipated any physical discomfort.

"How are you here?" Charlie murmured, his tongue thick in his mouth.

"I guess Dad was keeping tabs on me. He knew where to call." The blurriness of Charlie's vision extended the harsh fluorescents glaring behind his brother into long white lines, leaving the image of him as a vague, gray silhouette. This meant Charlie couldn't see his brother's expression yet, but he heard a discomfort in those words. His brother was conflicted by the display of his dad's care, even though it made Charlie feel completely warm.

He sank back into the plush hospital bed while his brother changed the subject: "Mom and Dad are just in the lobby getting coffee, by the way."

"Where were you?" Charlie asked, still floating in the thought of his dad knowing exactly where he'd been the whole time.

"I was just staying with a friend," his brother brushed off.

"Are you going to come home?" The fog was starting to clear around Charlie, and now he could recognize the state of his brother: pale, jittery, sweat beading on his temples, and faraway. His back stiffened against the hardening mattress, and he felt the sterile air tightening around him. He didn't bother asking if he was clean.

His brother sighed. "Don't worry, Charlie boy."

Charlie knew that answer was his brother avoiding the question. But he didn't want to dwell on it. Instead, he decided to focus back on the fact that their dad had been keeping an eye on his brother. He wanted to imagine their dad had followed his brother when he left, to make sure he wasn't sleeping on the street. When he saw him go into a real home, he probably sighed in relief. But that didn't stop him from writing the address down and making regular checks, going over there once a week or more and parking out front to make sure his son was safe.

That's what Charlie wanted to imagine anyway. And he wanted to imagine that when his mom and dad came back to the room, they'd all sit around his bed, holding each other's hands, and his dad would say how much he loved them all. That's what his dad did at hospitals. He'd say, *Charlie, I'm sorry it took us so long to get here. I drove straight home as soon as your mother called me, but I had to turn the house upside down to find your brother's address. When we leave here, there'll be a mess to clean up, but we'll do it together. I love you.* And to his brother, he'd say, *Come home. Stay. I love you too. I don't want to lose you, ever.*

There was a brief moment when Charlie thought getting sick might have been the best thing that could have happened. It might be the thing to finally bring his family together for good.

It must have been that he was still woozy from the morphine.

Their dad swung open the heavy, wooden door soundlessly and pierced into the constrained space, flooding it with a thickness like tar. He looked irritated and tired as he shoved a paper cup of coffee into his brother's hand. "Thanks for letting me know he had woken up." The sharp words cut through the heaviness like a torpedo. He didn't say anything to Charlie.

"He just woke up a minute ago. What did you want me to do, leave him alone and come running?" His brother dropped the full cup of coffee into the trashcan to demonstrate his disgust. The clear bag rustled at the impact, and dark brown liquid sloshed over the sides and onto the polished floor. The puddle went ignored.

"In the state you're in? I doubt you could run. What, did you shoot up in the parking lot before you came in? You look sicker than most of the people in the beds." Their dad took a severe sip from his own steaming paper cup, clutched tightly between his rough fingers.

"Fuck you," his brother spat over Charlie's hospital bed, who felt it ricochet off the metal footboard, not reaching their dad but settling on top of the stark white sheets pulled tightly over his little toes. "I'm here. Aren't I?"

"Well, gold star for you," their dad said sarcastically.

"What about you?" The lights above them seemed to double in their intensity, their subtle buzz vibrating the room. "I overheard the doctor say it was two hours before you showed up. What, you didn't notice he hadn't come home from school? Or were you off fucking some twenty-year-old?"

"I was working," their dad shifted his eyes defensively, his forehead covered in beads of sweat from the heat of the lights. "I came as soon as your mother gave me the message."

His brother continued in, relentlessly. "I'm shocked she got out of bed long enough to listen to the answering machine. You must really be taking care of her these days. Where is she anyway?"

"She wasn't feeling well. She headed home." He said it quietly, with his head down. There was a blink, and the lights appeared dimmer then, their glow hollow.

Charlie wasn't feeling well either. In fact, he was feeling quite horrible. Almost worse than before the surgery. The sheets were constricting him, and his insides felt cramped and tangled.

"Her son's appendix bursts and she can't be bothered to stick around?" his brother scoffed.

"You know she goes through periods like this. Probably doesn't help that one of her sons is a drug addict who's off trying to kill himself. Makes it difficult to want to answer the phone when at any point it could be the call that you've finally done it."

Tears started to well in Charlie's eyes. He didn't want to be there anymore, but he was bound to the bed by a number of wires attached to different parts of his body, and there was nowhere for him to go. The pain he was experiencing as a result of his surgery was nothing like the way the words passing between his brother and his dad hurt him. Nothing like the thought of his mom back in bed when he was here, still longing for her hug.

"Why don't you go run off and start a new family with one of your whores already?"

"And why don't you go shoot more poison into your arm and keep blaming us while you kill yourself?"

Both had their arms folded aggressively over their heaving chests. Both fired hostile scowls at each other as if in a standoff about to end with a ghost town of dead bodies. Charlie was caught in the crossfire, trying to burrow further and further into his cardboard mattress but completely exposed.

"I'm not the only one you make suicidal, you fucking prick," his brother shot.

The comment whizzed past their dad's face, grazing the burning tip of his left ear. And he immediately slumped out of his antagonistic posture. He didn't have a comeback. The features of his face fell, and he shook his head sadly. "You know, you could still come home if you're willing to get clean."

"I'm never coming back, Dad." His brother had not softened, his thin arms still crossed, his cracked lips still fixed in a frown.

Two perfect lines of tears fell down both sides of Charlie's face, but neither his dad nor his brother noticed. They were focused on each other, the hostility ebbing out of a crack between them that they had both decided to accept.

"Let me go get the doctor and tell him Charlie's awake," his dad said sensibly.

"I won't be here when you get back," his brother said, running his shaky hand through his oily hair regretfully.

"Okay," his dad said, his tone flat. He left the room as soundlessly as he had entered. And the crack became a chasm. The room sank into a dank, dreary cave, and in the dull walls, Charlie felt his upset echo.

But when his brother finally looked at Charlie and his tears, they didn't seem to penetrate the fog of whatever he was on.

"I have to go, Charlie boy," was all he said, his voice distant like he was already out the door.

"No, you don't," Charlie sniffled. The heartache resounded in his ears.

"I'm sorry." He said, "I love you," but it was too late for that to fix anything.

Then, he kissed Charlie on the forehead and wandered out the door. Charlie wouldn't see his brother again until the night he died.

The doctor was the first one to see Charlie's tears—really see them—and he asked if Charlie was in pain.

Charlie said he felt nothing.

17

ALONE

———

They had to keep him in the health center for a couple of days because he had come in severely dehydrated, and they wanted to make sure he was getting enough fluids. But that meant I had to be on my own, and I didn't know what to do with myself.

I went to my dorm room for the first time in weeks. There was a layer of dust over everything. The bed was unmade, but the folds and rumples had the staunch appearance of a military bunk—having held its tight position for so long. There were items of clothing scattered across the floor, crusty with dried sweat and ignored stains. They emitted a stale scent that felt thick in the stuffiness of the space.

I went to the window and cracked it open to try and ventilate the room. A subtle breeze scattered chalky gray dust from the ashtray across the nightstand. I picked up one of the bigger cigarette stubs and fell back into my desk chair, lighting it up. The smoke swirled in the thin stream of light entering through the cracked window, dissipating into the otherwise shadowed room. I hadn't bothered to open the blinds.

I found myself zoning out on the small square of yellow cast onto the carpet from outside. Ash fell from my cigarette end, and I wiped it quickly from the arm of my chair. Only a few minutes had passed, but it felt like hours.

An all-too-familiar sense of loneliness began to twist in my gut. It had been so long since I'd felt truly this alone—the last time I could remember was the first party we'd gone to together back at the beginning of the year. We had both gotten laid that night, and I had discovered he didn't drink. I remembered distinctly the way my stomach dropped—a gaping hole left in its wake that gnawed like hunger—when I realized how little I knew about him, how thick the wall was between us.

Now, I knew him well. I'd torn down his wall. I had seen the bottles scattered across his childhood home and the graves of those he had lost. Yet, that gnawing persisted, a noxious mixture of love and isolation. A new wall was forming, no longer his but mine. I now understood what past me had been trying so hard to figure out about him: He was afraid of connection, scared of intimacy, and against the idea of love for himself. But I had gone and fallen in love with him anyway. My feelings had become the barrier between us.

In other instances where I'd felt this alone, I had turned to my mom for comfort. I'd hop in my car, stop at the liquor store for a six-pack, and show up at her door, falling into her hug. The hippie would be at his call center job. We'd break into her secret stash of non-vegan gummy bears and demolish the beers while I ranted, and she provided sage advice.

Now even she felt distant from me, that alien hippie growing inside her. She would never just be mine again. Now, whenever I dropped by, there'd be a more needy child to tend to. Her attention would be split between us—but the majority of it would go to the cute baby who was fully a part of my mom's family. Unlike me, son of a fuck-up, guaranteed to be one himself.

A childish jealousy reared up out of me, and suddenly I was twelve again.

———

My dad had been in jail for two years. It was just me and my mom, who was working as a cafeteria lady at the high school, trying to get by without his endless stream of dirty money. She always came home beaten down. We would curl up together in front of a talk show rerun and devour tubs of chocolate chip ice cream with two spoons.

But there was this one night she brought a man home. He was a total greaseball with a receding hairline and a slimy smile. Apparently, he was one of the janitors at the school. And the whole way through dinner, she hung onto his arm, held onto every word he said, and generally, just ignored my presence.

After, she told me to go to my room. I could hear their muffled giggles in the living room and smell the skunky cloud of marijuana drifting in beneath the crack in the door. A little while later, she poked her head in and told me she was going to stay at his house that night since he had a bachelor pad all to himself, and would I be all right alone? I said yes, still clutching desperately to the idea my dad had put in my head before his arrest, that I was strong.

But I felt sick when I heard the front door close. I wandered out into the living room, dim and empty. The space in the couch where I usually sat had an unfamiliar butt imprint in its plaid upholstery, and I knew he had taken my spot. I didn't want to turn on the TV. So I sat on the shaggy carpet with my back against the couch and looked around the lonely home, experiencing that gnawing feeling for the first time.

And then I saw the half-smoked joint sitting on the glass coffee table in front of me. I was no stranger to the concept of drugs, what with my dad's charges and the fact that I was a middle school boy surrounded by wannabe badasses. But just like most of those boys who were all talk, I had never actually smoked weed.

Desperate to cloud the emptiness of the air, I stuck the joint between my lips and flicked the lighter over the tip until it glowed. Of course, I choked on my first puff, pulling way too much in and searing the back of my throat. But immediately, I experienced a dizzy feeling in my head that I enjoyed. So I took a few more controlled breaths until I got the hang of it, and then, I no longer felt lonely. The room was thick with smoke, and I felt warm.

———

Leaning forward in my dorm room desk chair, I stubbed out my cigarette into the bedside ashtray. I shook my head, trying to lose the growing hunger in my body. Had it always been about suppressing loneliness for me? I thought it had just been for fun. Had I been using it to fill myself up? I felt so empty.

I had already given up on the idea of sobriety at the beach two nights before, but I still hadn't gotten the opportunity to indulge. Now I was desperate for it.

There had to be a stash hidden somewhere in my room, even though I hadn't been there in weeks. I tore the cramped space apart looking: threw the sheets from the bed, ravaged the expired contents of my mom's care packages, flung books around, creasing their pages. I had just opened each of the desk drawers, hauling out their muddled contents, when its location came to me. My hand glided slyly beneath the desk and patted its way around until I struck gold.

I pulled out a plastic bag of pills. Sweet fucking relief. I didn't hesitate as I dry-swallowed two.

The next thing I knew, I was at the door to my ex-girlfriend's apartment, knocking. She answered in only a bra and panties, plus her socks. Of course, her socks—the little gray ones I loved so much.

"I knew you'd be back, Levi," she said coyly.

I was mesmerized all over again by her beautiful dark hair. My body was buzzing from the pills and the soft sound of my name on her tongue. In the long, slow pull of my wonky vision, her round lips bobbed up and down in a gentle rhythm that contrasted the time it took for the glow of her words to reach my burning ears.

"I'm in the middle of someone, but you're welcome to join us." Everything outside the outline of her figure was blurred into a dull oblivion as she sauntered away from me without closing the door. I watched her hips reverberate with each step, sending shockwaves through the creaking floorboards, which I couldn't actually hear because the thick, white walls were pressing against the sides of my head like earmuffs. I stepped over the threshold, each foot heavy to lift, and closed the door for her.

Immediately, I found myself in tow, as if a rope were wrapped around my waist and hers, dragging me along. My sneakers glided effortlessly along the dim hallway, and I still felt hugged by the walls, like the puffed-up sides of an inflatable obstacle course.

"I found a friend," she said to whoever was already in her room before I could see. When I slid to a stop in the door frame, I saw that it was a well-built, brown-haired man. He was tall and fully naked, lying on her bed with his hands resting behind his head, his feet hanging off the end of the mattress.

She hopped right back in to where she had left off, straddling and kissing him. I remembered when she did that to me. My body ached for it. But suddenly, I felt shy. The pills were making me feel small and ever-shrinking, as if I were at the far end of a tunnel of mirrors, casting a confused gleaming in my eyes. I felt out of my depth.

She got back off of him and came to take my hand. I let her lead me to the bedside. She slid a pill off the top of her dresser and placed it onto her tongue. Then, she kissed me delicately, slipping it swiftly into my mouth. She pulled away from me with a mischievous smile and began taking off my clothes, piece by piece. I watched her do this, hushed and curious and still buzzing. Every once in a while, my eyes would drift to him. He seemed to enjoy watching her strip me.

Once she had me completely naked, she fell back into bed, still holding my hand and taking me with her.

I didn't mind. I had given my body over to her, not feeling sure of myself in it anyway. Like when she went back to kissing him, I didn't know what to do. So she placed my hand on her chest for me without breaking their kiss. He kept peeking one eye open, though, noticing how lost I was.

He rolled over on top of her and made a smooth transfer from her lips to mine. It was so smooth, in fact, I didn't even notice at first that he was kissing me. And when I did realize, my eyes went wide, but they quickly closed again because he was an incredible kisser. The radiance of it ebbed into every vein, flushing my skin pink and thumping my heart into a bass drum. I was swelling with it, almost overwhelmed by the indulgence.

She helped ground me again as I felt her long nails snake down my abdomen. While he continued kissing me, rubbing his rugged hands through my hair, she began to pleasure me in other ways. I melted into the bed like a chocolate bar left in a hot car as they pressed their bodies into me, so different from each other but both beautifully sensual. Her, smooth and rounded, her movements viperous, her face severe. Him, rough and straight but plush around the edges, soft and loving.

I was floating blissfully. It was euphoric what they did for me.

Of course, I did things for them too. We did things for each other. It was without thought or insecurity. It was simply a journey for pleasure, and we all had our chances to drive and ride along. But together, we rose and rose into the cloud cover. The pre-formed droplets of rain waiting to fall tingled at our skin as the silky white puffs encapsulated us.

Whatever she had given me blended perfectly with what I had already taken, and I felt transcendent.

The peak of pleasure came when it was just him and me. The pills were in full effect, the entire room around me humming white light like a choir of angels. She sat back in her elegant red velvet, gold-trimmed chair like a queen, watching with her gray socks resting up on the bed. He entered me from behind. The initial pain morphed immediately into euphoria. And I cried out his name. Not the man behind me—I hadn't learned his—but the boy I loved, sick in the school infirmary. His name came out of me involuntarily.

But then it was in my head. That the person behind me was him. He was ramming into me with full force. And he was crying. This was the way he was finally releasing all his pain. He was giving it to me. And I took it gladly. I wanted to take it on for him so that he could come out the other side of our love more open, happier.

I told him to go even harder. "Give it to me," I cried out. "I want it."

He went as hard as he could.

And it was only once we both fell onto our backs, breathing heavily, that I truly realized it wasn't him.

The man leaned over to give me a kiss, and I felt nothing. I felt empty again.

I shook my head and got out of bed. I hurried to the bathroom and threw up. The pills that had at one point been working in perfect harmony were now fighting each other. I shivered on the freezing bathroom tile, the cold, gray walls spinning violently around me.

She came in with a blanket and wrapped my shoulders in it. Then, she propped me up against the wall and sat down beside me.

"You called out his name."

The lacquered tile of the bathroom's walls and floor pinged around the words, *his name,* in our ensuing silence. Every time it whizzed by my eardrums—fading with each pass like an echo—my eyes welled into a more complete blur. Until it could no longer be contained and spilled out of me: the truth. And I didn't have to spell it out for her in so many words. Even my cry was soundless. But she could read it off of the way my entire being released, brimming it had been with my suppressed feelings.

"You love him. That's okay." She wrapped her arm commandingly around me and squeezed me hard in objection to my upset. Her soothing tone counterbalanced the abrasiveness of her reassuring touch.

"I know," I said, nodding reasonably. I sniffed in roughly and bulleted the back of my hand across my bottom lashes, trying to recompose myself. "And it's not that I'm afraid of being in love with a man. I'm afraid…" my voice quivered unexpectedly, "of being in love with him." The tears burst back out of me. "I'm a mess. I can't burden him with that."

"Why don't you ask him before you go assuming?" she argued, still grasping my upper arm in determined strength. Her encouragement was so impassioned it came out heated, angry even. "He has the right to decide for himself. And I know he loves you too."

The brash fervor of her comfort was a relief. I couldn't fully digest her argument in the hazy beginning of my comedown, but I felt propped up if nothing else. Before, I had been flattened.

"Let's go get you some water." She helped me up off the floor and brought me to the couch. She put a glass of water on the coffee table in front of me and stroked my arm consolingly before heading back to the bedroom.

I lay on her couch for hours, staring from the cup of water to her bedroom door and back. She and the guy, whose name I still hadn't learned, were going at it again. I listened to their thump and the squeak of the bedsprings and mostly thought about him. Eventually, I fell asleep.

When I woke up, it was dark. I poked my head into her room and saw the guy had left and she was sleeping alone. I slipped beneath the covers with her, letting my toes find her sock-covered feet to bring myself some comfort. I snuggled my head into her chest.

"For the record, I loved you too," I whispered into the dark. The heat of her body pressed against mine crashed a wave of old feelings right through me. They hadn't been that far off, those feelings. Returning as if they never left. Clicking comfortably into my gaps. Just like her mattress, which molded right back into my body, recalling my old imprint—so many hours spent in this exact position, convinced it was where I belonged.

"I know," she said, patting my thigh tiredly, her long nails tickling my exposed skin before she shifted away to drift off. And then I also recalled the weeks leading up to our demise and how her bed began to devour me like tar. She'd roll over after getting herself off on me and start snoring immediately. And I'd lie on my back, depleted, the moon casting a ghostly sheen over the grime of my sinking body. Sometimes I tried to claw myself out, to no avail. I wanted to get back to him, to his bed, where I never had to question whether it would support me or suck me in. But I was too weak then, too tired.

It was much worse now: the aching, and the longing, and the desire. It swelled in me until I was bloated, brimming with need. Then it wrung me out with two hands, leaving me withered. That night, the sheer exhaustion slammed me into the pitch black of sleep.

She woke me up the next morning with a familiar pull of the blinds, abrupt and fierce. "I have to work. Are you going to go to class?"

I shook my groggy head like a cranky child, the light slicing the night's intrusive thoughts into bitter pieces scattered across the hardwood. I rubbed harshly at the gaping sockets of my thick eyes and tried to lift myself up from nightmare into normalcy. "I need to go check up on him," I said, reasonably, though I didn't move from my indent, once again comfortable.

She started to change into her uniform, and I lay in bed watching her shaved, petite legs slip into a pair of pants. She buttoned up her top over her small breasts and tucked it in so that the fabric hugged her sides, gapping at the center button and revealing a bit of her bra.

I rolled onto my back, sliding my arms casually behind my head. "Do you have anything?" I asked.

She pursed her lips in judgment but still dug into the pocket of a pair of jeans slung haphazardly over the hamper. She tossed a little vial of white powder across the room, and I sandwiched it between my palms in the air.

I sat up with the energy of anticipation and prepared a line on her dresser.

"You want any?" I rubbed at my nose, sniffling, and held out the open vial in her direction.

"It's 7 a.m." She snatched it back and twisted the cap on, shoving it into her bag. Then, she started for the door but turned back about halfway out. "I hope you tell him."

I waited a few minutes after I heard the front door close to get dressed. Then, I walked through the early morning chill, with no coat but feeling warm, toward the health center.

He was coming out the door as I approached the front walkway. He looked better than when I had left him but still not great.

"They already let you go?" I fell into step beside him because he didn't stop.

"My fever's gone down." His face was expressionless, and I was having a hard time deciphering why I perceived a distance between us.

"I missed you." I gave him a stupid grin, hoping to feel the gap start to mend itself.

"So, you gave up on sobriety then?" he guessed, his inflection still vague. He folded his arms over his chest to keep himself warm; he was sniffling.

"Yeah, it wasn't for me." I felt the urge to get him in a big bear hug so he could feel how warm I was, and maybe he could become so too. He felt so faraway and cold, my voice almost echoed in the blank space that kept us apart. "But listen to all the exciting things that happened to me." I tried to keep up my dwindling spirit by recalling the night: "I found a bag of pills in my room, and then I ended up in a threesome with my ex and a big, hunky man."

"I leave you alone for one day." He finally smiled at me. I wanted to snatch it up and keep it in my pocket. It was better than any high I had ever experienced, any lay. It alone felt like enough to satiate the gnaw forever. I almost indulged myself—it was ballooning behind my chapped lips—but then he asked, "Are you two going to get back together?"

I deflated. "No, no. I was just having some fun."

"I'm happy you're having fun." His posture contradicted his words. He looked sunken and beaten down. Just how I felt. He had lied to me. I had lied to him. Neither of us believed in the "fun" we had to bite our bottom lips to spit out. And the distance between us grew ten-fold.

We had made it back to his room. I plopped onto his bed and hoped he would sit at his desk so I could retreat into the familiar scene and forget our increasing estrangement. He put on a coat and began collecting his books.

"You're going to class?" I had to fight a quiver in my lip. My limbs were going numb.

"Yeah, you coming?" He didn't look up at me when he asked it. Just kept stacking the books in his bag in an orderly fashion.

I could feel my pulse racing in my neck. I could've jumped out of my body. There was no way I would be able to sit through a lecture. But there was no way I could spend another minute by myself. A thick glob of mucus bubbled at the back of my throat, begging him to stay with me, to never leave me alone, to lie in bed beside me and let me love him.

I hope you tell him, she had said that morning. But I just couldn't.

I shook my head.

"All right, I'll see you later then." His words were crisp, but in my ears, they rang. He slung his bag over his shoulder and headed out the door, shutting me inside the room.

The morning sun was streaming in. The empty cleanliness of the space made me feel hollow. It was silent. I found myself shaking, the gnaw of my loneliness ravaging.

18

AN ADDICTION

———

When I decided to give in, I really went for it. From the night at the beach when I'd first declared my surrender, six weeks passed in a blur of nameless bodies and arbitrary narcotics. I refused to let the silence settle in for even a second.

I started seeing much less of him. Days began passing between my visits to his dorm room. When I was there, we exchanged very few words. At first, I tried to tell him what I could remember of my wild nights away, but increasingly, what I could remember was very little. And anyway, I could feel him withdrawing more and more with each of my stories.

This was further proof I could not confess to him what I really wanted to—already our relationship starting to sag like the collar of a beloved T-shirt, washed too many times. But my feelings were not budging, especially lying in his bed, the syrup of his smell sodden into his sheets. And it was becoming impossible to separate those feelings from what I did in other beds.

I was exploring my sexuality. Going home with men from the club just as many nights, or even more, than women. The sex was an untrodden terrain, which made it especially provocative. I opened myself up to different positions, new sensations, unusual kinks. I was willing to try anything.

The same went for the drugs. I took whatever the man I was with had on hand. Half the time, I didn't even know what I was taking. An unmarked pill of yellow, blue, or pink pushed past my lips by a stranger's tongue. As long as it made me feel temporarily fulfilled. As long as the noise never ceased.

I got kicked out of school. Or really, I quit. The dean pulled me into his office one day, told me the end of the semester was approaching, and I was failing all my classes. He asked me what we were going to do about it—implying that he was willing to help me succeed. But I didn't want that. All I wanted was to pop a suppressant and go back to his dorm room, drift off into a haze of obscurity in his arms. I couldn't have it either way.

I didn't tell my mom that I'd quit. She was busy taking Lamaze classes and painting over the faded navy walls of my old room with a soothing lavender color. Sometimes she tried to call me, but I stopped answering. I knew she'd be able to hear the desolation in my voice, and I couldn't stand the thought of her putting down the phone and turning to the hippie to say, "He's just like his father."

The thought of her disappointment in me for being only half hers, and the thought of the wall building back up between us in his dorm room, meant I couldn't let myself think for a second without that damn gnaw rattling through me. So I didn't let myself think. I got high out of my mind and lost myself in the blur. I sleepwalked through six weeks.

When I finally woke up, it was in a room I didn't recognize, naked in bed next to a man I also didn't recognize. The space felt thick, the edges of the room foggy, and the walls were pulsing. There was cotton shoved inside of my skull. I felt heavy and dazed, and I tried to grasp on to something, anything—not just from the previous night but any night in the last forty. It was all a haze. I couldn't recall a single, specific thing. And this realization felt like the first clear thought I'd experienced in ages. I hated it.

So I used my clear, albeit lethargic mind to find something to take the edge off. It wasn't difficult. There were a couple of lines, like a little gift, already cut on the nightstand beside me. I didn't know what exactly it was, but I didn't exactly care, and I quickly snorted them before the stranger beside me could wake up and suggest we split them. He didn't stir, even though I held my breath in anticipation that he would.

I couldn't remember the extent of our sexual encounter the night before. I knew I'd done about it all, with a variety of men, but I didn't know what specifically we'd done together. And I didn't want to face him waking up and wanting to talk about it—and to talk about the next time. There'd be no next time for us.

I gathered up all my clothes and went to the bathroom to splash some cold water on my face. I looked in the mirror; I looked deteriorated. I looked behind the mirror and found half a bottle of Xanax. I popped one and shoved the orange container in my pocket. I also found a full bottle of cold medicine. I opened it up, took a hearty sip, and then put it back. When I closed the mirror, I decided I now looked passable. So I left with the pills in my pocket and the mystery boy still asleep.

I decided it had been enough time between my last visit to his dorm room—meaning an unclear amount resembling forever—that I could stand to rest there for the day.

On the walk back to his building through campus, I checked my phone. There were ten missed calls from my mom, with three voicemails, and four calls from him, with one voicemail. I didn't listen to any of them. I just shoved the phone back into my pocket.

It was a beautiful day. Summer vacation was just weeks away—for those still on a fixed timeline—and the weather reflected this in its balmy ease.

It was early. The sun had not yet risen, the birds were chirping, and the air was a little dewy. As soon as the sun came up, it'd be too hot, too humid. But now, it was perfect. And I was the only one out enjoying it.

I laughed at how silly everyone else was for sleeping through the best time of day. They'd come out of their caves at noon and complain about how hot it was. But a day didn't start at noon, and they had already missed the front half that was so beautiful. I shouted at all of them, "You're missing it, you idiots! You're missing it!"

It was no surprise, really. People always missed out on the best parts of life when they were sleeping away. Like that 3 a.m. shot of whiskey long after the last callers are already in bed, and the real fun is just beginning. Or that 4:30 fuck when your 4 o'clock ecstasy pill is finally kicking in, and there's an audience of cricket chirps funneling in through the window to cheer you on. Or this, a 5 a.m. "walk of shame" through the twittering of a hundred birds in the trees, their shrill music swelling like the crescendo of an orchestra.

I found the symphony to be soothing. My eyes were beginning to droop, and I felt tempted to take a quick nap in the grass. But I knew I'd wake up with the rest of them in the boiling heat.

So I carried on.

He wasn't in his room when I got there. He wasn't an idiot like the rest of them and was probably enjoying the morning with a run. I didn't worry about it. Instead, I cracked the window to let the bird-sounds flood the empty room and fell face-first into his bed, passing out.

When I woke up again, it was dark, and he was at his desk, writing. I sighed in the comforting nostalgia of it.

"You back at it then?" I croaked, my throat raw like sandpaper. A glass of water emerged in my peripheral. I shifted my neck to the nightstand, smiling, and gulped it down.

"Back at what?" he asked, spinning in his chair to face me when normally he would have kept on writing. I expected him to ask something more pressing of me since he hadn't seen me in days, but he just waited for my answer.

"Writing," I said as if it were obvious. "After your dad's funeral, you said you were feeling too overwhelmed to write."

He paused, eyeing me warily. "Yeah, I'm back at it. I started small, just like you suggested."

"Well, look at that. I can give some good advice." I got out of bed and noticed my ears were ringing. The cotton from that morning was beginning to crack my skull, trying to push its way out. I would stuff it back in. I went to the bathroom and crushed up two of the pills I had stolen from the stranger's medicine cabinet. I took them up my nose as a more direct *fuck you* to the cotton. I imagined the dust would find its way to my brain and dissolve the fluff like cotton candy under a tongue.

Out of habit, I checked behind his mirror, but of course, there was nothing.

Then I went back out and plopped myself right down on his desk. "Let's go to a party. For old time's sake."

"Levi, I need to tell you something." He was his same old serious self, only he was maintaining eye contact with me. It wasn't easy for him, indicated by the quiver of his irises trying to pull away, but they held out in order to win my attention.

But I didn't want to be bogged down with something important and serious. So I was the one who practiced avoidance.

"Come on! Don't make me go through this whole routine. We'll just go and get fucked up, and everything will be peachy." I wrapped my fingers around each of his upper arms. They didn't tense at all. They seemed wilted. I quickly became self-conscious, my stomach fluttering, so I took my hands back.

"Levi…" he tried again.

"What day of the week is it?" I popped off the desk and paced to the other side of the room, trying to settle the jitters building in my legs.

"Tuesday."

"Well, no problem. There's always a party out there somewhere." I spun back around and found him rubbing anxiously at the back of his neck. A cold sweat was beading on my own as I injected a false ease into my voice. "Sometimes, you just have to look a little harder. It'll be an adventure!"

"Levi," he sighed.

"What?" I was irritated. The Xanax was starting to kick in, and it wasn't hitting right.

"Your mom had the baby this morning."

There was a pause. He looked at me hopefully; I returned with a blank stare. "So?"

His shoulders sagged even further than they had already been. "She tried to call you last night when they were headed to the hospital, but she couldn't get you. So, she called me. And I tried to find you, but I don't know where you go anymore. I tried your ex's apartment, but she said she hadn't seen you in a week. I didn't know where else to check. So I just went to the hospital."

I couldn't look at him. I was staring angrily at the floor.

"Your sister—"

"Half-sister, at best," I muttered.

"Your sister is so beautiful." The glimmer in his eye—wonderment, sorrow—was detectable even in my attempt at avoiding his gaze. He stood like a bright-eyed child, in awe at the grandiosity of life as he was learning it. Frightened and dazzled by its alluring artifice. Intoxicated.

I wanted desperately to soften to him. To press his chest against my own and let the exhilaration swirl around us.

But I couldn't. I knew I would just start crying and admit everything. At which point, the open emotion I was witnessing in him would be closed to me fully.

I turned my back and began chewing nervously on my thumbnail.

Then I felt his hand on my shoulder, and I froze. "Your mom let me hold her. I didn't want to, you know. I was scared. But your mom made me, and I'm glad she did. Your sister, she's healthy, she's alive. She's beautifully unburdened."

I stepped harshly forward and glanced over my shoulder as his arm fell. My whole body was hot and shaking. "Be her brother then. I don't give a fuck."

"I'm not her brother," he said, firm yet affectionate. "You're her brother. And you're my brother. And you've been MIA a lot lately. I'm worried about you."

This triggered a reaction in me, and I whipped around. "Fuck you."

"Why?" he quivered, taking a stunned step back. He grew smaller, the full-press offense he had taken shriveling up as the features of his face shrank. Except for his eyes, which were big like a baby animal.

I shook away the unreasonable anger and breathed out slowly through my pursed lips to calm myself. "I'm fine." I tried to shrug my shoulders casually. "You don't have to worry."

"I do." His voice was minuscule. The room around us was an expansive vacuum. "You're not you. You're always high."

"But that *is* me!" I scoffed in disbelief, wavering on my feet and wanting something to lean on. "I was high when we met!"

"It's different now. You know it's different." He said it like a little boy, petrified of the dark.

I hung my head in shame. I knew it was.

"Your mom wants you to meet your sister. But she wants you to be clean," he tried to steer the conversation out of the pit we'd worked ourselves into.

I looked up and saw his cheeks were wet. I touched the dull tips of my fingers to my own and found the same.

"I want you to be clean too." The words were fragile, cracking as they scraped his dry lips on the way out. "You're scaring me."

I had to sit down on the floor because I couldn't seem to stand anymore. I grazed my hand along the spotless carpet. How could a dorm room floor be so clean? He hadn't allowed a single spill to stain the surface. The deeper ones caused by other occupants obviously couldn't be removed, but they were buried deep down. And he wouldn't allow anything new to mess up the well-kept appearance he had maintained for so long.

My head flittered back and forth faintly. "I don't…" I squinted hard, tapping at my forehead, trying to straighten out my racing thoughts. They were battering against all sides of my skull, no more cotton to keep them still. The carpet was too clean. There was a wall up between us that I thought had been demolished a long time ago. A confession was crawling up and down my arms. I couldn't look at him but desperately needed a hug. I had to keep up my facade. "I'm just having a bit of fun. I can stop anytime, but I don't want to right now."

He fell back into his chair, defeated.

I couldn't let myself feel guilty. And I had to believe myself when I said I was fine. So I popped back up with an energy that I had forced genuine. "A party then?"

"I can't go to a party with you." He was shaking his head vehemently. "Not like this."

"What do you mean?" I played dumb, not wanting to decide whether his passive criticism should illicit my anguish or outrage.

"I can't, Levi." His eyes begged me not to go either. And the genuine dread I saw on his face provoked a distinct reaction.

The unbounded anger I had pushed away bubbled aggressively back to my surface. All the time we had been friends, and never had my drug use been a problem. Only a short time ago, he had been the one convincing me I was fine. Why all of a sudden was he blowing it out of proportion? Why was it now something that would keep him from coming out with me? I hadn't changed. So, it was him. He thought he was too good for me. I went to his father's goddamn funeral with him. He cried in my arms at his brother's grave. And now he was unwilling to be there for me? He had the gall to judge me like a stain on his precious carpet? Bullshit. If it weren't for me, he'd be all alone. He had no one. He had nothing. Just his stupid little journal, full of masochistic variations on his past. He was obsessed with those stories. He was an addict for them. Fuck him. He was the addict between us. And clearly, I meant less to him than his drug. So why not find my own? I didn't need him to have fun. He needed me.

These thoughts came on with such rapid force, I struggled to believe they were even mine but for the palpable heat of animosity roiling through my bloodstream. It tremored within me, my entire body vibrating. So I doubled down in it.

"Fine then," I spat. "But I'm going."

He bounded from his desk, grabbing my arm as I started toward the door. "You don't have to."

I wanted to pull him toward me and kiss him with everything I had left—it wasn't much, but it would be enough to show him how I really felt.

Instead, I pulled my arm away and slammed the door behind me.

19

SILENCE

———

When he was young, Charlie used to lie on the floor in front of his bedroom door and whisper into the crack a silent plea for peace against the thundering war raging on the other side. Fighting, yelling, crying—it never stopped, even though with his own silence, Charlie begged. Now, he was thirteen. Everyone was gone. And the silence was unbearable. It was loss, that absence of noise, and it permeated every crack in the sad apartment. It emitted a heat that made the place stuffy, yet Charlie only felt cold. It was something like a fever, a sickness that clogs the ears and makes everything sound far away, if audible at all.

He sat on the edge of what was once his brother's bed, staring through the closed door of what used to be his sister's room, and heard nothing down the hall where his mom used to cry and his dad used to fight with the mothers of his children.

Charlie felt hollow, and the way the silence pressed against his empty shell made it seem like he was on the verge of shattering.

Usually, there was at least the sound of his dad stumbling around drunk, muttering to himself, to fill the void. But an hour ago, Charlie had heard the sharp crack of wood against wood five or six times alongside his dad's anguished grunts, and then the front door had slammed. Charlie snuck cautiously from his room and peeked inside the door of his sister's, which had remained shut—a shrine collecting dust— for two years. Now, the untouched crib lay in pieces on the floor, and beside it was one of the kitchen chairs, which had likely been wielded as a bat.

Charlie had trudged back to his brother's room. The space was stagnant—the same old furniture around him dull and lifeless—yet, he felt dizzy. Nothing around him had ever been stable. He had tried everything to take control, to stop himself from falling as everyone around him sank into the earth. All his efforts to stop their descent had been worthless. And each day, he felt himself lower and lower, tumbling endlessly behind them. There wasn't any pleasure in it. He felt drained and helpless. The silence congested his hollow chest.

He threw himself back on the bed and tried to think of a way to expel the absence, to fill himself up with something else.

That was when he noticed the drugs.

He didn't know what caught his eye—now, after five years, two living in this room. But suddenly, there seemed to be a spotlight on the edges of a plastic bag taped beneath the desk drawer. His sightline narrowed in directly on it as if someone had whispered where to look in his ear.

He took it in his hands like palladium, precious but poisonous. It was a little piece of his brother that had been hiding beneath his nose the entire time. But it was the piece that had taken him under. Charlie didn't know whether to set the bag on fire and send it swimming down the sewer line, or to place it under his pillow to help him sleep at night. There was nothing left to comfort him in that lonely home. That baggie of pink capsules was all he had left.

Then he thought of another thing he could do with them. Something he had watched his big brother do a hundred times, looking up to him. Back then, he had always felt disappointed to watch a pill disappear behind his brother's lips and slide down his throat. But he had just been a kid. He hadn't known what it meant to fall—not really. The closest he had come was rolling down the hill at age four. Even that, scary as it had seemed from the top, had just been child's play compared to the plummet he had taken since then—was taking.

For once, he wanted to take control over his lack of control. He wanted to choose the mess. He wanted to fall on purpose.

So he popped one of the pink capsules in his mouth and taped the rest back beneath the desk. Then, he lay back on his brother's bed and waited.

Charlie was under the assumption that it would come on quickly. He always thought people took drugs for their immediate relief. But he was still young and only knew what he had gathered from observing the farawayness that came from his brother's use when he had been even younger. But because his brother was faraway most of the time, it was often hard to tell when or how the drugs hit, especially for a confused kid. Even the time that stood out to him most—burned into his brain like a hot iron antidrug PSA—his brother had already been so high, there was no way for Charlie to tell what the new drugs did when they entered his system. Not until the next morning anyway.

For the first thirty minutes or so, Charlie just lay there, paying close attention to his mind and his body. He didn't really feel anything, but he kept thinking maybe his arms were tingling. Which he thought was fine, but not much—not what everyone built it up to be.

But just as that thought was on its way out, he really did start to feel something. It was a small buzz, and it wasn't coming from somewhere within him but under him. The floor was buzzing the bed, which was buzzing him. Charlie laughed. He didn't know why he hadn't thought about this solution before. Vibration: to shake up the stuffiness and buzz through the silence. It was brilliant really.

He also felt like everything inside him was loosening up. His own personal massage, courtesy of the floor.

He leaned over the edge of the bed to deliver an ironic, *thanks*, but what he saw down there was a chasm that had formed, miles deep. If he had called out his gratitude, it would have echoed.

He quickly pulled himself back up, scared of plunging over the edge to his death. It was clear the vibrating had been the earth around his bed sinking—or maybe just this once it was him shooting up higher. Whatever the case, he was now confined to his bed. The only escape would be to jump, and he was not yet desperate enough to risk death.

So he sat in the middle of the bed, holding his knees, as the room began to darken with the night. Even tripping, he knew the drop was an illusion, but he began to think of the consequences of seeing the world in such a cynical way and that scared him even more. It meant, for him, leaving bed would always be some sort of endless drop. And what came at the bottom was unavoidable breakage every time.

He didn't know where to go from there. And finally, realizing the sun had deserted him, he decided to lie back and stare at the ceiling in the hope that he could find something light up there, like stars. And even though he knew all he was looking at was the ceiling, there was a sort of twinkling going on. It got brighter and more prominent the longer he looked. Things began to click for him.

He understood why his brother had always been convinced that looking up was better than looking down. Down was a hole, inescapable. Up could be something beautiful. Charlie finally saw the world in the same way as his brother. Like the day they watched the clouds together, and his brother had seen affection. Or that night he looked up at the rotting roof of that stranger's porch in awe. He had seen this: something better than stars. It was beauty created by his own mind. And it made Charlie cry happy tears. The thought that maybe his brother saw something beautiful in the end. Instead of darkness, light.

And maybe that's what all of them saw before they left. Maybe dying was like an acid trip, and it felt warm and looked wonderful.

Charlie was warm. Not stuffy like before, but comfortable. The twinkling was radiating down and drying his tear streams into salty lines. Charlie basked in it. He understood why this was where his brother wanted to be. Did he wish his brother had wanted to be with him more than he wanted to be high? Of course. But at least he understood. And maybe now that he was alone, Charlie could do this too with no fear of the repercussions.

Then, he heard a drum. It was steady and low and sounded almost like a heartbeat. He thought it might be the pulse of the earth, reminding him that being alive happened much more often than death, and he had just pulled a bad hand.

But then it felt like some sort of arrival because, in line with the beat, the twinklings on the ceiling began to go dark until there was no more left, and Charlie was shrouded in black. He held his breath, afraid of what came next.

That's when things fell apart.

The dark was impenetrable, and instead of silence, it was the noise he couldn't escape. And that noise was unmistakably the voices of everyone he'd lost.

In the corner was the shadow of his mom, accusing him of being like his brother, begging Charlie not to leave her, but in a resentful tone, over and over, louder and louder.

And just beyond the cracked door was the sound of crying, but also the sound of struggling—the sound of suffocating, desperate and painful. Charlie knew it was his sister, but he was paralyzed in the bed, helpless to do anything.

He tried to turn his head away but was instead met with a whisper, lips right against his ear. "Not you, Charlie boy."

Charlie swallowed hard, squeezing his eyes shut tightly and refusing to turn toward the voice. But it persisted in his ear nonetheless, wet and hot. Like steam, hissing as it thickened the air and singed his skin.

"You're not allowed to join us." The distorted rejection was like a shard of glass—its two sides. Sharp, jagged, crystalline in its icy edge. But also fragile, emotionally transparent, and ever on the verge of shattering.

Charlie whimpered, his skin pimpled with goosebumps despite the heat of the words. "I won't."

"What is this, then?" the voice snarled, desperate and callous in its tone. He had never spoken to Charlie like that before. "Look at me," he hissed.

Charlie shook his head. Refused to turn. "I don't know."

"You won't do it again." Not a question but a command.

"Never."

"Look at me."

Charlie let out a fearful sob, his saliva stretching between his chapped lips, but still, he turned. And he was met with the image of his brother, just as he had last seen him. An empty shell. Ashen face with dark eyes open, fixed on the ceiling. Blue fingers stiffened into claws as if he had tried to dig his way out; blue lips and a bit of vomit on his chin, though mostly in a pool beneath his neck.

Just like the first time, Charlie tried to scream, but nothing came out of his open mouth, just streaming tears from his eyes as he turned back around and tossed himself over the edge of the bed into oblivion.

He might have fallen for miles, but he didn't come to until he was already at the bottom. By then, all the noise had ceased. He could only hear the sound of his heavy breaths. He tried to steady them. He welcomed the silence now. He held onto it desperately through the rest of his trip, staying on the floor and keeping his ear against the carpet, praying for the buzz to end.

That's where he fell asleep. It's where he woke up, head not quite clear but coherent enough to realize the hallucinations had just been the drugs. Although the fears behind them, the sensations that weren't imagined but were memories, still clung like tumors to his brain, all too real. He hadn't lost them in his spiral or learned to harness them in his attempt at controlling the chaos. They were still there; they always would be. All the drugs had done was spread the disease throughout Charlie's body, turning him into one big malignant mass, ready to latch onto another innocent victim.

He would never do it again. Any of it. Not drugs. Not alcohol. He had started smoking a couple of months back just to see if it helped any. He was giving that up too. He didn't like how it recalled all the pain of his past. He wasn't trying to move on, but he was trying to move forward—eventually move out. If he was the only one who got the chance to make it out alive, he'd do everything in his power to make it happen.

It started with throwing away the bag of pink capsules. They thunked to the bottom of the empty trash bin, and in their wake, the room's silence returned. The furniture was still, the bed frame grounded, the mirror's glass reflecting Charlie's determination. The drugs weren't a piece of his brother. He was. His messy brown hair, his tilted smile, his hazy blue eyes—Charlie became more an image of him with each passing day. And he had everything inside of him that his brother had been capable of, everything he could've done if he hadn't submitted to the instability of their family. Hadn't disappeared into the drugs.

Charlie showered the night off himself with scalding water. He came out of the bathroom red but accepting the silence as a perfect space to think in—to think about what was next for him.

He came back to the words. He always did. That was what his brother had pushed him toward, and he decided that was where he would go. He opened up the journal that had been closed for months and started in with his blue fountain pen.

20

NOISE

———

Cacophony. Lights rotate blue green red blue green red. Speakers vibrate an incoherent buzz into eardrums ringing. Shouting bodies bounce against the outside of the bubble I've created—of drugs and other numbing agents like denial. Inside, a hand presses against my skin, sensitive; a pill slips past my lips, desperate. And then our tongues intertwine. My body bounces, buzzes; the room rotates. The music grows, the lights turn, his hand lowers, I rise.

The room floods white, and everyone shouts. Him, in my ear, "Bathroom!"

I am bent over in a stall, hand on a grimy toilet seat for stability as he pounds his body into me, grunting with each thrust. I'm numb. I watch the water in the bowl reverberate slightly. I imagine what would happen with one flush. I reach out for the handle and watch myself swirl down the bowl. But I haven't moved, fingers gripping the seat, eyes locked on the ripple of the otherwise calm pond. It would be the perfect place to lose it. I can hear the sloshing against my walls, roiling stomach the antithesis to the subtle ripple of water. I can feel it coming up. And just as he climaxes, I spew my stomach contents, mostly missing the bowl and coating the seat—it dribbles down the sides and onto the floor—but a few murky drops land in the water to upset its peace.

He zips up his pants while I stand and wipe my mouth with the back of my hand.

"Got anything else?" I slur into his ear. The dull music of the club leaks into the bathroom and contorts my words into near incoherence.

But his own tipsiness straightens the sentence into an articulate thought. He pulls out a plastic bag with two pills and dumps them in my hand. Then, he puts his lips to my ear. "Clean yourself up and find me for round two." He bites my earlobe and grabs my crotch before leaving me alone in the stall.

I toss the pills in my mouth and swallow them dry as I work at my zipper, leaning into the sharpie graffiti of the stall to piss. My eyelids do a gentle bounce as they fight gravity, and I am still hardly upsetting the peaceful pool, contributing mostly to the messy seat.

I button my pants back up sloppily and stumble into the stall door, barely locked and clanging open at my impact. My hands automatically extend for the sink, and I splash cold water in my face. I look at myself dripping in the mirror. My eyes are smudged black from the eyeliner my ex put on me. Lost her as soon as we got into the club. My mouth has a red ring around it from where the stranger had been sucking on my lips. There's glitter on my cheeks, and I can't pinpoint where or when that's from.

My eyes begin to water. I'm afraid. And I wish I had his stoic presence beside me so I could put my head on his shoulder, and he could tell me it's all right. So he could take me out of this godforsaken place and back to his room, his bed, where I could watch him writing at his desk while he thinks I'm asleep. My body aches for him.

And then the pills kick in. I sigh at their relief. Close my eyes to reset and leave the bathroom.

Don't find the guy from the stall. Someone else. But it's the same cacophony. The lights the music the shouts. The hands and lips and tongue. Blue green red blue green red. The room spins and spins, and then the lights shut off.

———

Deafening. A drumbeat against my pillow. The wailing of my bloodstream. Echo of the lost hours, days maybe. Open my eyes to the smeared image of a yellow light and a white room. A strange shadow beside me breathing steady up and down up and down. He doesn't snore, but his quiet breaths still bat around my eardrums—their unfamiliar pattern.

I remember watching his lips on the beach and memorizing the way his chest moved. It's what I fell asleep to that night. I felt more peaceful than I ever had.

Moving the stark white covers off my body is like carrying the weight of my feelings for him times a hundred. My hand trembles with the effort. Beneath, I find I am still wearing my underwear. I strain to lift the covers higher. See that the shadow is also wearing his. That's all I need to know. I drop the covers and let my eyes fall back closed. Imagine it's him beside me instead of a stranger. *His* breathing.

But my fantasy is interrupted by a shrill voice: "You two haven't fallen asleep on me?" I open my eyes to a short girl with small breasts and big hips, evident in the skin-tight tube dress she's wearing. Though she slips it off after she has thrown a pencil case on the bed by my feet. Left only in her bra and panties. "Not while I was out getting our supplies."

I glance over at the shadow, who is now sitting up and fully man. I don't recognize either of them.

She crawls up between us, bringing the pencil case with her. She unzips it and begins taking out its contents: needles, cotton, lighter, rubber tubing, a spoon, and a small bag of brown powder.

"Levi, the water on the nightstand."

She knows my name?

Dazed, I hand her the plastic bottle. She goes to work. Sucking water up into a needle. Putting the powder in the spoon, the water; mixing it with the plunger end of the syringe. Heating it to a boil with the lighter. She tosses a bit of cotton in, which absorbs the poison. Then it's back up the needle.

"Who's first?"

He holds out his arm, and I don't object. She ties the rubber tubing around his bicep and taps two fingers against the crock of his arm. Then, the needle goes in—the poison—and he falls back against the headboard with a heavy sigh.

"Your turn."

She goes through the process again with the second needle. I'm wary but say nothing. And soon, the needle is in my arm, the concoction inside of me. Flush.

Noise blurs and swirls down the toilet bowl My weight sinks I feel heavy beautifully My burden is released I shiver with satisfaction like little lightning bugs Dancing across my skin Raising goose pimples Is the laughter mine or theirs It's a symphony of smiles Fluttering butterfly eyelids Kissing my lips I decide I love her Kissing him I decide I love men The outside world folds up into origami birds flown away The room is only ours Yellow light White walls It's all we have Not smeared but dripping As if I'm underwater again Him on shore Lips glowing What happened to the light What happened to him Where has he been and where am I Who am I with Their skin is clammy and not warm like the poison When it ends I sink beneath the bed beneath the ground and I recognize faces even though it's dark

———

I want to gasp awake, but instead, I stay completely still because there is someone on top of me violently pressing themselves into me over and over. Thump thump thump. Him into me. The headboard into the wall. And my heart. I feel it beating again, and I know it's tearing. But I make no sound. I lie completely still, and this time alone, I don't pretend it's him because he would never do this to me. But I do think of him, and the day we met, staring up at storm clouds. They seemed violent then. Not so much anymore.

Tears fall from the corner of my eyes. *Nothing that had been lost—*

Except life. Something he already knew. Something I am learning.

He is going faster now, his grunts thick and desperate. Their pitch rises as he approaches orgasm, into a hideous screech that rings in my ear long after he has blown his load and left the room. I remain unmoving for a while. All I have is the ghost of his weight on my back and the white stain dripping onto the sheets beneath me. Otherwise, I am empty.

I finally rise and clean myself up. Collect my dingy clothes one by one from their haphazard hiding places around the unfamiliar room, folding each neatly on the chair beside the bed as I go. Once I have reassembled all the scattered pieces of my appearance, I put my socks on first and then my underwear. One foot and then the other.

Fully clothed, I wander downstairs, where a group of strangers sits on stained furniture around a coffee table full of vice. But they know my name: "Levi!"

I can tell my aggressor by the sweat on his forehead. Plus, he doesn't say my name with the others but just gives me a sly grin, waving subtly with a massive hand attached to a monstrous arm.

I sit far away from him. The girl beside me puts a pipe to my lips, and I breathe in the pure white smoke. Soon, I'm staring at the ceiling.

all their noise rattling between my ears and the sound of his climax his thumping my heartbeat so rapid the whole room shakes fish swimming through my veins plunged underwater and gasping for breath nobody on shore all storm lightning bugs setting sparks beneath my skin and it's all violent buzz buzz buzz thump thump thump fuck fucking help me I scream but it seems no one can hear me under this dark cloud blue stains and words that are constantly being washed away nothing that had been lost nothing that had been lost except me losing myself he already knew and I am learning white light white walls white stain dripping flush me down flush me down flush me down you got anything else just words the stories I wish would wash away I'm lost but nothing that had been lost blue stains new words the noise is overwhelming Charlie please your blue ink I'm losing and the next day writing beneath lamp light nothing that had been lost nothing that had been lost nothing that had been lost nothing

"Someone call me a taxi!" I scream, bolting upright.

———

I lie back on the front steps, trying to find the stars so I can ask his brother some advice. All I see is the rotting wood of the porch.

A car horn.

I tell the driver to take me to his dorm.

21

TRUCK ARMS

———

It was late, but Charlie wasn't asleep. He was writing at his brother's desk beneath lamplight in blue ink. The scratch of his pen was the only sound in the apartment: The door slam and subsequent sniffles had come and gone hours ago. His brother's room had been empty for months. But Charlie was occupying it for the night because he felt lonely. He could settle into his brother's chair—at eight years old, just barely able to reach the desk to write, his feet dangling—and feel something of his brother. And of course, there was his scent: cigarettes. It brought a calm to the space, otherwise thick with absence. A calm that rested just atop Charlie's eyelashes, causing his eyelids to bob like fishing floats on a rippling lake. The grip on his pen loosened; his letters became long and faint.

The screech of the opening window jolted Charlie awake. A cold breeze disrupted the smell of cigarettes but also scattered the absence, and with it came his brother. One leg after the other as he flopped in onto the bed. His head ended up at the foot of it, meaning his aloof smile appeared upside down.

"Charlie boy," he murmured in delirium.

He wasn't clean, and Charlie knew that instantly. His head was stippled with sweat beads, and his gaze was distant. But it didn't keep Charlie from falling into his arms, relief flushing his veins.

"Is Dad home?" His brother pulled away from the hug, dazed, leaving Charlie's outspread arms exposed. His hands slunk back to his sides, dejected, as his brother began sifting through the dresser drawers.

Charlie sat down on the edge of the bed, shaking his head in response to the question but also in disappointment. Every time his brother came back into his life, he believed it would be different. It didn't matter how faraway he had been, Charlie always opened right back up to him. But it always ended the same: with Charlie, alone.

"No?" his brother confirmed. Charlie shook his head again, and his brother burst out of the bedroom. Charlie followed after him, watching him probe the dark apartment looking for cash. Charlie knew once he found it, he would leave. There was nothing he could say to make him stay. He had tried it all before.

Tonight, he tried something new. "Can I come with you?" Quietly.

"Hmm?" His brother hadn't stopped rooting around.

"I want to come with you." It was still low, but it was more confident.

"Aha!" His brother found some crumpled bills and shoved them in his pocket. Then he turned, finally acknowledging Charlie. "What? Come with me? I don't think…" He bent down and put a hand on Charlie's arm, preparing the bad news.

"I miss you." Charlie looked directly into his faraway eyes. And they became momentarily less far away.

His brother's face shifted from the tight scrunch of apology, loosening into tenderness, and landing in a big and silly grin. "Of course you can come with me, Charlie boy!" He gave Charlie a sloppy kiss on the forehead and stood up. He took Charlie's hand and led them out of the apartment.

The night was scattered with a twinkling of stars. His brother was walking with his chin up, his mouth open in awe. They drew Charlie in too, high and faraway as they were. A subtle smile cracked his somber face as he took in their light.

But where his brother's clouded eyes remained in the sky, Charlie's moved back and forth between the stars and his brother. He was trying to memorize this momentary happiness. Its gleam would be brief. By morning, it would be zipped up in a black body bag and carried away. But there was no way to detect such a thing in the fervor of his brother's smile. Charlie had never seen it so wide.

It spread a deep warmth beneath Charlie's skin. He slid his hand back into his brother's, and on cue, his brother produced a cigarette in the other. Its glowing tip was more mesmerizing than the stars.

Charlie got lost in it. It grew smaller and closer to his brother's chapped lips. And then suddenly, the stub was being pressed into a terracotta pot of dirt. They were on a porch, and Charlie's brother was knocking on the door. Charlie had forgotten there was a destination at all. Or he hadn't known. Maybe part of him hoped they would just keep walking forever. Long beyond the night and the blurriness in his brother's eyes. He had hoped they would walk until his brother was clean and he was old enough to understand the weight of their family history. But by then, they would have walked the past irrelevant and the future clean.

Instead, they had stopped on this strange porch, and a semitruck of a man opened the door. His upper arms were as big around as Charlie himself, and the skin stretched across the muscle as if on the verge of tearing and spilling out a grotesque inky sludge.

Charlie was at just the right height to watch Truck Arms dig his meaty fingers into his brother's bony butt cheek. They pressed their lips together vigorously. Charlie crossed one foot over the other and focused his attention on the cigarette stubs that should have been flowers.

Finally, Truck Arms pulled away from Charlie's brother and took notice of Charlie. It was only then that his brother remembered his presence.

"This is Charlie boy." The words were thick and distant. Charlie didn't like the way his name sounded on his brother's tongue after being inside the man's mouth.

He liked the man's hand even less as it extended for a handshake. Apparently, Truck Arms had forgotten he had just grasped his brother's butt with that same hand.

Charlie stared at it until the man was forced to take it back. His brother threw out an excuse: "He's shy."

Charlie felt tears welling in his eyes as the large man led them inside. His brother knew his quiet wasn't shyness, so telling Truck Arms that it was felt like a betrayal—where the stars they had just shared were consumed by the night. And Charlie was left alone in that dark as his brother walked obliviously ahead through the dingy hallway. The pale walls raised goosebumps up his spine as he sloshed through the sullied shag carpet. To arrive at a barren room: one beat-up leather couch with various drug addicts draped across the back like a slipcover and a glass coffee table filled with bottles, pills, powders, and ash. A lot of things Charlie recognized but still did not understand out of the context of his brother's blurry eyes.

"My brother," his brother introduced offhandedly as he draped himself across the couch with the others, somehow collecting one of the coffee-table bottles in his hand on the way down. Truck Arms took a seat on the floor, pulled up a line of white with his nose, and then yanked Charlie's brother into his lap. The impact of his fall made Charlie wince, but his brother just laughed as he pulled desperately from the bottle before continuing the porch's kiss. Charlie stood awkwardly in front of this display, eyes he'd forced dry stuck on the wretched carpet with all the other stains.

He was invisible to everyone in the room—including his brother—except for a girl whose skin was vacuum-sealed to her praying mantis limbs and whose eyes, smudged in ink, completed her skeletal vision. She hunched over in front of him, the notches of her spine sticking up like scales.

"What's your name, sweetie?" she cooed as if he were a toddler. The immediate interest of her horrific image grew quickly tired, and Charlie looked past her. His brother was letting Truck Arms slide his hand down the front of his pants while he pulled smoke from a glass pipe.

Charlie hated Truck Arms. Not because he kissed his brother or stuck his hand down his pants, but because he had taken away what might have been the only chance Charlie had to help his brother get clean.

"How about a Coke?" the girl offered, following Charlie's gaze to his brother and shifting her thin body to try and block the crude scene.

Charlie bit his lip and nodded.

She took his hand and led him to the kitchen. She smelled of cigarettes just like his brother, but on her, the scent was stale. She lifted him up onto the counter and grabbed a glass from the sink, rinsing it briefly with the tap's spurting stream. She tried to find ice in the freezer but was unsuccessful; she poured the flat soda alone into the glass, where it bubbled half-heartedly. Then, she pressed the glass into his hands and rustled his hair. He took a small sip, but it was sticky against the back of his dry throat.

She helped him off the counter and led him back to the living room. He saw the empty space on the floor where his brother and Truck Arms had previously been. His breath caught in the remnants of that sticky sip of soda, but he didn't dare display fear on his face. The girl saw it anyway. As she pulled him down onto the couch with her, she whispered a consoling, "They'll be back soon," in his ear.

It did nothing to pacify the panic scratching from behind his chest. He sat stiff-straight, eyes fixed on the staircase where he could hear a subtle thumping coming from the top, cascading down. He couldn't stand to drink the soda, so he just held it in his hands and willed his brother's return.

When he finally came down the stairs, he looked more dazed than before. He was hip to hip with Truck Arms, who had a possessive arm around his waist, leading him forward. As they sat back down on the carpet indent they had left behind, Charlie's eyes locked on his brother's throat, where a red handprint glowed as if he had been branded with a hot iron. Charlie tried to get his brother's attention with a look that screamed—brows raised, lips pressed desperately together, eyes bulging—but his brother was already too far gone.

So, Charlie shifted his gaze—brows down, lips pouted, eyes squinting angrily—toward Truck Arms, who looked grossly satisfied. This time, his look was trying to convey a message: *Hurt the brother I love, and I'll kill you.*

But again, it was ignored.

Truck Arms was too busy unzipping a black pencil case. He pulled out items one by one: a needle, cotton balls, a lighter, a spoon, and a little bag of brown powder. Charlie didn't know what any of it was, but he didn't like the hunger that burned in everyone's eyes as they watched Truck Arms put it all together.

What came next was a scene that imprinted itself in Charlie's brain, like the handprint around his brother's throat. The sound of the spoon bubbling. The smell of burning metal. The mesmerized silence of everyone in the room and the sticky taste of soda and mucus collecting in a ball at the back of Charlie's throat. Truck Arms reached his hand back to his brother's waist to take off his belt. But instead of slipping his hand into his pants, he resituated the belt around his brother's arm, so tightly his taut skin spilled over, and the vein at his inner elbow jutted out. Truck Arms took up the concoction in the needle. And then he pierced his brother's vein, pressing the poison in.

His brother's eyes glazed over, and he let out a sigh of ecstasy, his eyelids drifting shut as he fell back against the carpet, now one of its stains.

Charlie stared so hard his eyes trembled. Tears welled at his bottom lids, but he couldn't allow his eyes to blur, and even more, he couldn't let the tears fall. He had to be the strong one. His brother looked so fragile, like a cracked pot heavy with dirt.

The needle made its way around the room, and all the others went down in much the same way as Charlie's brother. Except after a few minutes, they all rose again, sluggish and dazed, but with eyes open. Truck Arms even went in for a second hit, and it still didn't put him down. But Charlie's brother didn't rise. And Charlie grew increasingly afraid. Inside, he was coming unhinged, his heart thumping outrageously in his ears, battering around his chest like the carbonation in a bottle of soda that's been kicked down a flight of stairs. On the outside, however, he remained completely unaffected, his facial features calm as he continued to balance his tears.

Time itself held like the tears, unmoving.

And then suddenly, it all moved again: time, and the tears he was finally able to blink away, and his brother, who rolled over on his side and threw up.

And that's when Charlie returned to reality and realized nobody else was concerned for his brother. Not Truck Arms, or the girl who had gotten him a Coke, or any of the other horrifying faces of the room. It was up to him.

He went to the kitchen and called a taxi. Then he came back and pulled his brother away from Truck Arms, who was pressing a pill into his brother's mouth with his tongue.

Charlie dragged his brother out to the porch to wait. He stood, tapping his toe impatiently with his arms crossed. His brother slumped down on the top step and then fell onto his back. He looked up with the same awe as earlier. Only now, he wasn't looking at the stars. Just the rotting wood of the porch's awning.

"Come look at the clouds, Charlie boy." He laughed deliriously.

Charlie stayed where he was, wiping his wet eyes with the back of his fist.

"It's ridiculous. Births, and deaths, and sex—so much sex. It's just in our nature to fuck and fuck up. The clouds say it all." His brother paused and then abruptly began to cry.

Charlie's gut twisted in pity, but he didn't move to console his brother. Instead, he stared hard at the boards beneath his feet and counted each case of stain.

He was at thirty-six when the taxi arrived in front of the house. Charlie pulled his brother up by the arm.

"What do you see, Charlie?" he sobbed.

Just the same old story, he wanted to say. Instead, he said nothing because he never did say much.

When they got back to the apartment, Charlie tucked his brother into his bed. He crawled in beside him. Took back up his hand.

"Will you stay this time?" he asked in a whisper, still—after everything—wanting to believe.

"Sure, Charlie boy." His brother was hardly there. But Charlie squeezed his hand tighter and moved closer to feel the heat of his body.

"Will you get clean?" he begged, his throat shaking with the words.

"Mmm," his brother grunted.

That wasn't good enough. Charlie shook his brother's shoulder. He snorted awake and rolled onto his back to look at Charlie.

"Will you get clean?" Charlie asked again, desperately searching the farawayness of his brother's eyes in the dark for the truth. "For me?"

"Anything for you." A serene smile spread across his face, and he closed his eyes again, his breaths becoming steady and gentle as he drifted off.

Charlie fell asleep simply after that. Those three words brought him peace.

He woke up pleasantly. He felt his brother's body still next to him and knew the night's promise had been pure. He sighed, calm. He turned.

And there was his brother, cold and empty. His eyes were open, staring up at the ceiling, more faraway than they had ever been. His skin was dull. His lips were blue and spilled dried vomit down his chin. The joints of his fingers were extended and stiff; clearly, he had tried to claw his way from whatever it was that had taken him. Although his hands remained reaching, he was gone.

Charlie tried to scream. Nothing came out. He flung himself off the bed, away from the vacant body. He darted back against the wall, tears raining from his eyes, still no sound escaping his open lips. He stared at the body unmoving as his eyes rained and rained.

Eventually, he ran out of tears. Nothing in the room was moving. The apartment was quiet. Still, he stared.

And then he stood. He walked back over to the bed, the body, his brother. He crawled in beside it. And he reached for one of the hands that clawed at the sky. He interlocked their fingers and pulled it to his chest, then to his nose. He breathed in the cigarette smell still lingering from the night's last smoke. And he stared up with his brother, hoping to see clouds, or stars, or stories. All he saw was ceiling.

22

BAD TRIP

———

Where am I? The hall around me appears familiar—all worn wood and stifling silence—but still, I don't recognize it. I'm seeing it from new eyes. Who am I? The door before me becomes a one-way mirror, where I can see through to the other side. He is there. Writing like he always is. I want to lie in his bed and watch him. I am afraid to knock. What if I have lost him? I've already lost myself in the grotesque arms of addiction, which clung to me in what at first felt like an embrace but is now more like a strangling hand around my throat, suffocating. It leeched onto me, consumed me, swaddled my skin, and made me believe I would never be alone again while it simultaneously blocked out anyone close to me. A wall. A closed door. A bulging closet where I've shoved all my shame like dirty laundry. I can't open it—can't reveal to him the true and utter mess I've made. He'd be horrified.

The thought of it makes me sick. I feel brutally sick. Sicker than I have ever felt before. And more alone. I grab my upset stomach and fall against the door. I fall to the floor. I bring my knees to my chest and let out a whimper. Everything is spinning out of control. Spiraling. Floor, wall, ceiling, door—all mixed up in the grimy tub of my mind and running down a dark drain. Soon I'll be dried up.

But then, here he is, pulling me back.

"Levi?"

I jump up, forgetting my sickness and my shame, and assault him with a hug. He is quick to wrap his arms around me, pressing his body into mine as if to check that I am solid instead of an apparition. Although I may have been mist just moments ago, in his arms, I feel real for the first time in months. His touch is something I have been craving more than anything. I breathe it in. I hold it in my lungs, even after he pulls away.

"Levi," he murmurs, concern clogging his throat and making my name come out almost like a hiccup. He looks me up and down, a terror in his eyes similar to the last time we saw each other. How long ago was that? I don't even know, but suddenly all that I have done between then and now comes swirling back to me. The men, the women, the drugs. The monster who had been slamming himself into me only hours before. I feel sick all over again.

"I'm sorry," I moan, before I've thrown up all over myself and the floor right outside his room.

He places his hand gently on my shoulder. It is the only center of heat in my bleak body. I can see the red flames emanating from his five fingers while the rest of me is shrouded in blue. I will his fire to spread. I will him to hold me fully until the red erupts from my own fingertips, my toes, my lips. I will him to kiss me, even though there is vomit on my chin. I would thaw completely. I would feel so warm.

He just leads me to the bathroom and sits me down on top of the toilet seat, which is a glacier when he removes his hand—all remote and icy. He takes off my soiled shirt and my pants, tossing them in a pile on the floor. Among the vomit is a number of other stains I didn't realize were there. I can't remember the last time I changed or showered. I feel so unclean. He must know.

I am shivering in just my underwear, exposed. He waits for the water from the tap to heat up. And he's not saying anything.

"I'm sorry," I sob, growing more hysterical with each silent second that passes. "I'm so sorry."

He wipes the vomit from my lip with a wet rag. He holds the back of my head so gently as he does it. I'm searching his face for disappointment. All I see is empathy in his flushed cheeks. Warmth. I search even further for affection. But his features are beginning to blur. I'm still sobbing.

"You don't need to apologize," he says to me. His voice is soothing. But I also hear a little quiver.

He leaves the room, and I'm swooning at the harsh lights bounding against the glossy tile on the floor. He returns with some of his own clothes, which he dresses me in. Then, he leads me to his bed, the room around it shrouded in a chilling indigo. He tucks me under the comforter, but I can't stop shivering. My teeth are chattering dramatically. The sound of bone against bone makes me think I might be a skeleton. I might already be dead. I can hear the song of my funeral procession. It sounds like a thunderstorm.

"I'm afraid," I say to him, cold tears streaking my cheeks. It's the rain of my storm. It's brutal. I feel waterlogged and heavy. I feel flashes of lightning running through my limbs. My insides are thundering. "Lay with me," I beg. I feel so alone.

He crawls beside me from the bottom of the bed and slips his hand into mine. I can feel him shaking too—ever so slightly.

"It's going to be okay," he whispers. It's for both of us.

On the ceiling, I can see a scattering of stars. Far off, I can hear someone other than me crying. Beside me, I feel him letting go of his fear with a sigh. But when I turn to look at him, it's someone I don't recognize. But there is an obvious resemblance.

"You're not allowed to join us," he says to me.

I rain and I rain and I rain. He holds my hand the entire time. I can feel myself completely drenched. This storm is violent. I clench his hand and cry blue ink all over his bed. It blurs into meaningless stains. The hours also blur, but I'm still sure that the entire time, he holds my hand.

And then I can feel the sky clearing.

I whisper something to him.

"What?" he asks.

"I love you, Charlie boy." It doesn't sound like my voice, but the words are definitely mine. I've been wanting to tell him.

He holds his breath. He doesn't say it back before I drift off to sleep.

I have horrible nightmares.

I wake up beside death, and I'm paralyzed, hands clawing at the ceiling. I can't move. I can't scream. I can't fight him as he jams a needle into my arm and flushes me with warm, flat Coke. He looks a lot like the man who assaulted me earlier—same sly grin and those arms. Like trucks. Death has me. And I know I'll never escape.

I try anyway, flinging myself off the bed. But I fall for miles, the chasm beneath growing darker and darker as I plummet. The flickering stars above me start to extinguish one by one, and then there's a drum. Accompanied by a chorus of suffering. I prepare for my crash.

I land back in bed, but now it's white, and the lights are fluorescent. Like a hospital. But my eyesight is blurry—the world is spinning—and the sounds around me are muffled. My side aches. It feels like the gnaw of loneliness amplified, but each time I try to reach out to those who are supposed to love me, they turn away. And at my bedside, a ghost. Pale and shivering. I'm so cold.

I'm lying almost naked in the snow. Flakes melt against my skin, and I feel completely numb. My fingers turn blue, and I reach out for my baby sister—the one I haven't met yet—hoping to hold on to the only source of warmth still in my life. But because of me, she also turns blue. I get a backhand across the cheek so hard it turns my skin red in the shape of my father's hand.

Who I've told my deepest secret. I can't hold it on my own any longer. I want to be strong, but it's heavy. It's deteriorating my body. Just like the drugs I've been using to avoid the truth. At first, they helped my heart feel stronger, like steel. Now my heart is melted strawberry ice cream, and I hold it out, hoping my father will accept me. He's disgusted by the mess. The carpet beneath our feet is stained. Just like the concrete outside where I'll be living.

Now I'm moving. And I assume the box truck is full of my things, but when I open up the back, there's nothing but potted plants. Everything sentimental to me rots in the city dump or below the ground. I have to fill my home with green when all I can see is red. No longer recognize my parents' bed. And at the back of the box truck, a crib. I'm too terrified to look.

But I'm forced to look inside the coffin and what I see
is a body. What I can't tell is if it's my dad, my mom, my
sister, me, or Charlie. But they're dead all right, whoever it
is. I can't stay. I run away. I run outside and smoke an entire
pack of cigarettes. I can smell them on my hand. I can't hold
down my pancakes. Blue ink is leaking down my leg. I want
it to leak from my eyes, but it seems I can no longer cry. I'm
completely out of tears, but I'm still trembling.

Someone takes my hand. It's him, and I feel safe. He leads
me to the grassy hill where we met and points up at the
clouds. "You see the stories too. Don't you?" he asks.

And I nod. I do.

23

CLEAN

———

I wake up, and he is not at his desk. He is lying beside me in bed, holding my hand. He is studying the steady up and down motion of my chest, and every so often, he glances at my lips. They're so dry, I can feel each crack like a ravine. My mouth is full of sand, and my entire body aches.

I'm beyond my bad trip, but I already feel sick with withdrawal. I can't even remember how long it's been since the night on the beach when I decided to give up on sobriety.

I'm too scared to ask. So I ask him something else, similar but not quite as jarring.

"How long was I out of it?" It's dusty and fragmented from my lips, but I don't have the will to clear my throat.

"Eight hours." He is still holding my hand, and it doesn't seem like he will take it away soon. I am sticky with sweat, wrapped up in one of his sweaters, tucked beneath his comforter, and pressed against his body, emanating heat. But I don't dare move.

I squeeze his hand subtly. "And you stayed up that whole time, watching me?"

Our faces are inches from each other. His hot breath breaks against my listless eyelids, and now I'm the one caught up in his lips, straight and sultry. But despite the intimacy of our intertwined position, his voice is detached. "I was scared if I went to sleep, you'd stop breathing."

I want to laugh. It's a joke. Right? It has to be—the way he's delivered it so matter-of-factly. I'm youthfully immortal. I get extra lives for my recklessness. My second chances play on loop. I'm in my fucking twenties, and this is just what we do: test the limits of our boundless existence.

The calcified corners of my mouth break into a grin. But I scan his face, and he looks deadly serious.

Dismayed, my entire body sags. His silent defense against my theory of earthly eternal life is an immense weight. It is also a button of fear that pins itself to the back of my skull.

"I'm sorry I scared you." I fall into his eyes for a few seconds, now feeling teary, especially with his fingers still intertwined with mine, our bodies so close together in this shitty twin bed. I feel on the edge of telling him the truth, thinking it might be easier to digest in the quiet of our close proximity. But I pull back at the last second, a coward, tearing my hand away from his. I sit up with a grunt, letting the covers fall off of me, and find a cigarette on the nightstand to put in my mouth.

"Smoking now?" I ask him as I stretch. Across my limbs are tight balls of cramping muscle that pull taut and twinge. It's as if I've been contorted inside a coffin for months on end, and I just dug my way back to the surface.

I pop the window open and wince at the bright day. Still thinking I'm too hot, I take off the sweater. It's gray, and there's a wet ring around the neckline from my sweat. I'm not wearing pants—they're in a ball on the floor. I must have taken them off in the night. I bunch both pieces of clothing together and toss them across the room to the hamper. I just barely miss, and the pants hang halfway out of the bin; the sweater is sprawled across the carpet.

He doesn't move from the bed to pick it up.

I light my cigarette and offer it to him.

He nods, taking it. "Only on tough days."

I sit down on the floor with my back against the abandoned bed parallel to his and bring my knees to my chest. Now that I'm only in my underwear, I feel a chill from the open window. A shiver crawls from my lower back, up my spine, and to my head, where I'm made fully aware of a rattling headache. Which then morphs into a dull throb that's sent back down through my body but concentrates in my gut, especially as I gaze up at him blowing out smoke in the ray of sunlight penetrating through the window. He has dark bags under his eyes, and his face is set in worry, but he is beautiful.

He turns his head to me and stretches across the four feet that separates us to hand back the cigarette. I reach out and take it without looking, having shot my chin downward so as not to implicate myself staring, longing. I lock onto the carpet, clean as ever.

"I'm feeling a bit sick," I say to the ground. I shrug my shoulders casually. "I sure could use something stronger than nicotine."

I glance up, and he looks like I've just knocked the wind out of him. I am similarly breathless, the guilt sitting heavy on my chest. But sitting on guilt's shoulders even heavier, desire. My mind, my body, my veins, begging.

"You're not gonna get clean?" he squeaks out, his voice small and fragile, as if he hasn't spoken in months and is only just rediscovering the ability.

"Why would I?" I still have the cigarette, and I'm puffing on it selfishly, looking at his alphabetized shelf of books; at the sleeves poking out of his closet, all neutral colored but for his army green coat; at the blaring red journal on his desk. Anywhere but him.

"Because you could've died last night."

It cuts through my avoidance, severe, assertive, ominous. Each syllable thunks against my turned cheek, enticing me to look. But I cross my arms and hold out stubbornly. It's like I'm a pouting child, getting scolded by a parent. It's never as serious as they want to make it out to be. They just want to scare you into submission from their out-of-touch moral high ground. Yet, the terse worry of their set jaw and the chagrin wrought in their authoritative tone is always enough to make you question, *Could I have really hurt myself, and by proxy, hurt them?*

I have to bark that thought away like a defiant teenager.

"Don't be dramatic," I grumble dismissively, rolling my eyes.

"I'm not." He pauses long enough to fool me into looking in his direction. He's staring at me, his back stick straight, his hands folded in his lap cordially, his face expressionless. He is the picture of composure. But there are two distinct lines of tears falling down each cheek. His wet eyes have locked mine. My resolve is shaken.

"Levi…" His head swings back and forth, the tired pendulum of an ancient grandfather clock striking its last midnight. He wants to say more, his tongue pressing against his teeth, forming the words, but he holds them back. Hides them, buries them, and cements himself shut. As always.

I can't take it anymore.

"What?" I shout at him defensively. Even though I know. I don't want to admit it. I don't want to admit anything to him—who flinches at my unexpected outburst—or to myself. So instead, I keep lying, and it pours out of me as an attack against him. "Say it! Say what you think of me. You think I'm a goddamn mess. You think I'm a dirty fucking addict shooting heroin in some back alley. Tell me how disgraceful I really am. Except you're so wrong. It's not like that at all!" The untruth spews. "I'm just enjoying life, same as I always have. And I have total control over it. So I'm not gonna to stop using. I don't see why I would. I'm having too much fun basking in the beautiful messiness to get clean."

He trembles at my escalation—my emboldened, misguided conclusion. I wish he would shout back so that we could really get into it, spitting in each other's faces, pushing roughly at each other's chests until one of us tackles the other, and we're rolling on top of each other in the spotless mud pit. I want to feel his heaving chest on top of mine.

He hasn't moved, sitting respectfully on the bed, knees pressed together. He releases a shaky sigh to disarm my aggression, tears still dribbling sensibly, silently, but steadily down his cheeks.

"You won't even get clean…" *for me?* I beg him to finish, but he bites his bottom lip, cutting off the sentence.

I try so hard to find reciprocal feelings inside the unspoken end to his question. I would surrender my act immediately if I knew he felt the same. A simple confirmation from him, and I'd be on my knees admitting, *I do have a problem. I don't know how to stop, but I will goddamn give it a shot if I get to hold your hand through it all.* But there's no way to tell with him. He's a brick wall. Has been since the beginning.

So I go back on the offensive, pretending his wet beautiful face doesn't affect me and asking bitterly again, "Why would I?"

He slides down from the bed like a flimsy paper doll, joining me on the carpet—its two stains.

His neck extends oddly forward, like an abandoned duckling, and his shoulders rise in tension as he chokes on his reason and suppresses an audible sob.

"This is how my brother died," he pushes out through gritted teeth, his voice cracking. I feel myself cracking too. My lips splitting me open into a dark chasm; my feelings dripping from the sharp edges, echoing in the pitch-black well of my heartache.

I'm so cold. I flashback to the night, to the warmth of his hand on my shoulder. I want it again.

Now I'm spilling. The shards of my hollow shell dig into my swollen heart. It could be blood pouring from my eyes. But when I wipe at them roughly with my palm, it comes away clear. Still, I have to bite my tongue to keep the confession from coming out of me, and I can taste copper running down the back of my throat. I feel weak.

"I can't stop," I weep. My first admission.

He is also crying openly now. He can't hold the sound of his tears back any longer. His heavy shoulders hiccup with each short gasp in, and the involuntary moan emitted during the exhales is so vulnerable.

"I can help you," he says. "I can get you help. I'll do anything for you."

"It's not that." My throat is thick with mucus, and I'm choking on the truth.

"Then what?" His volume finally escalates in an exasperated wail. "Please, Levi! I don't understand." It's impassioned, his desperation. It's messy fucking need. He's shaking all over, and so am I. The two of us have suppressed too much behind our facades, and now it's bursting out. I'm completely undone by the sight of his undoing.

I crawl across the carpet toward him, and I place my hand on his cheek. I kiss him. It's difficult because we're both crying. And at first, his lips are stiff with surprise. But he doesn't pull away, and I kiss him with everything I have. My second admission.

When I'm empty of all that has built up inside of me the past year, I push away and dart backward across the room on my palms, bringing my knees to my chest once I'm propped against the vacant bed and crying even more than before. "Charlie, I love you. I'm sorry."

Now he won't look at me. He's searching the carpet for stains that aren't there. Meanwhile, my stomach is a pit. I've ruined everything. I wish I *had* died in the night. Even more, I wish I'd never found him outside, looking up at the clouds. He was better off without me.

"God," I shake my head. I'm so disoriented. The veins in my body pop like fireworks and then oscillate between a fierce burning and a tight, freezing pinch. "I'm sorry. I'll leave. It's just, I feel horrible. I mean, about feeling this way, but also, I actually feel horrible. God…" I clutch my uneasy stomach and swallow hard. I'm shivering, but I can also feel sweat beading in droplets on my forehead.

He still won't look up from the floor.

"Please say something," I beg. I feel like I've lost him for good.

He shakes his head as if coming back from somewhere faraway. Finally, he looks up at me. "I'm sorry."

"It's fine." My teeth are chattering. I could melt.

"I'm just—" he stutters, "I didn't know. You caught me off guard."

"It's fine," I repeat. I've already accepted his rejection and the fact that our friendship is over. I can't even feel the hurt of it right now because there are so many other pieces of me screaming out in agony. I just want to curl up in a ball.

"I love you too—"

"—but not like that," I finish for him. "It's fine." I cross my arms tightly over my aching chest, trying to close the gaping wound.

The stream of light from the open window has drifted over the course of our conversation and is acting as a spotlight on him. The tips of his messy brown hair are golden, the right side of his damp face glowing. His elusiveness appears ethereal.

But also in that stream is a glass of water on the night-stand I didn't notice before—too familiar, that act of care, it was rendered invisible to me. The sun reflects off of it now like a magnifying glass, right into my eyes, singing them. I can feel the balls searing in their sockets, watering all over again. I am also burning in the hell of rejection. My renewed loneliness is a red-hot ball of lead in my stomach. I cringe, a sharp cramp slicing into my side.

He rubs at the back of his neck, probably trickling sweat from the spotlight beam and my desperation, steaming up the tight room. "No, I do—I mean, I might." He cringes too, but just because he's struggling to find the words. "I'm afraid."

"Me too." So afraid. Not of loving a man, not of how the world would perceive us walking down the sidewalk hand in hand, but of the way I would perceive us. We walked so differently. I would be in constant fear of us falling out of sync. I'd always have to worry about me stumbling and him pulling away. I'd be ever-afraid of my mess darkening our relationship like storm clouds to a blue sky.

"I'm afraid because I've lost everyone I love," he admits like a sigh, the burden of his entire being released in one simple sentence, now hanging heavily over the already thick room like a stifling humidity.

I breathe out densely, "You're not going to lose me."

"But are you going to get clean?" he counters immediately. All the emotion has drained out of him, and he bores me down as serious as I have ever seen him: eyes upright and locked, chest open toward me.

I feel like screaming myself out of my own body. Why can't he just hold me and dispel all my pain? Then it would be easy to say yes to him. Easy to take on withdrawal and recovery and amends and all that miserable-sounding bullshit that's supposed to come after rock bottom. But with the way I feel in this tumultuous pit, all desperate need and ravaging emptiness, I don't know if promising him I'll be clean is a lie.

I start to break down again. "I'm in so much pain."

Loose snot is leaking from my nose, coating my upper lip in a viscous sheen, same as my blotchy cheeks, angry with more tears. I'm losing myself to the torment. It's so overwhelming, I almost feel numb. But not really numb at all because I endure every jolt, sparks going off across my nervous system like extinguishing stars.

"I know," he says without sympathy. He doesn't move toward me to comfort me like I need him to. He's sat firmly in his spot, the pressure of his question barreling me down relentlessly. "Will you get clean?"

"Will you be with me if I do?" I'm getting restless. My stomach is churning like a washing machine, and my body is quaking like a dryer with a few too many screws loose. The dirty laundry of me is anything but clean, and I can't see how it ever could be without him.

"It doesn't work like that. You have to want to get clean for yourself." There is a hint of his earlier exasperation—his passion, his need—in his voice, although he tries to remain strict and collected. "We can't talk about being together until you're stable in your sobriety."

"Charlie," I whine. I cover my face in embarrassment. "I don't *want* to be clean." I make sure it's muffled by my hands, hoping he won't be able to decipher what I've said. It's my final admission, and I'm ashamed.

I smush my hands as hard as I can against my face, hoping to break through the layer of thick skull so I can turn around my backward brain. Who could devote themselves to such an uncertainty? Who could stand behind something so likely to fall? Who could love someone so fundamentally broken? Drugs are the only thing that deserve me. Maybe death.

I hear him stand up, but I don't move my hands to look if he's left the room. Better for him to leave me here in my shame anyway.

But I don't hear the door open or close. And then I feel his body close to mine—the warmth of him.

I part my hands like an automatic door and see his journal held out over my lap. I take it in my fingers like a fragile artifact. I turn to him to ask if he's sure, but he's looking away from me, hugging his knees and smoking a new cigarette.

I stare down at the cover—bright red self-destruct button, glaring red help signal. His throbbing red heart. I'm holding it in my hands. And it's all I've ever wanted, to pry the layers back and look inside, but suddenly I'm terrified. What makes me worthy of reading the words I've watched him pore over every day for the last year? My desire to know him—to read these words—has always been a wholly selfish one. I wanted to fill my own holes, the blank pages of my own book. I didn't want to be alone and empty anymore. I wanted to be consumed in someone else's story, for it to intertwine with my own into one beautiful and complete image: Two boys holding on to each other for dear life.

I push the journal back in his direction. The words are his. I don't want to ruin them.

He shakes his head solemnly, the muscles of his face serene. "You need to read it," he says, unfaltering. Then he rests his left ear on his knee, taking a pull of the cigarette and blowing smoke in my direction, watching me.

I resituate the journal against my thighs and let out a heavy breath, as someone who knows they're entering a life-altering moment might.

Then, I peel back its red leather cover. I am delicate and tentative with each turn of the page. All the torment of my withdrawal is momentarily dulled by the steady shape of his blue letters. I read each of the stories like they're my own memories. They feel close and real, yet I feel further removed from myself with each one. I'm in his childhood apartment, listening to his parents fight. I'm at his mother's funeral, seeing her in the casket. I'm carting pots up the stairs, moving his dad's girlfriend in. I'm racing his brother down a hill; he just keeps falling. So do I. I hold his baby sister in my arms. I endure violent sickness but recover. I try drugs for the last time. I ask his brother to get clean, he agrees. But then, he dies.

I had assumed my tear ducts were all dried up. They are not. A heavy, cathartic cry seeps out of me.

I don't want that to be me. I am racked with a realization like lighting that I experienced this suffering the night before—I truly could have died—and it was worse than anything I could ever endure getting clean. It is not just because of him that I am convinced. Not just because he does not deserve any more death, although that is a big reason. But it is also for me. I want to wake up next to him in the morning. I want to feel loved and fulfilled and clear.

I close the journal delicately and set it on the ground between us. "Will you help me get clean?"

He looks at me gratefully and wipes a tear gently from my clammy cheek with his thumb, even though his own eyes are getting misty. I have never felt closer to him. I feel myself inside of him. I feel him inside of me.

"Of course," he says, still serious because he wouldn't be him otherwise, but there is a gentle smile on his lips that is unwavering. It's got all the strength I need wrapped up into it.

"Okay," I nod to reassure myself, already a seed of doubt sprouting from the drizzle of withdrawal's rumbling ache rolling in fast. Getting clean will be the most difficult thing I have done in my life. I already know. But I want to do it for his brother. I need to do it for me. And I will do it for Charlie.

He slips his hand into mine. I feel safe. I bring his hand up to my lips and kiss it.

Then, I just hold it there. And I breathe him in. His fingers smell like cigarettes. They're smudged in blue ink.

ONE MORE HAPPY STORY

The faded mossy fabric of the waiting room seat is unraveling, probably picked at incessantly by some nervous finger unable to stifle the anxiety of the four white walls pressing in on their body. Bleach-based disinfectant saturates the air with a sharp bite, giving each breath in a subtle twinge, like a hand squeezing its fingers around the lungs. But Charlie finds it almost comforting, like a hug after a cold shower.

It is a clean space. Behind the swinging door that leads to the main facility, the sneakers of orderlies squeak against the tiled floor. In the left corner of the waiting room, a wispy-haired janitor is mopping. There is something serene in the steady swish-swish of the mop across the tiles. Every so often, he lifts the mop and thrusts it in the bucket of dingy water with an enveloping squelch. Then there is the pitter-patter of rain as he wrings the mop out and starts again on the floor.

When they first entered, he had given Charlie an encouraging nod. Now, Charlie watches his assured movements, trying to draw from his peaceful demeanor.

But the flap of the swinging door has Charlie whipping his head frantically away from the janitor. It is just a nurse, taking her lunch break—brown paper bag in hand and purse against her hip. She stops at the receptionist's desk, and the two giggle some sort of gossip back and forth for a minute before the nurse, in her white tennis shoes, squeaks across the room and out the front door.

Disappointed, Charlie moves his eyes away from the sole square of light peeking in from the front door's glass and onto the baby girl cooing in the stroller beside him, awash in the fluorescents above her. There is spittle on her rosy lips, and she's reaching toward the speckled ceiling with her little fingers.

Charlie gives her his pointer. It's a good distraction from his urge to pick at the seat's fabric in his own nervousness. She accepts the finger graciously, bringing it to her lips, and immediately a calm washes over him like the mop tendrils dragging a clear wave through the tarnished flooring.

Her mother puts a stable hand on Charlie's thigh, smiling between the little girl and him. Her other hand is intertwined with the hippie's, who, despite the wooden peace symbol hanging around his neck, looks the most on edge of the group. For some reason, Charlie finds that reassuring.

The sound of the swinging door beats through the air again, and Charlie is slower to look, content in his place among this family.

But when his eyes do make it to the door, they meet a bright, clear pair.

"Levi."

"Charlie."

They approach each other hesitantly, stiff from the forced distance that has been between them. But when their arms wrap around each other, all the anxious anticipation dissipates. Their fractured edges fit together perfectly. They become melted strawberry ice cream in each other's tender grasp—the stiffened muscles of their limbs softening, their rose-tinted skin becoming one unencumbered mass.

They are both slow to pull back from the intimate moment but smile knowingly at each other before fully releasing their arms.

Levi moves down the line, pressing his nose into his mom's shoulder as she sways them back and forth. This is the first time she has held him since they filled out the check-in paperwork ninety days prior. Then, she had been holding him up, the thin and cowering shell of him. Now, he is full and firm in her loving arms. She is so proud of her son. It is displayed in the brightness of her plump cheek grazing his as her upturned lips whisper in his ear. She ends the interaction with a sloppy kiss on his forehead and a grin.

Levi is beaming, and so he even slides his hand respectfully into the hippie's, who gives it a firm shake and a nod of approval.

Then, Levi's attention falls on the stroller—its black, umbrellalike fabric. Charlie can see his breath catch in unease. He turns back to Charlie, his usually laidback features straining toward the red tips of his ears. His body begins to curve in on itself, wrought heavy with guilt.

Charlie mouths, *it's okay*, and absolves Levi.

So Levi turns back to the stroller and peers inside, going soft again the instant he sees his baby sister. He squats down and lowers his finger to gently bop her nose. She giggles wildly, and he pops back up, looking over at Charlie again, elated.

The hippie claps his hands together to tear the tender moment back to reality. The ticking circle clock on the wall reads lunchtime, and just down the way is a newly opened vegan diner.

But there is no gnaw in their stomachs. They are content.

So they decide on the park instead. It is a beautiful day.

They head for the door just as the janitor plops his mop in the bucket with a definitive splash. He has finished cleaning. The floor is spotless. He waves pleasantly at Charlie.

Once outside, Levi lights up a cigarette, and Charlie grabs for his hand. They walk along the sidewalk together, their steps falling into a steady rhythm. The sky above them is a bright blue.

ACKNOWLEDGMENTS

At one point, this story was nothing but an idea, budding inside my head and my head alone. I hadn't even spoken it, afraid that as soon as it touched the air, it would shrivel. If I had attempted to keep it to myself like every other story I've written, that's exactly what would have happened.

Instead, I received help from so many people. Each one peeled back the layers of petals I had locked over this story, blooming it into what it is today: my first published novel.

First and foremost, I would like to thank Eric Koester, who granted me the opportunity to fulfill my lifelong dream of becoming an author at just twenty-two. Without his incredible Book Creators program, this story would still just be a rinky-dink Word file on my laptop.

I would also like to thank my editors.

Thank you to Margaret Danko, who always asked the exact right question to open a chapter up to its true potential during the development stage. For as many tailspins as her brilliant prodding of my story caused, twice as many revelations were made under her guidance.

And thank you to Bailee Noella, who provided me much needed words of encouragement throughout the difficult revisions phase. Despite my nagging belief that everything needed to be changed, she reassured me of my story's merit while helping me pick out the strategic places that would polish my book off.

I would also like to thank the beautiful souls who took the time to provide me with edits even though it wasn't their job to do so: my beta-readers. Thank you to Vincent Gabriel, who made sure the story I told—so much different than my own lived experience—was accurate and sensitively written. Thank you to Austin Huber, whose thoughtful and detailed feedback pushed me to improve my story that much more, right near the end. Thank you to Laci Durham, whose lovely compliments gave me the confidence to submit my manuscript, happy with what I had produced. And thank you to Abby Blakeney, who offered to give it one last read to calm my nervous expectation that I would miss something significant before it went to the printers.

Thank you also to the very first person who read an early draft of this book—who begged me to let her read it before I was even ready to share: Carly Baker. Your early encouragement of this story made me believe it was worth sharing.

Thank you to the English Department at the University of Northern Colorado, who let me submit many of these chapters as assignments and gave me early feedback in the form of A's. Specifically, thank you to Lisa Zimmerman, who not only advised me through my college creative writing journey but also taught the poetry class in which the inspiration for this story struck. And thank you to Andreas Mueller, who ran the department in a way that allowed me to explore, and now pursue, both the creative and professional sides of my passion for writing.

Of course, I have to thank my parents for being supportive of this crazy pipe dream. Having an artist for a kid may not always be easy on the nerves, but I appreciate their willingness to believe I'll land on my feet, even if the journey isn't always stable. Thank you to my mom, Melissa Riggs, for spending hours on the phone with me every week throughout the process, listening to me ramble on about my every fear and insecurity. And thank you to my dad, Scott Riggs, for pushing my campaign over the edge, making this whole journey a reality.

On the topic of my presale campaign, I want to thank my beautiful artist friends, who helped me produce some absolutely incredible artwork to pair with the first sales of my book. Thank you to Clark Ellis for converting your sweet collage records into postcards that fit into my front cover. Thank you to Leah Petrie for using my words as inspiration to design two harrowing posters. And thank you to Jordan Burgmeier for rapidly turning out some adorable tote bags to go along with my story.

Thank you most of all to my entire author community, who supported this book before they could even hold a physical copy in their hands: Gary Hays, Paula Burright, Mark Fenton, Traci Wuerstl, Katelyn Jensen, Natalie Bollig, Maddie Riggs, Paula Ramsey, Amelia Palmer, Charlotte Nunnallee, Nancy Beebe, Janice Warren, Norma Jean, Tammy Allen, Taylor Zangari, the Kleins, Rachel Weir, Lisa Zaborsky, Austin Divine, Belinda Sutherland, Michelle Deines, Dalana Peterson, Julie McGough, Angie Jensen, Zoey Benham, Sarah Lukins, Andy Riggs, Hunter Conway, Aran Coll, Tresha Stevens, Jim Word, Gaylyn Fraiche, the Troschers,

David G. Tholl, Ingrid Daniel, Malinda Keck, Freda Dreiling, Linda Love, Cheryl Grubbs, LyNysha Foss, Susan Hart, Kyle Shoemaker-Webster, Collin Eagen, Nikki Lester, Bonnie Benham, Audrey Moreau, Wendi Sidney, Colin Jones, Angela Mombleau, Brett Steward, Katie Kroeker, Adam Elder, Jessyp Brown, Maddy Benham, Julia Letzig, Mitchell Bollig, Kaitlyn Brink, Sydney Small, Marc Cañizares Andres, Julia Thompson, Dionna Alverson, William James Boswell, Sandra Smith, Kandee Khodl, Amy Molina, Tara Langness, Skyler DeYoung, Justin Macon, Donna Faulkner, Dillon Lind, Cynthia Williams, David James Wheeler, Theresa Bickel, Mary Jo Elder, Tracey Winter, Eric Canuel, Allison Kalbach, Patrick Trujillo, Kyra Harris, Anna Tapia, Monica Vogel, Amber Whetstine, Anonymous, Daniël-James van den Berg, Christy Knouf, Tena Stacy, Jovana Caicedo, Gabrielle Kallina-Tran, Abigail Burg, Gavin Hall, Tommie Harden, Leslie Klamm, Erin Scherger, Erika Siebring, Victor R. Aves, Mary Hopper, Mindy Abbott, Mindy Fleming, Melissa Morganthaler, Cecilia Metcalf, and Micah Miracle.

This book would not exist without each and every one of you.

APPENDIX

AUTHOR'S NOTE

Duran, Eric and Brooke Sopelsa. "More Harvard, Yale freshmen identify as LGBTQ than as conservative." *NBC-News*, September 14, 2018. https://www.nbcnews.com/feature/nbc-out/more-harvard-yale-freshmen-identify-lgbtq-conservative-surveys-find-n909781.

Juergens, Jeffrey. "Drug Abuse and College Campuses." *AddictionCenter*, June 15, 2021. https://www.addictioncenter.com/college/facts-statistics-college-drug-abuse/.